When They ALREADY Know It

*How to Extend and Personalize
Student Learning in a PLC at Work®*

Mark Weichel • Blane McCann • Tami Williams

Solution Tree | Press

a division of

Solution Tree

555 North Morton Street
Bloomington, IN 47404
800.733.6786 (toll free) / 812.336.7700
FAX: 812.336.7790

email: info@SolutionTree.com
SolutionTree.com

Visit **go.SolutionTree.com/PLCbooks** to download the free reproducibles in this book.

Printed in the United States of America

Library of Congress Cataloging-in-Publication Data

Names: Weichel, Mark, author. | McCann, Blane, author. | Williams, Tami, author.
Title: When They Already Know It : How to Extend and Personalize Student
    Learning in a PLC at Work / Mark Weichel, Blane McCann, and Tami Williams.
Description: Bloomington, IN : Solution Tree Press, [2018] | Includes
    bibliographical references and index.
Identifiers: LCCN 2017046579 | ISBN 9781945349621 (perfect bound)
Subjects: LCSH: Professional learning communities--United States. | Teaching
    teams--United States. | Effective teaching--United States. |
    Individualized instruction--United States.
Classification: LCC LB1731 .W393 2018 | DDC 370.71/1--dc23 LC record available at
    https://lccn.loc.gov/2017046579

Solution Tree
Jeffrey C. Jones, CEO
Edmund M. Ackerman, President

Solution Tree Press
President and Publisher: Douglas M. Rife
Editorial Director: Sarah Payne-Mills
Art Director: Rian Anderson
Managing Production Editor: Kendra Slayton
Senior Production Editor: Tara Perkins
Senior Editor: Amy Rubenstein
Copy Editor: Evie Madsen
Proofreader: Jessi Finn
Cover Designer: Rian Anderson
Editorial Assistant: Sarah Ludwig

Acknowledgments

As we worked to develop this book, it was clear to us that we needed to work with other educators, share ideas, and see how elementary- and secondary-level teachers utilize the five elements of personalized learning and five instructional strategies for responding to question 4 that we champion in this book. The following educators offered expertise to the writing team in many ways. We visited or interviewed many of them to gain ideas to support our narrative regarding one or more of these elements or methods.

Crystal Bonin, Bow, New Hampshire

Karen Calcaterra, Wildwood, Missouri

Brittany Castellano, Wauconda, Illinois

Bay Cunningham, Olentangy, Ohio

Paul Darvasi, Toronto, Canada

Ric Dressen, Edina, Minnesota

Andrew Easton, Omaha, Nebraska

Amy Eide, Pewaukee, Wisconsin

Gara Field, Providence, Rhode Island

Brett Geithman, Manhattan Beach, California

Marcia Gentry, West Lafayette, Indiana

Maria Harley, Sewanhaka, New York

Erin Heiman, Pewaukee, Wisconsin

Kristen Hogan, Omaha, Nebraska

Jenny Klemme, Pewaukee, Wisconsin

Jill Lizier, Sanborn, New Hampshire

Kristin Marconi, Olentangy, Ohio

Julie Martin, Manchester, Connecticut

Mike Matthews, Manhattan Beach, California

Marie McCann, Omaha, Nebraska

Kate Perardi, Edina, Minnesota

Crystal Phillips, Charlotte, North Carolina

Rebecca Reagles, Pewaukee, Wisconsin

Joe Renzulli, Storrs, Connecticut

Jim Rickabaugh, Whitefish Bay, Wisconsin

Julie Schmitz, Omaha, Nebraska

Enid Schonewise, Omaha, Nebraska

Julie Schonewise, Lincoln, Nebraska

Shorewood School District, Shorewood, Wisconsin

Kristin Shrout, Lee's Summit, Missouri

Katie Sindt, Omaha, Nebraska

Randy Smasal, Edina, Minnesota

Paul Tessmer-Tuck, Edina, Minnesota

Tara Thomas, Long Beach, California

Jill Thompson, Charlotte, North Carolina

Jonathan Vander Els, Sanborn, New Hampshire

Nicole Waicunas, Storrs, Connecticut

Westside Community Schools staff, Omaha, Nebraska

Additionally, in the fall of 2015, Blane and Mark worked with a small team of educators over the course of two days to, among other things, help define and develop the five elements of personalized learning. While other lists exist, the five elements we present in this book resonated with this writing team. We would like to thank the following educators for serving on that team: Greg Betts, Michelle Patterson, Lynn Spady, and Rebecca Kratky.

Solution Tree Press would like to thank the following reviewers:

Jay Billy
Principal
Slackwood Elementary School
Lawrenceville, New Jersey

Elizabeth Bruening
Principal
Shimek Elementary School
Iowa City, Iowa

Karen Calcaterra
Associate Principal
Lafayette High School
Wildwood, Missouri

Charles Folsom
Instructional Coach
Waukee High School
Waukee, Iowa

Maleea Gannon
Fifth-Grade Teacher
Greene County Intermediate School
Jefferson, Iowa

Jennifer Gates
Assistant Principal, Pine Mountain Middle School
Assistant Director, Teacher & Leader Effectiveness
Cobb County School District
Marietta, Georgia

Beth Houf
Principal
Fulton Middle School
Fulton, Missouri

David Jones
Superintendent
Bonsall Unified School District
Bonsall, California

Derek R. McDowell
Secondary Science Coordinator
Frisco Independent School District
Frisco, Texas

Bruce Mellesmoen
Vice-Principal
Waldheim School
Waldheim, Saskatchewan
Canada

Jennifer Nauman
Principal
Shields Elementary School
Lewes, Delaware

Jon Schultz
Assistant Principal
Francis Howell High School
St. Charles, Missouri

Megan Thomsen
Instructional Coach
Stillwell Junior High School
West Des Moines, Iowa

Visit **go.SolutionTree.com/PLCbooks** to download the free reproducibles in this book.

Table of Contents

Reproducible pages are in italics.

Chapter 3

Instructional Strategies That Support Question 4 Students

Chapter 4

Knowing Your Learners

Chapter 5

Allowing Voice and Choice

Chapter 6
Implementing Flexibility **121**

Chapter 7
Using Data **151**

Chapter 8
Integrating Technology **179**

Chapter 9

Bringing It All Together **207**

References and Resources **219**

Index **233**

About the Authors

Mark Weichel, EdD, is assistant superintendent for teaching and learning at Westside Community Schools in Omaha, Nebraska. The district has received local and national attention for its commitment to collaboration, innovation, technology integration, and personalized learning. Mark and his team developed collaborative systems that have been written about in various journals, and they host visiting districts and attend state and national conferences.

Previously, Mark was director of secondary curriculum, high school building administrator, and junior high school social studies teacher at Papillion La Vista Community Schools in Nebraska. He and staff implemented Professional Learning Communities at Work® strategies and failure rates plummeted while standardized testing measures such as ACT, PLAN, and state writing assessments confirmed high levels of student learning. Mark and his leadership team at Papillion La Vista South High School presented at conferences nationwide, and their work was featured on AllThingsPLC.info and in *Principal Leadership* magazine. They received the 2008 Ethel Percy Andrus Legacy Award for Innovation from the American Association of Retired Persons (AARP). Mark also taught in the graduate schools for Peru State College and the University of Nebraska Omaha.

He earned a doctorate in educational administration from the University of Nebraska Omaha. To learn more about Mark's work, follow @westsideweichel on Twitter.

Blane McCann, PhD, is superintendent of Westside Community Schools in Omaha, Nebraska, and former superintendent of Shorewood School District in Wisconsin. In both districts, Blane led cost-effective strategic planning efforts and initiatives around personalized learning, professional learning, and integration of technology, which allowed each district to close achievement gaps while maintaining excellence.

Previously, Blane served as a teacher, coach, assistant principal, and elementary and middle school principal, as well as executive director for K–8 instruction. He has taught leadership courses at Cardinal Stritch University and is a member of Phi Delta Kappa, Learning Forward, the American Association of School Administrators, and the Nebraska Council of School Administrators. He serves on the boards for Methodist College, Wellness Committee of the Midlands, and Nebraska Council on Teacher Education.

Blane's honors and awards include Outstanding Educational Leader by Phi Delta Kappa chapter #0116 at the University of Nebraska Omaha (2017), Lexington Education Leadership Award Fellowship (2015), U.S. Department of Education's ConnectED Summit Future Ready White House participant (2014), and Kenosha Unified School District Administrator of the Year (2001).

Blane earned a bachelor of science in secondary education from Miami University in Oxford, Ohio; a master's in administration and supervision from the University of North Carolina at Chapel Hill; and a doctorate in educational policy and leadership from Marquette University in Milwaukee, Wisconsin. To learn more about Blane's work, visit *Blane McCann's Blog* (www2.westside66.org/wcsblog) or follow @BlaneMcCann on Twitter.

Tami Williams, EdD, is an assistant professor in the educational leadership department at the University of Nebraska Omaha. Tami has been a teacher, behavior interventionist, assistant principal, and district administrator. She is former director of assessment, research, and evaluation at Millard Public Schools in Nebraska, where she supervised buildings and led assessment innovations, program evaluations, data storage and reporting, and data professional development.

Tami is a member of Phi Delta Kappa. She was selected for the PDK Emerging Leaders class in 2012 and received the 2010 Linda Gehrig Educational Leadership Award from the Metropolitan Reading Council. Tami has presented on social justice, program evaluation, and school improvement at several local and national conferences.

Tami received a bachelor's degree in mathematics and a teacher endorsement in secondary education from the University of Nebraska–Lincoln. She earned a master's degree in educational leadership, a principal certificate, a doctorate in education, and a superintendent certificate from the University of Nebraska Omaha.

To learn more about Tami's work, follow @tamijwilliams on Twitter.

To book Mark Weichel, Blane McCann, or Tami Williams for professional development, contact pd@SolutionTree.com.

Introduction

What would schools look like if educators invested energy and time into thinking about what they do for students who already know the material and content when they walk in the door? Concurrently, what would it look like if educators' ideas of who these students are were flexible and evolving? What if teachers deliberately and intentionally thought about lessons, units, and activities that could make learning experiences personal for the students who would benefit from extension and challenge by staying engaged and continuing to learn more? We authors believe that teams in such schools would be privileged to work in a culture that valued supporting the needs and talents of every student, where the norm was highly engaging and effective learning. In this book, we aim to offer a framework and resources toward creating such a culture, consistently addressing the needs of students who are of high ability and high potential, thinking flexibly when determining which students fit these criteria, and encouraging collaborative teamwork to meet these goals.

The results of this type of system would be a sight to behold. Imagine walking through various classrooms in a school district where students, particularly those who already know the material, are engaged, enthusiastic, and energetic as they work together with their teachers. A first-grade team develops centers with student choice, writing workshops, and performance assessments based on the achievement levels of the students. Another first-grade teacher uses gradual release of responsibility as students work in strategy groups based on their understanding of the content from the previous day. A third-grade teacher uses digital tools to help students work at their own pace in mathematics. Another elementary teacher works with students to choose their own learning pathways and assessments in mathematics based on their understanding on a pretest. Two sixth-grade teachers have their dividing wall torn down so they can team teach, continually pretest, and then set up stations where students have choices in their learning paths, based on where they are in the learning process. A middle school English teacher who knows her students well uses data to push students further in extending their learning. A middle school team uses student pretest results for student placement in stations that ultimately determine whether they earn entrance tickets to an upcoming assessment. A freshman English teacher employs a system in which students have ten goals to complete in ten days. Each goal requires different cognitive and collaborative skills, and students choose to work on the ten goals in the order of their preference, based on their ability. A high school social studies teacher uses a game where high-achieving students have forty-eight to seventy-two hours to complete a mission, which allows them to learn more about the Roman Empire. A high school science team develops an assignment where students choose their own final assessment tool while the teacher checks their work against certain benchmarks along the way. Teachers in this district are using a great variety of ways to lead students toward clear objectives while allowing already-proficient students to learn in a more personalized manner.

We've seen such classrooms and can attest that, if you walked into each of these classrooms and talked to the teachers leading these activities like we have, you would also feel the passion of both the students and the teachers that comes from this type of learning environment. If you talked to the students, you would learn that this type of learning makes time in class go quickly and doesn't feel like learning. You would also learn that in these environments, learners perform just as well as—if not better than—in traditional classrooms such as those we described previously. Not only that, but students are being challenged, feel a great deal of efficacy, and are highly engaged. Perhaps not surprisingly, these students also stretch themselves further than their teachers might have been able to stretch them. Such a learning culture encourages a mindset that students can grow their intelligence and stretches the limits of what might be traditionally expected of students. And, the beauty of it is that the stretching and growth are internal; students are achieving because they want to. All of these classroom examples we describe are based on real examples we have seen or learned about through our conversations with educators from all over the United States. We describe all of them as examples of *personalized learning*.

Personalized Learning

A theme that runs through each of the ideas, instructional strategies, and stories in this book is that of personalized learning. Throughout this book, we will seek to define personalized learning and to examine the five elements we have identified that comprise it: (1) knowing your learners, (2) allowing voice and choice, (3) implementing flexibility, (4) using data, and (5) integrating technology. As we will discuss further in chapter 2, students today have grown accustomed to personalization in most aspects of their lives, as advances in technology increasingly adapt to our preferences and needs. It only makes sense that we would adjust our approaches to teaching to similarly reflect personalization of students' learning to challenge and engage them. When working with students who are of high ability and high potential (and all students for that matter), a key piece to the planning process is the need to allow room for the student to determine his or her own learning plan. This type of thinking and release of responsibility are firmly aligned with the elements of personalized learning. To us, the best platform to incorporate this work and make this vision a reality in your classroom, school, or district is not to go about this work alone but rather to use the well-established Professional Learning Communities at Work® model.

The PLC Model

As authors, we first learned about professional learning communities (PLCs) when education giants Rick DuFour and Robert Eaker's book *Professional Learning Communities at Work: Best Practices for Enhancing Student Achievement* (1998) was published. Thanks to this book and the calculated efforts of educators it has influenced to share best practices, many schools are regularly functioning as PLCs.

According to DuFour, Rebecca DuFour, Eaker, Thomas Many, and Mike Mattos (2016), PLC work is "an ongoing process in which educators work collaboratively in recurring cycles of collective inquiry and action research to achieve better results for the students they serve" (p. 10). School leaders start this process by convening the staff and working through collaborative approaches to determine their mission, vision, values, and goals. Experts suggest thinking about the foundation of a PLC as resting on four pillars—the mission, vision, values, and goals (DuFour et al., 2016). When building leaders focus on why they exist, articulate a compelling and understandable sense of direction for the work, identify the specific actions the group will take to achieve the mission and vision, and determine how they will know whether or not students achieve success, the likelihood of success magnifies (DuFour et al., 2016). Following the development of these four key pillars, teams use the three big ideas and the four critical questions of a PLC to make their work come alive.

The Three Big Ideas of a PLC

According to DuFour et al. (2016), the three big ideas of a PLC are:

1. A focus on learning

2. A collaborative culture and collective responsibility

3. A results orientation

These three big ideas do not represent a program, a series of documents, or a project to complete. They represent a way of thinking and doing business in a school. With the first big idea, we ensure that we, as educators, are willing to examine everything to ensure that nothing is misaligned with promoting high levels of learning for all. Big idea number two ensures a collaborative culture exists. This means that all staff members, regardless of assignment, are on a collaborative team that shares norms; common goals driven by timely, user-friendly, and relevant information regarding student learning; common frequent meeting time during the school day; and protocols to guide the work. Members of a team are committed to holding each other accountable. Big idea number three ensures that team members regularly seek out evidence for student learning and use this information to improve the practice of the individual teachers and collaborative teams as they work toward goals, and to respond to the needs of students through intervention and enrichment.

The conduits to much of this work are the four critical questions of a PLC. By examining the four critical questions, teams are doing the necessary work to ensure that they are embedding these three big ideas of a PLC into their practice.

The Four Critical Questions of a PLC

In PLCs, grade-level or same-subject collaborative teams spend considerable time and energy discussing the four critical questions (DuFour et al., 2016).

1. What do we want all students to know and be able to do?

2. How will we know if they learn it?

3. How will we respond when some students do not learn?

4. How will we extend the learning for students who are already proficient?

These questions become the focal point and driving force for collaborative time, as members work to ensure that they are constantly discussing and considering them. This ongoing cyclical process utilizes data to inform the team's work and ultimately ensures all students learn at high levels.

While all four questions and the work of a PLC are important for this book, this fourth question is our focal point. We seek to provide a way for teams to address students who are already proficient when they walk into the classroom or who quickly gain proficiency early on in an instructional unit or lesson. There are a few different ways that you will hear educators refer to this population, including:

- Students who already know it

- Students who are already proficient

- Students who need to have learning extended

- Question 4 students (or Q4 students)

- Gifted and talented students

For the purposes of this book, from this point forward, we will refer to this population of students as *question 4 students*. Note that we do not endorse only considering students identified as gifted as question 4 students; this is not a "gifted book." This is a question 4 book that addresses high ability and potential, which is flexible and evolves based on what is being taught. We authors have seen it's possible that one student might be considered a "question 4 student" one week but not necessarily the next. For example, a student who is not under the "gifted and talented" label but shows high potential during a pretest would benefit from the instructional components we advocate in this book.

Teams often report to us that the four questions are addressed in order, one through four, with the last question typically skipped due to time, priorities, or lack of know-how by the collaborative team members. When this happens, question 4 students' needs are not being met. We contend that in order to truly consider the fourth question, teams need to address how they plan to extend learning for question 4 students much earlier in the process. If teams wait until a formative assessment is administered to make this determination, it is too late, as instruction has already occurred. This conversation needs to take place at the beginning of a unit to ensure that teams take the needs of all students into account.

The Challenge With Responding to Question 4

Because question 4 very specifically uses the word *extend*, as we begin a discussion about question 4, we feel it is important to define the difference between enrichment and extension. We have seen these terms commonly used interchangeably when discussions emerge about question 4 and what to do for question 4 students.

Enrichment is a term used to describe "the subjects traditionally taught by specials or electives teachers (such as music, art, drama, applied technology, and physical education) and the activities often used to enrich learning (for example, field trips and assemblies)" (AllThingsPLC, 2016). *Extension*, by comparison, is:

> when students are stretched beyond essential grade-level curriculum or levels of proficiency. Extension can be achieved by asking students to demonstrate mastery of essential standards at a level beyond what is deemed grade-level proficient, providing students access to more of the required grade-level curriculum that is deemed nonessential, or providing students access to curriculum above their current grade level. (AllThingsPLC, 2016)

The strategies described in this book reflect *extension*. We are providing tools for teachers to extend and stretch students' learning, particularly for question 4 students. From our experience, question 4 is a question that the classroom staff rarely answer. Teachers and educators in general tend to work through questions 1–3 chronologically, stop at question 3, and not move forward to answer question 4. Many teachers and educators focus on the struggling students (who are the subject of question 3) and their deficits and work toward progress on district, state, or national tests. We often hear educators call students who are just below proficient *bubble students* and spend time and energy moving them to proficiency. This type of work and conversation often trumps the rich conversations that would otherwise take place around question 4.

However, we can't just ignore question 4 students. It is easy to assume that these learners will be fine and will adapt to whatever is given to them. This isn't the case. Experts share that students, when not challenged, will (1) get by and try not to bring attention to themselves (and not be intellectually challenged), (2) zone out and find a different activity to engage their brain (such as doodling), or (3) act out with behaviors that draw negative attention to them (Long, 2013).

Many might look at these three items and think that as long as the result isn't the third option, things will be fine. We are really short-changing students with this mentality, as studies show the great things that are possible when educators intentionally design instruction to respond to these students. Researchers at Vanderbilt University have been working on a fifty-year longitudinal study of students identified as gifted from 1972 to 1997 (Park, Lubinski, & Benbow, 2013). They have been conducting follow-up studies with the former students at various intervals to learn about how gifted education practices have impacted their lives. Gregory Park, David Lubinski, and Camilla P. Benbow (2013) find that the students in their cohorts have gone on to be top scholars, scientists and inventors, and leaders. One key finding from this study shows that pushing gifted learners by allowing grade skipping resulted in a 60 percent higher likelihood that the students would go on to earn doctorates or patents and be more than twice as likely to get a PhD in a STEM field (Park et al., 2013). The researchers also point out that while this does not happen in most schools, even modest interventions have a demonstrable effect (Clynes, 2016).

Park, Lubinski, and Benbow's (2013) study shows that question 4 students benefit when we determine how to meet their needs and implement the identified interventions. The problem is that school leaders and teachers in some PLCs often skip this question in their team meetings. Consider the following statements. Does this sound familiar?

> *If we are going to work together and be able to talk about what we are doing instructionally, it stands to reason that we should be on the same page with at least the standards that we will be teaching. From there, it also makes sense that, as long as we are teaching the same curriculum, we should have common assessments. For one, it will help us work smarter by not needing both of us to make separate tests if we are teaching the same content. This leads to a guaranteed viable curriculum. And, as long as we are giving the same tests, let's see how our kids are doing. This then generates wonderful discussion about what we see in all of our students' collective work. I could ask you great questions about how you are getting your results and vice versa. Then, let's take a look at what students struggled the most and have a conversation about how we can get them up to at least minimal proficiency.*

For many teams, this is where the process stops. We authors wanted to know why, so we asked participants at a PLC Institute, "Why is it so hard to get to critical question 4 in your collaborative team?" The answers ranged from time to priorities to a lack of resources explaining what to do with question 4. All three of these themes are understandable and predictable in many ways.

Time

In panel discussions at PLC Institutes, Rick and Becky DuFour have shared that a strong team needs a minimum of forty-five to sixty minutes of meeting time per week. The school's culture must support this need and keep this time sacred. This time goes by quickly, as it takes a great deal of time to have conversations around essential learnings, to develop common assessments, and to analyze data. Teachers report that after doing these items, they don't have time to talk about anything else. Elementary teachers have shared with us that if they had enough time after completing this process with one subject area, they would move on to the next. If reading is the focus, for example, any "extra" time would go toward conversations about mathematics. Use the reproducible "Collaborative Team Discussion: PLC Critical Questions" (page 16) to reflect on your team's current reality of time usage surrounding the critical questions and support collaborative conversations and learning in your collaborative team.

Unfortunately, this book will not be able to provide more time to teachers. Although we sure wish that it could, we have yet to work in a school or district where teachers have an amount of planning time that enables them to not have to stay late, work at home, or come back to school later in the evening to get their work done. We know this because we have also done it as teachers and administrators our entire work life. In order to address question 4 without the gift of additional time, we have to *make* the time during our collaborative meetings, even if it is a short amount. I saw one team make a team norm for the year of spending at least ten minutes per meeting on the needs of question 4 students. This small amount adds up over the course of the year. By sticking to this norm and acting on its growing list of ideas, before this team knew it, it was doing things for these learners that it never had before. In fact, the classroom examples we highlight throughout this book are activities that have occurred as a result of this type of collaborative work. Collaborative teams will need to make the time to include question 4 as part of their ongoing conversations.

Priorities

For many, collaborative teams look at their work with the critical questions as a hierarchical system. Question 1 leads to question 2 leads to question 3 leads to question 4. Question 4 gets assigned the last spot on the priority list for collaborative teams. Similar to this hierarchy, Parry Graham and Bill Ferriter (2008) outline the following seven stages that teams pass through in their development.

1. Filling the time

2. Sharing personal practice

3. Planning, planning, and planning

4. Developing common assessments

5. Analyzing student learning

6. Differentiating follow-up

7. Reflecting on instruction

In our considered opinion, stages six and seven require the dialogue necessary to arrive at critical question 4. If it takes teams time to pass through the prior stages, it is likely that new teams will not get to stages six and seven early in the school year. In our experience, when teams do get to these steps, their conversations are usually more centered on the interventions and not extension or acceleration. This is especially true if the school's culture does not expect or promote activities around question 4. To avoid this, throughout this book we offer a different way to look at the fourth question, and provide suggestions for how to prioritize it to ensure addressing it does not fall by the wayside. To really develop a plan for question 4 students, teams need to address and discuss question 4 at the same time that conversations begin around question 2, "How will we know if they learn it?" Not only should teams have the traditional conversations about assessments given after instruction, teams would also talk about preassessments prior to instruction.

Resources

Teachers also report that they don't know what to talk about with regard to question 4. If the resources aren't at hand and question 4 students are content to work on other things like reading a book or working on other homework assignments during down time, there is not an imminent need to change practice. In fact, we once had a teacher share with us that as long as the gifted students have something to work on, he didn't need to spend much time thinking about them; they kind of take care of themselves. Even if the student is considered proficient, this is not a scenario we should be proud of; we need to create systems where the needs of all learners are being addressed and commit to overcoming what prevents us from doing so. We don't want students to "kind of take care of themselves." We want to push, inspire, and intentionally stretch all students' learning. The reality is that there aren't a ton of great resources focused on question 4 students out there to help teams with this struggle. It is our hope that this book provides a wonderful entry point for this work.

Instructional Strategies

While resources on ways to shape school cultures and processes in a way that prioritizes responding to proficient students may be sparse, there are a plethora of individual instructional strategies available from various books, journals, and articles offering advice on how to work with the student who already knows the content. While the following list is not meant to be all-inclusive, it represents the five strategies we feel collaborative teams who are just beginning to work in this area will have immediate success with: (1) curriculum compacting, (2) flexible grouping, (3) product choice, (4) tiered assignments, and (5) multilevel learning stations.

Note that an argument could be made for how each could fit into a different personalized learning element. We will expand on these connections in chapter 3 (page 47). The great news is these are strategies teachers can begin employing in classrooms right away. We provide examples throughout the book showing what this implementation might look like in the classroom.

How to Use This Book

This book is for collaborative teams at all grade levels working in a PLC to better address the fourth critical question—How will we extend the learning for students who are already proficient?—through personalized learning to maximize student achievement and engagement. Implementing the five personalized learning elements may require a significant departure from some traditional methods. To that end, chapter 1 will focus on reframing some common beliefs readers may hold about curriculum guides or maps, the teacher's role in the classroom, and the nature of collaborative conversations. In chapter 2, we will provide a definition of personalized learning and a detailed explanation of how it meets the needs of high-ability and high-potential students. Chapter 3 will focus on five specific instructional strategies that work well for question 4 students. Chapters 4–8 will each examine one of the five elements of personalized learning and how it will serve your team in extending proficient students' learning and maximizing their achievement and engagement. Chapter 4 will consider how teachers can intentionally take steps to learn about these students and act on what they know. Chapter 5 will look at inviting, respecting, and considering student voice—their perspectives, opinions, and preferences—and offering students choice regarding the ways they engage in learning. Chapter 6 examines implementing flexibility in mindsets, grouping, and space. Chapter 7 considers how using student learning information can help teachers make decisions about learner growth related to an instructional standard. Chapter 8 explores how integrating technology tools and technology-based practices into daily classroom routines can support personalized learning. Finally, chapter 9 outlines specific detailed steps you can take to make PLC critical question 4 and the five elements of personalized learning a regular part of your collaborative team meetings and classroom practices.

Personalized Learning Stories

At the end of each of chapters 4–8, we provide classroom scenarios based on observations and interviews Mark and Blane conducted for this book, inspired by real teachers' classrooms across the United States in schools that have begun to implement personalized learning approaches. In these stories, we illustrate one elementary and one secondary example of a personalized learning element in action while also highlighting at least one of the five key instructional strategies for addressing question 4 students. These stories not only illustrate how a teacher might practically use personalized approaches to extend the learning for question 4 students but also show how this can realistically occur in a classroom where a teacher is simultaneously responding to *all* students' varied needs.

While we will focus on one main element in each classroom story, the reality is that to fully extend learning, all elements play a role, so you will see multiple elements being utilized throughout these stories. In fact, we believe that at least two elements need to be present to extend learning, personalize learning, and design engaging learning activities. The same can be said for the gifted instructional strategies. You may see a blend of various components, and that is OK. The important thing is that you are able to see practical examples of these strategies being implemented. As we authors have worked with educators to implement innovative ideas, one thing we have learned is how beneficial it can be to access specific examples to make the ideas more tangible. That is our intent with these stories, so we are hopeful that readers will be able to make connections between the stories and the work they do in schools.

While some of the examples we provide may seem advanced, be assured that these teachers did not begin teaching in this manner the first day they started. They tried a few activities and ideas, watched how students responded, made some tweaks, expanded some ideas for the next unit, and continually moved forward. That is exactly what we are asking you to do in your teams as well. Not only is it OK to start small, it is also recommended. Before diving in and ultimately trying these ideas in a lesson, an activity, or a unit, we suggest you and your team consider the sample steps to begin your work that we outline in chapter 9 (page 207).

Individual and Collaborative Team Reflections

This book is a hands-on guide and reflection journal you and your team should use while gaining knowledge of personalized learning and how it will help you and your team extend learning for students who have demonstrated competency with the instructional content. As a collaborative team working in a PLC focusing on your own learning, be prepared to engage in thoughtful and meaningful discussion after each chapter. As you read about each element, take time to answer the various questions and participate in the reflection opportunities. At various intervals throughout this book, you will be asked to individually reflect on readings from the text. When you get to these points, you will see the following image.

This will be your cue to stop and reflect on what you just read. At the end of each chapter, you will be asked to look back at what you individually reflected on and have a collaborative team discussion about your findings. For this type of reflection, you will see the following image.

This structure is intentional. The individual reflection allows you to internalize the content and honestly reflect on current practices. Individual reflection also allows for personal creative thinking that is specific to your students and thus most actionable. Additionally, learning is social. So, after you have the opportunity to internalize the content and creatively apply it to your students, the collaborative team discussion occurs in a safe, professional space where you can share your own thinking, receive feedback, and try new approaches with the support of your peers.

With this book, K–12 educators working in collaborative teams can engage in nine collaborative book study meetings. We offer the following sample collaborative team schedule (see table I.1), which you may choose to use in addition to your regular norms and ways of operating as a collaborative team.

Table I.1: Sample Collaborative Team Schedule

Collaborative Meeting	Topic	Items to Complete
Premeeting	Addressing critical question 4 of a PLC through personalized learning to extend learning for question 4 students	Prior to first meeting, read the introduction and chapter 1. Complete the reproducible "Individual Reflection: Teaching Approaches" (page 26) while reading.
1	Review of introduction and chapter 1	Discuss individual reflections and complete collaborative team discussion. Assign chapter 2.
2	Review of chapter 2	Discuss individual reflections and complete collaborative team discussion. Assign chapter 3.
3	Review of chapter 3	Discuss individual reflections and complete collaborative team discussion. Assign chapter 4.
4	Review of chapter 4	Discuss individual reflections and complete collaborative team discussion. Assign chapter 5.
5	Review of chapter 5	Discuss individual reflections and complete collaborative team discussion. Assign chapter 6.
6	Review of chapter 6	Discuss individual reflections and complete collaborative team discussion. Assign chapter 7.
7	Review of chapter 7	Discuss individual reflections and complete collaborative team discussion. Assign chapter 8.
8	Review of chapter 8	Discuss individual reflections and complete collaborative team discussion.
9 and ongoing	Developing plan for implementation	Begin implementation and plan for ongoing use of collaborative time for addressing PLC critical question 4 through personalized learning to extend learning for students who are already proficient.

Please note that we are not suggesting each topic will take up an entire meeting. We wrote this book to support readers in making individual connections and reflections before meeting with the full team. We encourage you and your team to be thorough and complete this work, but to do so in an efficient manner that does not take away from the other important work you do in your teams. As with all teams, we know time is always a factor.

One Final Thought

We authors hope to spark a movement in all districts, schools, and individual classrooms throughout North America, in which conversations about engagement, extension, building on learner strengths, and pursuing all learners' interests are standard. When engaging in this work, it will be important to have a common vocabulary with your collaborative team members as you move forward in your own learning. From time to time, you may need to pause and review the foundation for this work. As you reflect on what you know about PLCs and collaborative teams and learn more about personalized learning and strategies for teaching question 4 students in the upcoming chapters, we offer a quick cheat sheet for remembering key concepts connected in this book. Everything in this book centers around the following.

- **One** goal:
    1. Extending learning for question 4 students to maximize their achievement and engagement

- **Two** key philosophies:
    1. Professional learning communities
    2. Personalized learning

- The **three** big ideas of a PLC:
    1. A focus on learning
    2. A collaborative culture and collective responsibility
    3. A results orientation

- The **four** critical questions of a PLC:
    1. What do we want all students to know and be able to do?
    2. How will we know if they learn it?
    3. How will we respond when some students do not learn?
    4. How will we extend the learning for students who are already proficient?

- The **five** elements of personalized learning:
    1. Knowing your learners
    2. Allowing voice and choice
    3. Implementing flexibility

      4. Using data

      5. Integrating technology

- The **five** instructional strategies for question 4 students:

      1. Curriculum compacting

      2. Flexible grouping

      3. Product choice

      4. Tiered assignments

      5. Multilevel learning stations

Being clear on these items will keep you grounded while you work toward addressing critical question 4 of a PLC through personalized learning.

Collaborative Team Discussion: PLC Critical Questions

Without exceeding 100 percent for the four critical questions, what percentage of your team's time do you spend in each of the following areas (DuFour et al., 2016)?

1. What do we want all students to know and be able to do?

2. How will we know if they learn it?

3. How will we respond when some students do not learn?

4. How will we extend the learning for students who are already proficient?

What was your highest number?

What was your lowest number?

What surprised you?

What percentage did you place for question 4?

CHAPTER 1

Reframing

I t is human nature to integrate new information into existing mental models (Senge, 2000). Our personal experiences as students, our teacher preparation and experiences, and the test-driven memories of our most recent history all influence our consumption of new information. However, piling new on old doesn't allow our minds fresh thinking opportunities. Instead, adding new to old simply adds more quantity to the boundaries and parameters of our original learning that already confines us. Thus, for the subject at hand, we offer the following mental models to reframe your thinking to prepare you to engage with the personalized learning ideas and accompanying strategies we will discuss in this book.

For us, the path to personalizing learning required us to reframe our thinking around three areas: (1) curriculum maps, (2) the role of the teacher, and (3) collaborative conversations. In this chapter, we will look at each of these areas and discuss how reframing them enables us to extend learning for students who have demonstrated proficiency with the instructional content. You may have already been thinking of these items in ways that resemble what we describe in our reframing; we are not suggesting everyone reading this book will need to change their thinking or that we are offering thoughts others have never considered. If you read one reframing idea and you are already doing it, you can enjoy knowing you'll need to expend less mental energy on that idea and move to the next.

Reframing Curriculum Guides or Maps

Many of us remember our first days of teaching and entering our first classroom or new teacher induction program with wide eyes, eagerly anticipating direction on what we would be expected to teach students. The three authors of this book all had very different experiences in their first roles, and we suspect that everyone reading this book can relate to one of the three. One had a very detailed curriculum map and pacing guide that teachers were expected to follow in great detail. Another was handed a one-page document and the district-approved textbook for the course. He found that the one-page curriculum document was simply a list of the chapters in the book and was told to teach it however he saw fit. The third was given a detailed curriculum map and pacing guide but was informed that this was just a guide and that he had plenty of freedom to make it work for him. Three brand-new teachers, three different guidelines, and three different sets of expectations.

We propose that you and your collaborative team have a conversation and add those to whom you report in order to gauge where your school or district falls within these three scenarios—or perhaps there are other scenarios we haven't considered here. Your collaborative structure and curriculum expectations are unique to you. Before you continue, please review your curriculum map and any school or district non-negotiables that could impact your classroom actions.

In many school districts, we have seen very specific curriculum maps that lay a foundation for a guaranteed and viable curriculum. A *guaranteed and viable curriculum* ensures that every student, regardless of the teacher, principal, or school he or she is assigned to, has the same opportunity to learn from a highly effective teacher because schools set the systems in place to ensure this occurs. This includes determining the most important standards to be taught across grade levels and courses that are tied to an established and aligned assessment plan (Marzano, 2003).

The research is clear about the importance of a guaranteed and viable curriculum, and personalization is not intended to distract from it. Institute for Personalized Learning senior advisor and personalized learning author Jim Rickabaugh refers to this and other non-negotiable items as "load-bearing walls" (J. Rickabaugh, personal communication, September 21, 2016). To do this work, you need to identify the non-negotiable walls (standards, indicators, district assessments) and those you have the ability to alter (small-group work, intervention and extension time). Interestingly, load-bearing walls in one district or school can look different from those in another. In fact, our research for this book finds that tolerance for personalized learning looks very different from one building to the next. We want to make sure you are fully aware of your circumstances as you begin this work. Identify the most flexible places, or non-load-bearing walls, in your curriculum map and instructional model (see figure 1.1).

	Load-Bearing Walls in Our District or School	Non-Load-Bearing Walls in Our District or School
Individual Reflection		

Figure 1.1: Identifying load-bearing walls.

*Visit **go.SolutionTree.com/PLCbooks** for a free reproducible version of this figure.*

In one district, we reviewed a language arts map, which included standards, indicators, suggested materials and resources, common assessments, and pacing available for all teachers. Within the eighty-six-minute block, there were items recommended for the whole group which may take fifteen to twenty-five minutes per day and would not be considered as prime for personalization. The rest of the allotted time had room and flexibility for personalization. In this example, there was a great deal of time for personalization, while also providing guardrails for what is required and non-negotiable. In another school, this one a gifted focus school, teams found that extended learning for students needed to be built around the district-mandated and time-sensitive common standards and assessments that occurred after each four- to six-week unit of instruction. Around this load-bearing wall, the school could build its teaching strategies that would best suit the many question 4 students in an innovative way that worked for them.

The last thing we want is for readers of this book to be in a position where they have to defend the use of personalization. We contend that by being very clear about load-bearing walls with others in your environment, your success at implementation will be far more likely. Consider the guaranteed and viable curriculum, required assessments, school and district tolerance for trying new things, and other mandatory components to your position when identifying load-bearing walls.

Reframing the Teacher's Role

For some, the teacher's role may be the most difficult area of reframing we discuss in this chapter. It seems everything we have been taught in our profession has put us, as educators, at the center of the learning process. We think back to our own formal teacher education training and reflect on the phrase we heard repeatedly, which was intended to be a guide for how we—as teachers—should develop lessons: *from sage on the stage to guide on the side* (King, 1993).

Alison King (1993) uses this phrase to challenge college professors to instruct differently. In her article, King (1993) states that the day and age of the instructor being the sole source of knowledge and pouring information into the empty vessel of the learner is no longer effective. She then provides specific examples of how educators should change to being the ones who facilitate, orchestrate, ask questions, and provide resources in order for the learners to think up their own answers (King, 1993).

Sometimes, when we authors were new teachers, we felt guilty when the class was engaged in learning but we were not specifically lecturing or at the front of the class and leading the lesson. We privately wondered if this was cheating. However, with this "guide on the side" way of thinking, not only was it acceptable but it was also encouraged. We should intentionally and deliberately think about ways to promote active learning and facilitate activities such as think-pair-sharing, generating examples, developing scenarios, concept mapping, flowcharting, predicting, and developing critiques.

While we still support the "guide on the side" thinking, personalized learning adds yet another wrinkle. Many of these activities to promote active learning that we have mentioned are still very teacher driven and developed, even when the teacher is not lecturing from the front of the classroom. Rickabaugh (personal communication, September 21, 2016) describes the next shift and transformation in learning: "Don't just be the sage on the stage or the guide on the side, be the mentor in the middle."

We love this quote as it relates to personalized learning. First, we appreciate the use of the words *don't just*. What that tells us is there is a time to be the sage on the stage and a time to be the guide on the side, but don't be *just* that. Also be the mentor in the middle. It reminds us that in a personalized learning environment, it isn't always going to be one way or the other. There will be times when it is most appropriate for a teacher to stand up and be the sage on the stage. When students are misusing potentially dangerous equipment, for example, we want the teacher to provide very specific knowledge and content for safety's sake. We don't want our students to learn in a self-directed way. There will be other times when being the guide on the side is the most appropriate. For example, if the standard calls for using mathematical representations of Newton's law of universal gravitation and Coulomb's law to describe and predict the gravitational and electrostatic forces between objects, the classroom activities may look more facilitated than personalized. Most students aren't going to know this on the first day of class. However, if this teacher has students in class who, for some reason, are well familiar with these laws and can prove this understanding on a preassessment, the teacher could allow these students to conduct an experiment they find interesting that proves the laws to be true. Or perhaps a team of students work together to develop a video clip of movie scenes that demonstrate Newton's laws that they could later share with the class.

Rickabaugh's quote also reminds us that when you aren't *just* being a sage or a guide, you are stretching yourself to do more. To be the mentor in the middle, you are taking on a very different role. Mentors, by nature, are experienced and trusted advisors who support mentees on their personal journeys. When we authors think of our own mentors, our relationships with them started with the mentors being good listeners and co-developers of the necessary actions and steps to meet our goals. To us, this role is much different from guiding or facilitating because it makes it personal, which is what all learning is.

Being the mentor in the middle can be a little uncomfortable. As the teacher, you are letting go of some of the responsibility and shifting it to the learners. If you are starting to fidget a little bit while reading this book, remember this is why we are discussing mentoring in the context of *reframing*, and we are advising you to start slow. We think the following example helps illustrate the mentor in the middle, as this teacher was literally in the middle of the classroom as students worked on the perimeter and he gave immediate feedback to support their work.

A fifth-grade science teacher shared that, for the most part, before he began using personalized learning, every day he arranged students in neat rows. Because he taught the one elementary grade level in which students are assessed on the state test in a three-year band, he felt a great deal of responsibility to make sure the students not only were proficient at what they learned in fifth grade but also remembered what they had learned in the previous grade levels. At the start of each class, he followed a pretty familiar pattern for his lessons. He wrote the objectives of the lesson on the board, and students would start with a short quiz on the previous night's reading assignment. He would lead a lecture or discussion, and an activity with some sort of hands-on feature would follow. Last, he grouped students in teams and assigned a sort of review game for them to play, which would include items from third and fourth grade that might be on the state test. When asked what students would do if they already knew the material, he shared that they could always pick up one or two new ideas in class that they hadn't considered before.

However, after this teacher made a commitment to extend learning for question 4 students, the classroom looked very different. When the students entered the room, this teacher asked them to complete a short preassessment that gave students three leveled options for responding to a question on the topic the class would be exploring. Students could read over the three choices and complete the task they felt most comfortable answering. The teacher jokingly called it "a poor man's adaptive test." Based on students' level choice and the accuracy of their responses, the teacher could identify the question 4 students for the upcoming learning target and extend their learning. The teacher would meet with these students and have a collaborative discussion about the extended tasks that the students could do around the topic. Then, after whole-group instruction each day, the students worked on the project they decided on as a group.

What we love most about this activity is the willingness of the teacher to be vulnerable—to take a risk to engage students so they might own their learning. This teacher will tell you that the mood, environment, and energy levels far outweighed those when teaching the same standards just one year prior for both the students who already knew it *and* the students who did not. Students who already knew it owned their learning, wanted to learn, and were more confident while working at their own pace. Students who didn't know it yet had more teacher attention and could shine while answering the questions and leading the small-group activities. Classroom duties and leadership roles were redistributed.

Reframing Collaborative Conversations

When we think about the ways that we have known teachers to approach teaching question 4 learners, we consider their various options for strategies on a type of continuum ranging from the least amount of energy for the classroom teacher on one end to the most amount of energy that exceeds the normal routine of a typical classroom on the other.

The strategy that has the least effect on the classroom teacher is, of course, to do nothing additional. Teachers stick to the course guides and scope and sequence and vertical alignment documents they have developed for the entire class and apply these with all students. We do not promote the idea of plan, instruct, assess, and move on to the next unit and allow the student who already knows it to be a part of the regular class. The research we share in this book suggests that this method can actually have adverse effects on students (Long, 2013).

The next options on the continuum involve pull-out services provided by trained gifted education teachers. During this pull-out, these teachers stretch students' learning in ways that engage and challenge students. Slightly further along on the continuum, we find similar strategies to the pull-out strategies, but with the gifted staff coming into the existing classroom during scheduled times.

Moving along on the continuum, the next options involve more energy and planning on the part of teachers. They consider those students who have been identified as gifted using approved district measures throughout the course of a given unit. In this arrangement, for example, all students receive an assignment to work on after the whole-class instruction. The few gifted students might be asked to meet the teacher at the front of the room and are then challenged to take the assignment further or do more in the time that other students are engaged in the original activity.

Finally, options toward the far right of the continuum, which include using data, are less common but are the ones we most advocate using. To begin moving further along on the continuum and implementing more robust options for responding to question 4 students, teams will need to reconsider what they discuss during collaborative conversations. Teams should also consider what "already proficient" means to them. Does it refer to students who show proficiency after a common formative assessment? Or does it refer to students who already know the material before you begin instruction? To us, these two topics have major differences and need to be considered by all teams.

How teams define proficiency will require additional adjustments to collaborative conversations that they may not be accustomed to. For example, if a team identifies students as proficient based on performance on a common formative assessment, the collaborative team really needs to make certain that its learning plans and pacing guides include flexibility to respond to these students. The team would need to have conversations around developing specific, additional lessons that meet the needs of students at regular intervals that would take place after each common formative assessment. Realize, however, the drawback with this approach is that the students who knew the material when they walked in the door would have still been involved in the same instruction as all of the students in the room up until this formative assessment occurred, even if they already knew the information. In addition, based on the most typical concern we hear from teachers, we know time is of the essence. It can be difficult to identify a time in the school day to allow for this type of teaching following a common formative assessment but before beginning teaching the next set of content. These are issues a collaborative team will need to discuss and decide how to respond to.

If teams identify students as proficient before beginning instruction, they'll need to decide what criteria to use to determine this proficiency. Without some sort of preassessment, question 4 students would still be a part of the traditional instruction of every student in the room at least until a teacher gives and reviews a formative assessment to determine who does and does not know the material. If teams define already knowing it in the context of *before* the lesson, they need to have conversations to create measures and procedures to learn what understandings and abilities students have *before* instruction occurs.

In our personal experiences and in reading the work of the experts in gifted education, there are various ways to go about this task. This includes using information that you have learned about the students from work in the class in a previous unit or assessment, offering an opportunity to complete a project, and, probably the most common, providing a preassessment (as we described in the example of the fifth-grade teacher in the preceding section, Reframing the Teacher's Role [page 20]). The preassessment doesn't have to be long or look exactly like the final test that students will be completing at the end of the unit; it needs to be something that informs the teacher about how this student will have his or her time best utilized over the course of the unit.

A shift to offering a preassessment and then thinking about the various options for differentiating the instructional activities may pose a need for some teams to reframe their processes, procedures, and the way they think when they have conversations about how to logistically use and respond to preassessments within their workflow. Regardless of where your team falls on the continuum, you need to know what you are going to do with question 4 students *before* you begin instruction, so you must reframe your collaborative conversations to address this.

For teams who have not previously considered preassessments, this will likely create a wrinkle in what you are used to your agendas and team meetings looking like. To help make a smoother transition to this shift in the way team conversations are framed, we offer some questions for teams to discuss: How do we make sure that the needs of all students are met, which means determining who already knows the material? How do we, as a team, want to preassess students? As a result of this preassessment, how do we plan to personalize learning? While incorporating these instructional strategies, how will grading be impacted? Collectively answering these questions prior to the start of a given unit will provide teams with an intentional and deliberate approach to addressing question 4 with a small reframing of their collaborative team time.

We suggest teams also consider deciding to change their typical agendas to discuss question 4 along with question 2. Many teams we have worked with assume they must follow the four questions in chronological order in their collaborative meetings, which is likely one reason question 4 is often omitted. By the time many teams get to question 4, it is too late. By reframing their conversation structures to discuss these two questions concurrently, teams will be equipped to address this item. We think this will serve as a reminder to teams that if you are truly going to do something for question 4 students, it must be considered at the start of the ongoing cyclical process of a collaborative team.

Next Steps

As you continue reading this book, consider how you and your collaborative team will make a shift toward moving within your load-bearing walls, being this mentor in the middle, while reframing how you think about the curriculum and the teacher's role, as well as how you discuss and develop ways to respond to question 4 students as a collaborative team. Before you move on to the next chapter, use the reproducible "Individual Reflection: Teaching Approaches" (page 26) to reflect on your individual approach to the teacher's role. Then, as a collaborative team, use the reproducible "Collaborative Team Discussion: Reframing" (page 27) to reflect on your team's current reality and support collaborative conversations and learning in your collaborative team.

Individual Reflection: Teaching Approaches

Rank the following three phrases from first to third in terms of how comfortable you are when instructing your learners.

_____ Guide on the side

_____ Sage on the stage

_____ Mentor in the middle

Did your ranking surprise you? Why or why not?

Collaborative Team Discussion: Reframing

As a team, use your individual work to develop a master list of load-bearing and non-load-bearing walls for your collaborative team.

	Load-Bearing Walls in Our District or School	Non-Load-Bearing Walls in Our District or School
Collaborative Team Reflection		

Collectively, when looking at the following three phrases, how did your individual rankings compare to your team's? How did your rankings reflect your teacher education programs, schools you have worked in, and personal backgrounds?

Guide on the side:

Sage on the stage:

Mentor in the middle:

CHAPTER 2

Personalized Learning

Educators are beginning to use the term *personalized learning* more and more frequently. In fact, our colleagues note it is not uncommon to see a reference to personalized learning in district strategic plans, journal articles, and books. As we have worked with and for school districts that have implemented approaches that deliberately put students at the center of learning and intentionally plan for how they will respond to proficient students, we have seen engagement and achievement flourish. Teachers and administrators who have embraced concepts such as personalized learning, Genius Hour, and schoolwide enrichment have an advantage in addressing PLC critical question 4 because they have had practice in using these methods that are beneficial to question 4 students' extension. Therefore, we believe the five elements of personalized learning serve as a wonderful foundation for framing how your collaborative team addresses question 4. In this chapter, we will clarify the concept of personalized learning by defining the term, address misconceptions, outline the five elements we identify as comprising this approach to teaching and learning, and discuss the research and realities that support using this approach in your classrooms and schools.

Definition of Personalized Learning

Personalized learning can mean many different things to many different people. Is it a free-for-all where students come in and do whatever they want? Is it using a series of packets that students complete one after another? Is it a personal learning plan? Is it offering classes online with 24-7 access? A grandparent at a community forum we attended may have summed up the confusion best when she asked, "If my grandson wants to learn about clowns all day, can he just do that and forget about math?" To her, personalized learning sounded loose and unstructured, with little direction, and not tied to the standards and indicators of the content being taught. We can assure you that this is not the type of personalized learning we espouse.

Take a moment before you read any further in this chapter to reflect on what your definition is for *personalized learning* (and, please, leave out any references to clowns). When you reconvene with your collaborative team, share your definitions. In what ways are your definitions similar or different?

INDIVIDUAL REFLECTION

Without reading any further in this chapter, how do you define *personalized learning*?

If you struggle with a definition, you are in good company. In fact, EdSurge columnist Alex Hernandez (2016) writes that personalized learning is so difficult to pin down, perhaps we should stop trying to develop a definition. We, however, would argue that developing a common vocabulary and set of elements has truly been the key to our growth in this area.

Also, if yours is like other teams, your conversations may reflect a difficulty in determining the difference between traditional differentiation, individualized learning, and personalized learning. Personalize Learning, LLC, founders Barbara Bray and Kathleen McClaskey (2015) offer a wonderful chart and exercise in their book *Make Learning Personal: The What, Who, WOW, Where, and Why* (see table 2.1). They (Bray & McClaskey, 2015) break down the differences between differentiation, individualized learning, and personalized learning into ten categories.

Individualized instruction is what takes place when the teacher provides accommodations and customization to the individual learner. Even when individualization takes place with technology in an anytime, anyplace format, it is still the teacher who assigns the tasks (Kallick & Zmuda, 2017). *Differentiated instruction* is what takes place when the teacher provides accommodations and customization to groups of learners. Again, the teacher still assigns the tasks. *Personalized learning* is what happens when the teacher provides groups and individuals with accommodations and customization but the learners help drive their own learning.

Table 2.1: Differentiation Versus Individualization Versus Personalization Chart

Differentiation	Individualization	Personalization
The Teacher . . .	The Teacher . . .	The Learner . . .
Provides instruction to groups of learners	Provides instruction to an individual learner	Drives his or her own learning
Adjusts to learning needs for groups of learners	Accommodates learning needs of the individual learner	Connects learning with his or her interests, talents, passions, and aspirations
Designs instruction based on the learning needs of different groups of learners	Customizes instruction based on the learning needs of the individual learner	Actively participates in the design of his or her learning
Is responsible for a variety of instruction for different groups of learners	Is responsible for modifying instruction based on the needs of the individual learner	Owns and is responsible for his or her learning that includes voice and choice on how and what he or she learns
Identifies the same objectives for different groups of learners as he or she does for the whole class	Identifies the same objectives for all learners with specific objectives for each individual who receives one-to-one support	Identifies goals for his or her learning plan and benchmarks as he or she progresses along his or her learning path with guidance from teachers
Selects technology and resources to support the learning needs of different groups of learners	Selects technology and resources to support the learning needs of the individual learner	Acquires the skills to select and use the appropriate technology and resources to support and enhance his or her learning
Supports groups of learners reliant on him or her for the learning	Understands the individual learner is dependent on him or her to support the learning	Builds a network of peers, experts, and teachers to guide and support his or her learning
Monitors learning based on the Carnegie unit (seat time) and grade level	Monitors learning based on the Carnegie unit (seat time) and grade level	Demonstrates his or her mastery of content in a competency-based system
Uses data and assessments to modify instruction for groups of learners and provides feedback to individual learners to advance learning	Uses data and assessments to measure progress of what the individual learner learned and did not learn to decide next steps in the learning	Becomes a self-directed expert learner who monitors progress and reflects on learning based on his or her mastery of content and skills
Uses assessment of and for learning	Uses assessment of learning	Uses assessment as and for learning with minimal assessment of learning

Source: Adapted from Bray & McClaskey, 2015, pp. 9–10.

Even though this chart (see table 2.1) highlights differences, we should note that these three concepts are deeply connected. Carol Ann Tomlinson (2017), *the* guru on differentiated instruction, refers to personalized learning as a type of differentiated instruction. Andrew Easton (2016), a teacher who works for a midwestern school district as a personalized learning collaborator, offers an interesting perspective on the relationship between these three key themes. He explains that personalized learning is differentiated *and* individualized instruction on steroids (Easton, 2016).

The key distinction between personalized learning versus differentiation and individualization is students have voice and choice in what they are learning. To us, the linchpin of personalized learning is *voice and choice* (one of the five elements we discuss in the next section) and how teachers use it in conjunction with the other elements. That being said, our definition of *personalized learning* is this: an instructional approach designed to nurture learners to discover and broaden the ways in which they learn best so that they become independent learners committed to their learning by encouraging student choice, voice, and interests to master the highest standards possible in a relational environment.

A Misunderstood Concept

As we've noted, *personalized learning* can mean many different things to many different people. While there is a great deal of momentum around personalized learning, Benjamin Herold (2017) explores in an *EdWeek* article three main critiques educators and policy makers have expressed regarding this learning philosophy: (1) the hype outweighs the research, (2) personalized learning is bad for teachers and students, and (3) big tech + big data = big problems. We'd like to offer our perspective on the points this article raises.

The hype outweighs the research. Some educators are unreceptive to personalized learning because there is not a definitive set of research to demonstrate its effectiveness. While the RAND Corporation has done some research in this area, it has not developed studies to cite conclusive evidence. Also, this topic becomes hard to study because the term *personalized learning* means different things to different people.

While there is not a definitive set of research on this topic, Herold (2017) highlights that there is a great deal of research that supports the fundamentals of personalized learning, which include giving students control over their own learning, differentiating instruction for each student, and providing real-time feedback.

Personalized learning is bad for teachers and students. Many educators are under the impression personalized learning is really just putting learning on the computer where tasks are broken down into smaller segments and students quietly proceed through a program until they reach completion at their own pace. They are concerned that if this is what personalized learning is, it does not offer an inspiring education experience. Herold (2017) notes that until personalized learning can figure out "the appropriate role for software in the classroom, how much autonomy is best for student learning, and the challenge of maintaining high standards and social interaction when every student is pursuing his or her own path," these concerns will remain high.

We agree that personalized learning is an often misunderstood topic. The difficult thing is that one person might feel it *is* a computer program that students work through at their own pace and another feels it is a way of thinking when designing classrooms, activities, or units in a way that works in parallel with the teacher, and they are both correct. There is not one universally agreed-on definition. However, to us, personalized learning is the latter of these two conceptualizations. It is teachers philosophically and collaboratively developing instructional strategies that incorporate concepts such as knowing your learner, allowing voice and choice, providing flexibility, using data, and integrating technology. Personalized learning is not, to us, students working on a computer program on their own in the corner of the classroom.

Big tech + big data = big problems. To some, personalized learning means a large emphasis on data hardware and software, which involves technology companies. For example, Mark and Chan Zuckerberg have pledged to invest millions of dollars into the initiative. With this type of involvement, Herold (2017) notes there are concerns about sacrificing student privacy and asks, if students are entering detailed information about their thoughts, preferences, hopes, and fears, is that something we are OK with? Herold (2017) also raises the question of whether it is appropriate to have formulas and algorithms to determine what students are learning.

Big data and algorithms are not a part of any conversation regarding the personalized learning that we promote in this book or the schools and districts we highlight throughout this book that are using this approach. It is a philosophy and way of thinking for classroom teachers and is not intended to replace the teacher in any way.

It is important to note when studying personalized learning that there are many misconceptions and misunderstandings around this topic. In the following sections, we will describe in detail our view of this concept to ensure that all readers understand *personalized learning* as we envision and intend it.

The Five Elements of Personalized Learning

While working with groups of teachers implementing personalized learning, we reached a key turning point when we broke down the definition and understanding into smaller parts we call the five elements of personalized learning. These elements serve as the framework for the subsequent chapters in this book.

1. Knowing your learners

2. Allowing voice and choice

3. Implementing flexibility

4. Using data

5. Integrating technology

It is important to note that implementing one of these elements in isolation is not personalized learning. Typically, it takes combinations of the elements to come together to create personalized learning. Grouping students or rearranging furniture does not make a lesson personalized; however, it might be if you discover where students are in their learning with a preassessment and then establish opportunities for voice and choice by offering tiered learning activities to meet the learner at his or her level based on how he or she performed.

Teachers working in collaborative teams will be able to better address critical question 4 if they make it a regular part of their time together and frame their critical question 4 conversations around the five elements of personalized learning. In most cases, question 4 students have likely proven through various traditional methods that they are ready for extension by their performance in class. When this occurs, customization for the individual learner is just a natural fit as their learning needs to move beyond what the teacher intended and planned for every student. Personalized learning provides the framework and discussion starters for teams looking to determine what to do for this type of learner. It further encourages a classroom culture in which students are encouraged to stretch their learning, ingraining in students what Carol Dweck (2006) refers to as a *growth mindset*—a belief in the idea that intelligence can be developed rather than simply inherited. This philosophy and type of thinking goes beyond asking students to read quietly, help a struggling student, or just hang out while others get caught up. Personalized learning (and its five elements) is a wonderful tool to ensure question 4 students in every grade band from kindergarten through senior year are successfully extending their learning beyond the learning targets.

The Case for Personalized Learning

When leading conversations about why we advocate for personalized learning and its connection to question 4, we enjoy starting with a simple activity in which we ask participants to recall a time when they, as teachers, had students who were totally tuned out and unengaged with a lesson because they already knew the content, and a time when a student was ecstatic about and very engaged in what he or she was learning because the teacher respected what the student knew about the subject matter. For example, one author, Mark, remembers his first year of teaching eighth-grade American history. As perhaps many first-year teachers would, he wanted to follow the rules and be seen as a good teacher. Many of his units were geared around discussions and lecture about the textbook readings, which would typically be followed up with some sort of activity or simulation, and conclude with a type of assessment. There was one student who was an American Civil War enthusiast. When it came time for the units and activities around this topic, Mark didn't quite know what to do with him. He would routinely interrupt the classroom conversations to share cool and interesting facts and bring in various artifacts he had collected. While the student was able to share his excitement and knowledge in some ways, there is no doubt that he was bored or at least not given an opportunity to shine or extend his learning. Looking back, we authors realize offering personalized learning opportunities based on the elements and strategies we feature in this book would have been far more valuable for this one student.

INDIVIDUAL REFLECTION

Think of a time when, as a teacher, a student you were working with was tuned out and unengaged with a lesson because he or she already knew the content.

We would argue that, like many question 4 students, Mark's student played along with what the rest of the class was doing even though he personally didn't get much out of it. He could have been far more engaged if his teacher had worked with a collaborative team that intentionally and deliberately planned for ways for him to extend his learning since he already knew the content. Perhaps this student could have presented on a certain battle or chosen an independent project to work on and develop over the three-week unit.

Conversely, we recall an example of heightened engagement when Mark was working with his son, who was learning about force and motion in his fourth-grade classroom. He had previously passed the classroom assessment, which covered the material during whole-group instruction. Not needing additional direct instruction, his son had the opportunity to extend his learning with an activity that was very similar to one done by sophomores in that district's high school. The son brought home a balloon and said that by the end of the week, he needed to use household items to make a vehicle, and students would win prizes for the vehicles that went the farthest distance. The balloon would ultimately serve as the one energy source that would provide propulsion to the vehicle that he would be creating. For three days, the author watched his son perform various trial-and-error activities to get things just right. After using just the right aerodynamic box, pencils to serve as axles, and old CDs as wheels, the son proudly obtained a third-place finish out of about one hundred fourth graders who completed the activity. The boy profoundly commented, "I was just really proud of myself. I don't know why. I want to do more of that kind of thing." Interestingly, the next day, his kindergarten-age brother saw the excitement and energy in his older sibling and was busy making his own vehicle out of household items. Mark's son was given an opportunity to show that he knew the material (which involves personalized learning elements of knowing learners and using data), was allowed to extend his learning, was given voice and choice in how he wanted to construct his vehicle (which involves voice and choice), used technology to generate ideas (which involves integrated technology), exercised a growth mindset as he went about multiple trial and errors to make sure his creation would be competitive (which involves flexibility), and got to share his final product in a competitive environment. If we can provide personalized learning opportunities like these to question 4 students, everyone wins.

INDIVIDUAL REFLECTION

Think of a time when a student you, as a teacher, were working with was excited and engaged with the content because he or she was allowed to extend his or her learning.

It's likely that student you thought of in the preceding individual reflection was one who, when he or she was engaged, just worked—not because the student had to, but because he or she wanted to—and time passed quickly for the student. Learning didn't just happen to this student; he or she took command of it. This is what researcher Mihaly Csikszentmihalyi (2008) calls *flow*. Csikszentmihalyi (2008) finds that our best moments occur when we are completely absorbed in an activity, particularly when those activities help us explore our creativity. *Flow* describes that feeling people get when they are totally locked into a task and make progress with what feels like effortless movement (Csikszentmihalyi, 2008).

As educators, we know what *flow* is, but it is a challenge to get to it. Using the five elements of personalized learning and making them a regular part of collaborative team discussions is a wonderful way to intentionally and deliberately create opportunities for students to be more engaged and extend their learning. In our experience, question 4 students who aren't being challenged or given additional opportunities typically just play along to just get by with minimal effort, or find something else to keep their mind occupied. As educators, we would never allow this with struggling students. It is our job as professional educators to give all students an intentional and engaging learning plan.

With any change in an organization, it is important to start with the *why* (TEDx Talks, 2009). Along with our personal experiences of being engaged and unengaged, the reality that no student is average, the technology- and personalization-rich era in which today's learners have been raised, the ways in which emotions impact learning, and the connections of personalized learning to deep research help make a strong case for why we advocate for personalized learning as a tool to extend learning.

The Myth of Average

The myth of average presents a compelling case for personalized learning. In a 2013 TED Talk, Todd Rose, a Harvard professor and former high school dropout, describes the design principles that guided the work of the U.S. Air Force in the early 1950s (TEDx Talks, 2013). The Air Force used fighter jets with cockpits made for the *average* pilot from the year 1926. Thinking that perhaps pilots were just bigger than they used to be, it was determined that new specifications for planes would be needed, based on ten different physical traits. Air Force researchers, at a base in Ohio, measured thousands of pilots to find this new average. In the end, not one of the 4,063 pilots was average in all ten categories. This finding transformed the way the Air Force began to builds jets (Rose, 2016).

The pilots might have been above average in some areas, average in others, and below in still others, so the manufacturers had developed jets for literally nobody. In a bold move, the Air Force called for companies who built planes to no longer build for the *average* but to *design to the edges*, which called for designing planes that could be personalized for pilots, so pilots of various sizes could fly (TEDx Talks, 2013). Because of the new cockpits, pilots were more successful and the pool for pilots expanded. Rose's (TEDx Talks, 2013) presentation gets to the point:

when you design for the average, you design for no one. Rose (TEDx Talks, 2013) then connects this story to education, noting that classrooms are the "cockpits of our economy."

Often in education, we plan our instructional activities around what we consider to be the average. Teachers we know have shared with us that, realistically, in typical learning and lesson plan creation, whether alone or as a collaborative team, conversations center around average students who have struggled to learn the material. Hardly any mention is given to the question 4 student. When we plan in this way, we are not really planning for anyone. To further illustrate the myth of average, use the tool in figure 2.1 to rate your aptitude on several characteristics educators tend to value in students.

Individually, reflect on how you would rate yourself in each of the following categories, with a score of 1 being very low and 5 being excellent.

	1	2	3	4	5
Memory					
Language					
Knowledge					
Reading					
Vocabulary					
Curiosity					
Perception					
Cognition					
Interests					

Now, add up your columns and divide by 9. What is your average?

How many items did you rate yourself as average (3)?

Figure 2.1: Personal rating exercise.

*Visit **go.SolutionTree.com/PLCbooks** for a free reproducible version of this figure.*

When we do this activity with groups of educators, it is interesting to see that those who consider themselves to be average are, like the pilots, not average in many areas. For those with an average overall score, it is not uncommon to see only one or two individual areas that actually represent the average. Our students are no different. So, like Rose (TEDx Talks, 2013) suggests, when we plan for the average or the middle, we are not serving the needs of anyone. Personalized learning is a wonderful way to consider *designing to the edges*.

Our Students' Immersion in Technology

As of 2018, all K–12 educators teach students born after the year 2000. What are some personal characteristics you believe to be true about students today that are different from when you were a student?

The students of this generation have much different backgrounds and upbringings than many of the people reading this book. First, because these students have always had access to technology that quickly responds to their needs, they have had their entire lives personalized; they have been able to access anything they want at a moment's notice in the way they want. A colleague of ours has a daughter with a 1998 birthday who is a college freshman. His daughter was born the year Google became available for public use. Students in college have literally not been alive for a day when they couldn't just google the answer to a question. In fact, many young adults live their entire lives through social media; it didn't happen if it wasn't published to the world. Unlike this book's authors' generations, these students have full-text articles and books, and experts on social media just a click away.

Educators reading this book probably remember watching television shows like *The Brady Bunch*, *Happy Days*, *Family Ties*, or *The Fresh Prince of Bel-Air* with their families and also watching whatever their oldest siblings were watching. We remember when there was one TV in the house and the family watched together. Then, the youngest child in the family didn't have a say in what to watch and was not allowed to change the channel to something else. Now, because of handheld technology, in some families the youngest doesn't even use the main TV in the family room. They are watching another TV or are using their own devices, watching the shows they want when they want, with no commercials. Tom Murray (2017) calls this generation the *Netflix Generation*, a term to describe students who use newer platforms like Netflix and YouTube for entertainment. Murray (2017) makes the connection to this idea by calling out a challenge to our profession: "If our existing mindset is that our job (as teachers) is content delivery, we have to realize that we are being outsourced by YouTube."

Nearly everything else with technology is personalized as well. We authors remember, when we were much younger, buying our music on tapes, records, and CDs and trying to enjoy all the songs that came on the album with the one hit song we actually liked. However, when we choose songs we like on iTunes, we don't have to order the rest of the album, and as the app begins to learn our tastes in music, it shares potential songs to buy based on what it knows about us. If someone does a search for a product that he or she finds interesting, that person will suddenly see many ads appear with these items when he or she uses other sites such as social media. Netflix similarly recommends shows for us to watch based on what we've already viewed. Whether it is watching television, ordering products, or listening to music, we are all used to and expect personalization.

Emotions and Learning

As authors, we had the chance to sit in on a series of conversations with Mary Helen Immordino-Yang, associate professor of psychology at the Brain and Creativity Institute at the University of Southern California. Mark and Blane enjoyed professional opportunities that allowed them to meet with Immordino-Yang on multiple occasions from 2015 to 2017 and speak with her personally on the topic of emotions and learning. In these conversations with us, Immordino-Yang convincingly shares that all learning is emotional (personal communications, 2015–2017). When educators recognize that people only think deeply about things they care about, it becomes clear that asking students to recite or recall facts may not be the most effective strategy. In fact, in her studies on individuals with certain brain injuries, Immordino-Yang (2016) finds that when learning is devoid of emotion, being able to apply what was learned in a novel situation does not happen (Damasio, 1999; Fischer & Bidell, 1998). In other words, proficient and advanced students who learn how to play the school game, sit quietly, and get through the traditional tasks of schools as quickly and efficiently as possible are likely going to struggle when it is time to apply their learning outside of school. Teaching and learning with the end goal of a good grade on the material from the book is less effective and lacks the emotional aspect of learning. This embodies the old saying that someone is "book smart, but not street smart." To challenge and push learners, especially those question 4 students, it is our job to make learning emotional and to connect their learning to what they will need to know and be able to do outside of the classroom.

Emotion and cognition go hand in hand. In education, we ask students to learn, pay attention, remember, make decisions, motivate, and collaborate with others. Emotion affects all of these important learning factors. The question isn't whether we should pay attention to emotions. For educators the question becomes, How do we leverage the emotional aspects of learning in education?

Immordino-Yang (2016) shares another key finding: the *toggling* that takes place when the brain is *looking out* (actively learning) or *looking in* (resting). While we all know the brain is never truly at rest (it is always working to keep us alive and manage biological functions necessary for life), we do have times when we turn off external stimuli and rest our brains to a certain degree. Daydreaming, reflecting, and just thinking are key components of what takes place when we turn off the external stimuli. In listening to and reading study after study (Buckner & Vincent, 2007; Esposito et al., 2006; Fox et al., 2005; Raichle et al., 2001; Seeley et al., 2007) cited in Immordino-Yang's (2016) work, it seems logical to suggest that it is important for educators to consider providing students the opportunity to spend time *looking out* and *looking in*.

While we certainly don't want to make a claim or post the headline that says, "Neuroscience says personalized learning works," we do feel validated because what we know about the connection between emotions and learning supports the personalized learning strategies we describe in this book. In personalized learning, teachers give students opportunities to emotionally connect with what they are learning and time for self-reflection. Based on all that she has done in the field, we asked Immordino-Yang what her ideal classroom would look like. She shared that her ideal classroom, which would of course look different in each environment, would be one where all students are engaged and generally willing to share what they are doing. Students may say they are doing great, not doing great, or just doing OK, but they would know *why* this is so and *what* it would take to do better (M. Immordino-Yang, personal communication, April 2017). Immordino-Yang also said in her ideal environment, the teacher would be able to tell you one thing about which each student is an expert. To us, this sounds a lot like personalized learning.

Research on Personalized Learning

While there is not a great deal of research about personalized learning, the limited extant research is promising. Some specific studies include a 2014 Bill and Melinda Gates Foundation report featuring RAND Corporation research and a 2015 follow-up report (Pane, Steiner, Baird, & Hamilton, 2015). The two-year study

(Bill and Melinda Gates Foundation, 2014) includes five thousand students attending twenty-three charter schools that began implementing personalized learning in 2012. There are some promising results, as gains in mathematics and reading scores are significantly higher than a comparison group's. Effect sizes are .41 in reading and .29 in mathematics (Bill and Melinda Gates Foundation, 2014). Note that effect sizes allow researchers looking at others' work to compare their results, even if they used different statistical measures. Effect size predicts whether or not the strategy would work and it helps predict how much range in the scenarios.

In a 2015 follow-up report, the RAND Corporation uses a larger study of sixty-two schools involving more than eleven thousand students, which again reveals gains in mathematics (.27) and reading (.19) when compared to control groups (Pane et al., 2015). Perhaps even more promising, the 2015 report states the schools in the original study continue to see gains, and those who had the most growth are students who began with lower achievement levels. A 2017 report (Pane, Steiner, Baird, Hamilton, & Pane, 2017) notes that schools that were awarded funding through the NGLC (Next Generation Learning Challenges) experienced positive achievement effects in mathematics and reading, with statistical significance in reading, and that levels of achievement relative to grade-level norms appeared to benefit.

Additionally, Jim Rickabaugh shares impressive data about work from districts in Wisconsin (J. Rickabaugh, personal communication, March 4, 2017). He notes that in an unpublished report from the Institute for Personalized Learning, where he serves as senior advisor, there are specific examples from three different districts showing increases in projected growth in areas such as mathematics and reading on Northwest Evaluation Association Measures of Academic Progress tests after incorporating personalized learning strategies. In the study cited in this report, all seventh-grade students were evaluated by how they performed on the Northwest Evaluation Association (NWEA) Measures of Academic Progress (MAP) assessments. This is significant, as even the top-performing students were measured for academic growth. In this example, 73.6 percent of the students saw growth in their own learning. In another middle school implementing personalized learning strategies, a significant number of students completed top-level mathematics courses and were ready for precalculus when they entered high school. In yet another middle school, a district with scores typically above the eighth-grade norm-referenced test, data indicate that at each grade level at the middle school, students, even the top performers, showed an average 25 percent growth in college readiness in English, mathematics, reading, and science. The report also shares qualitative findings that reference the power of personalized learning.

While it would be wonderful to have a broader range of research that specifically ties to personalized learning, the best case for the topic comes from Professor John A. C. Hattie's (2009, 2015) work, which includes a great deal of deep research that reflects the underpinnings of personalized learning. Hattie, who many consider to be the most influential education researcher, regularly updates a ranked list of the influences that impact student learning (Visible Learning, n.d.b). Of the top items, we find the ones in the following list to be in direct alignment with personalized learning. Note the numbers in parentheses are the effect sizes. Hattie determines that the average effect size of all the strategies or interventions is 0.40. The list ranges from 1.62 (teacher estimates of achievement) at the top to −0.9 (physical influences of ADHD) at the bottom.

- **Teacher estimates of achievement (1.62):** Teachers knowing their learners, developing a plan to ensure student success, and then following the plan

- **Self-reported grades (1.33):** Teachers getting to know learners by learning what the students' expectations are, and then working with the students to exceed them

- **Cognitive task analysis (1.29):** Instructional strategies that require a lot of cognitive activity from the learner and include items such as decision making, problem solving, memory, attention, and judgment

- **Strategy to integrate with prior knowledge (.93):** In order to acquire deeper learning, deliberately activating prior knowledge and then making relations and extensions beyond what students have learned at the surface phase

- **Teacher credibility (.90):** Students' perception about whether or not the teacher is high quality

- **Teacher clarity (.75):** Teachers providing a clear explanation about what is expected of students (goals and success criteria) before providing instruction

- **Feedback (.70):** Teachers providing immediate feedback, which aligns very closely with formative assessment, to learners to maximize student learning; this also includes feedback from the student to the teacher

While these items do not specifically mention personalized learning, the teacher actions they describe are in close alignment with the five elements of personalized learning you will learn about in the upcoming chapters. It is hard to argue against personalized learning when deep research so clearly aligns with this work.

Further, in conversations with teachers who are implementing personalized learning, we continually see and hear about how it ignites student learning. It is hard to measure what a teacher is telling us when she says, "I just feel it"; the students' energy, engagement, and excitement to learn are palpable.

Just as important, the students aren't the only ones who benefit from this approach. In reference to personalized learning, one teacher we spoke with stated, "The spark is back." The teachers we talk to are enjoying their roles as mentors and team members in the learning process. Not all learning has to come from the front of the classroom.

Next Steps

At this point, you and your team have developed some common definitions and understandings around personalized learning and why you should consider implementing it. In the upcoming chapters, you will learn specifics about each of the five elements of personalized learning to better support your understanding of this topic, which will provide you with tools to address PLC critical question 4. Before you move on to the next chapter, use the reproducible "Individual Reflection: Ranking Reasons for Personalized Learning" to reflect on the arguments this chapter makes for using personalized learning. Then, as a collaborative team, use the reproducible "Collaborative Team Discussion: Personalized Learning" (page 46) to reflect on how your team defines personalized learning, your examples of engagement and lack of engagement, and your thoughts regarding the arguments for personalized learning.

Individual Reflection: Ranking Reasons for Personalized Learning

Rank the following items that argue for implementing personalized learning from first to fifth based on which you think makes the best case.

_____ My own examples of being engaged or unengaged

_____ The myth of average

_____ The age of our students

_____ Emotions

_____ Research studies

What resonates with you about your top-ranked item?

Do you think your top-ranked item also resonates with others on your team?

What item did you rank last? What is it about this item that causes you to provide a low ranking?

Collaborative Team Discussion: Personalized Learning

Definition of Personalized Learning

How did your collaborative team members' definitions of personalized learning compare? How are they similar? How are they different?

Engaged and Unengaged Examples

In the examples the authors provide of their own experiences with students being engaged and unengaged, there is a profound difference between a student (such as the Civil War buff) sitting and waiting for an opportunity to explore and be challenged in an area of passion, and a student feeling pride in his or her accomplishments. List the differences your team sees in your own examples.

The *Why* of Personalized Learning

Collectively, when looking at your rankings of arguments for personalized learning, how did your rankings compare to others' on your team?

Does your team think the arguments in this chapter make a strong-enough case to continue to learn about how personalized learning relates to PLC critical question 4? Why or why not?

CHAPTER 3

Instructional Strategies That Support Question 4 Students

When students who are already proficient walk into our schools and class-rooms, we contend that elements of personalized learning are going to have to be in play. Without them, even the best-intentioned teachers may fall back on practices that we would call "low-hanging-fruit activities" as a way to engage students who demonstrate proficiency, such as peer tutoring, correcting papers, or other teacher-assistance tasks, or they merely assign more work but do not extend learning in any significant way. With these as the options, maybe students are best left to do what the rest of the class is doing. What these items lack is any engagement or new learning or skill development on the part of these students. The question, then, is what instructional strategies to pair with these personalized learning concepts.

When considering instructional strategies that are especially relevant for teaching question 4 students, we authors turned to Jacqueline Grennon Brooks and Martin G. Brooks's principles of constructivist theories. Brooks and Brooks (1993) explain that students need to seek deep understanding of a topic by using prior experiences and construct their own meaning from those experiences. They also argue that students should be able to apply these understandings to build on new classroom learning experiences. They further emphasize students' ability to transfer knowledge from these experiences to new situations, demonstrating that they have actually learned the information. What this tells us is for question 4 students to transfer and under-stand the content, they must become critical thinkers and own their learning.

INDIVIDUAL REFLECTION

How do you currently extend learning for your question 4 students?

While there are hundreds of instructional strategies that may lend themselves to one or more of these ideas, we found ourselves continually going back to Colleen Willard-Holt's 2003 article that outlines five impactful strategies for gifted instruction: (1) curriculum compacting, (2) flexible grouping, (3) product choice, (4) tiered assignments, and (5) multilevel learning stations. To ensure that these were indeed the areas where we should focus our energy, we sought out some of the nation's top researchers and presenters on gifted education. Through email correspondence with Joseph Renzulli (J. Renzulli, personal communication, January 30, 2018), Marcia Gentry (M. Gentry, personal communication, January 31, 2018), Gara Field (G. Field, personal communication, January 31, 2018), and Nicole Waicunas (N. Waicunas, personal communication, January 31, 2018), they agreed that this would certainly be the list to focus on. These five strategies align well with the five elements of personalized learning.

While these five strategies are commonly intended for use with gifted students, recall our note in the introduction not to limit question 4 extension to only the gifted students. While question 4 students could be gifted, the group of students considered question 4 students may change from week to week and by content area. Please don't limit yourself to those students named on the district-identified gifted list. We encourage collaborative teams to use the strategies discussed in this chapter to extend learning in personalized learning environments for any proficient students with high ability and high potential.

This chapter provides you with background information on each of these five strategies, including definitions, explanations, a description of its impact, and clarity on how it connects to personalized learning. We also outline and share these strategies in the stories at the ends of chapters 4–8.

Curriculum Compacting

Sally M. Reis and Joseph S. Renzulli (n.d.) note that curriculum compacting is an instructional technique that is specifically designed to make appropriate curricular adjustments for students who are capable of mastering the regular curriculum at a faster pace in any curricular area and at any grade level. This procedure can be used for students who display a strong understanding and knowledge of the subject matter and mastery of the standard or benchmark the class is working toward achieving. Students who compact out of a standard or benchmark are those who have demonstrated that they know the material. The collaborative team should use PLC question 4 to determine the academic activities it should provide to these question 4 students who are ready to go deeper into the standard and benchmark. During instruction time, these students pursue different learning activities from the rest of the class that are often more authentic and project oriented, and usually more independent and student directed. The teacher must use his or her professional judgment to determine if the student already knows the content. The process includes three steps: (1) identifying the standards and indicators to be taught and eliminated, (2) identifying students who would be candidates for compacting through previous tests, classroom participation, and preassessments, and (3) determining a suitable replacement activity for the standards that will be compacted. A curriculum compactor tool could be used as a sort of contract between the student and the teacher to ensure that both sides are clear on the expectations of the learning activities that will be taking place. Visit https://bit.ly/2JXdTeA for an example of such a tool. Visit **go.Solution Tree.com/PLCbooks** to access live links to the websites mentioned in this book.

There may be slight differences in the ways teachers use curriculum compacting in elementary versus secondary classrooms. In the elementary classrooms, teachers may rely more on pretests and common assessments whereas in a secondary classroom they may rely more on their previous experience with a student. Since the secondary content may be more difficult and mastery may not be evident in a pretest, a teacher can use his or her observations and knowledge of individual students to determine which students are able to digest and master the content more quickly than others.

Students identified for compacting are then able to engage in a variety of activities to extend and direct their own learning. Activities could include alternative reading assignments, independent investigations, and independent projects that are related to the standard but that might also integrate other content areas and standards. For instance, a mathematics assignment on making change using U.S. currency could be extended to include a project comparing U.S. currency to that of other countries.

The extant literature and our own experience conclude that curriculum compacting increases student and in most cases teacher engagement. Lisa S. Stamps's (2004) study reflects that first graders who experienced curriculum compacting exhibited positive attitudes toward school. In fact, they shared more information about what they were doing at school with their parents than other students not experiencing curriculum compacting. According to the National Association for Gifted Children (n.d.), curriculum compacting can help high-achieving students avoid frustration and boredom that may lead to underachievement. Further, they mention that there are no differences in the academic outcomes for those who skipped curricular assignments and those who completed each assignment. Students who had mastered the content and whose teachers eliminated assignments and provided extended learning opportunities said their learning was more rigorous than it was before their teachers used compacting. Finally, practitioners across the United States have personally told us over and over that their students who experienced curriculum compacting developed a mindset where they felt they could accomplish their goals and were willing to work harder to be successful. Student efficacy and student ownership for learning increased when student learning was extended through curriculum compacting. Before moving on to read about the next instructional strategy, take a moment to reflect on table 3.1, which highlights how curriculum compacting directly relates to each of the five personalized learning elements.

 Table 3.1: Curriculum Compacting and Its Connection to Personalized Learning

Personalized Learning Element	Connection to Curriculum Compacting
Knowing Your Learners	Identifying the students who would best benefit by being given the opportunity to have the curriculum compacted in order to benefit by extended learning requires knowing your learners. This is done by intentionally learning about and observing each student to understand his or her strengths, interests, and talents.
Allowing Voice and Choice	The teacher and student, together, determine the extension activities that will meet and allow for a deeper understanding of the required standards, benchmarks, and indicators for the lesson or unit.
Implementing Flexibility	The teacher and student work in a flexible manner to co-develop the best learning plan for the individual student. Grouping and work space could be flexible depending on the chosen activities.
Using Data	Teachers make data-informed decisions based on students' performance on past assignments, preassessments, or classroom observations in real time when choosing which students will participate in curriculum compacting.
Integrating Technology	Technology integration makes compacting by providing ways to modify and redefine learning. Students will be encouraged to think critically while creating new content and then communicating it locally, regionally, nationally, and globally using technology.

Flexible Grouping

Flexible grouping provides opportunities for students to participate in a range of instructional groups that may be organized as homogeneous or heterogeneous groups in a whole-class setting or in small groups or learning partners. In flexible grouping, assignments may also vary from very specific to very independent and may be student selected or teacher selected (Cox, n.d.; Wisconsin Department of Public Instruction, 2011b). The idea of grouping students is a strategy that has been used for generations and has evolved greatly in the last generation. In the late 1980s and 1990s, the idea of ability tracking fell out of favor. Heterogeneous grouping became a favorite strategy because it was clear that ability grouping limited access and achievement of those labeled low achievers, and that those labeled high achievers could function very well in heterogeneous environments. As those of us working in schools strived to create more access, we began to understand that students were not all the same (Oakes & Lipton, 1990).

The evolution of ability grouping included flexible grouping within classrooms that allowed like-ability students to be together for at least part of the day and also increased access since different students would be grouped based on ability and skills identified through classroom formative assessments. Today, we see the idea of grouping taking several forms, but the underlying motive of this practice is to increase access and achievement of all learners. In this book, we'll concentrate on applying this to question 4 students or students who already know the content and are able to be grouped together based on the content area. As you read this section, recall Todd Rose's ideas about the myth of average (Rose, 2016; TEDx Talks, 2013). We do not know any "average" students.

Flexible groups should be based on several data points so that all students have the opportunity to demonstrate knowledge and at some point be grouped in the high-ability group. We authors first saw this occur in the use of enrichment clusters, which is part of the Schoolwide Enrichment Model (SEM; Reis & Renzulli, 2016; Renzulli & Reis, 2016), a concept that calls for students to be grouped together based on their interests, talents, and strengths. In addition, this model also groups staff members in a similar fashion and asks them not to create a lesson plan but to facilitate students driving their own learning as they connect to state and district academic standards. See chapter 4 (page 61) for a deeper discussion of enrichment clusters and the SEM.

Flexible grouping allows collaborative teams to group students in ways that accommodate the high-achieving students but also allows teams to group all students in ways that meet their needs. Marcia Gentry (2014) points out the many benefits of clustering and grouping students. She highlights that students are challenged at all levels of learning and, in the case of question 4 students, given rigorous activities that push them deeper into the content area. Another benefit is for students with like ability to be grouped together and interact and push one another's thinking. Further, students learn to collaborate and work as a team—something future employers will value (S. Myer & K. Hughes, personal communication, 2018). Finally, the number students labeled as low achievers is reduced and those viewed as high achievers is increased (Gentry, 1996). The benefit for teachers is that this also narrows the range (or gap) of achievement in the classroom, allowing teachers additional time to devote to question 4 students to increase their achievement and engagement. They are able to be much more efficient and are more willing to differentiate their instruction. Flexible grouping is critical, as there is no one-size-fits-all approach because there are no average students. Before moving on to read about the next instructional strategy, take a moment to reflect on table 3.2, which highlights how flexible grouping directly relates to each of the five personalized learning elements.

Table 3.2: Flexible Grouping and Its Connection to Personalized Learning

Personalized Learning Element	Connection to Flexible Grouping
Knowing Your Learners	Flexible grouping requires teachers and collaborative groups to understand their question 4 students and their readiness to move to more challenging tasks.
Allowing Voice and Choice	Flexible groups of students are able to self-select groups of similar interests. In addition, along with their instructor, they may determine the types of assessments, projects, and ways to demonstrate their knowledge acquisition.
Implementing Flexibility	Flexible groups allow students of similar interests, talents, and academic skills to work together at least part of the day. This increases student engagement and may provide a sense of accomplishment to those students.
Using Data	Teachers use data to group students based on academic skills, interests, and talents.
Integrating Technology	Technology allows students to be grouped virtually and for their learning to take place anywhere, anytime with their peers.

Tiered Assignments

Tiered assignments is a strategy in which all students are working toward the same learning goal, standard, or concept, but the assignment or assessment is designed toward each student's level of understanding and academic skills. This strategy is best used when question 4 students are studying similar standards and benchmarks that the rest of their classmates are studying (Heacox, 2002). Diane Heacox (2002) explains teachers may tier assignments in six different ways, but each approach is focused on helping question 4 students to remain stimulated and engaged with classroom activities. Let's look at the six ways assignments can be tiered.

1. **By challenge level:** Teachers who tier their assignments according to academic challenge use Bloom's (1956) taxonomy as a guide and can design lessons at various challenge levels from similar content. At the lower level, lessons are designed for knowledge and comprehension whereas higher-level activities incorporate activities that synthesize and evaluate the content being studied. For example, a social studies teacher might ask students to evaluate the similarities between the American Revolution and the Vietnam War and discuss the similarities and differences.

2. **By complexity:** Teachers focus on student readiness and design lessons for some students that are introductory in nature. For other students, the lesson is designed to be more abstract and considered advanced work. Teachers must guard against merely assigning more work for question 4 students and focus on open-ended assignments where these students are able to construct meaning while using their strengths and interests to complete the assignment.

3. **By resources:** This strategy is employed mostly with reading levels, so students are able to find their zone of proximal development—what Lev Vygotsky (1978) identifies as an individual student's challenge zone based on what he or she can do without help and what he or she is capable of learning with some guidance and instruction—but are participating in the same or a related learning activity (for instance, literature circles where students read leveled books on the same topic).

4. **By outcome:** Teachers usually ask students to use the same materials (such as mathematics manipulatives), but what students do to demonstrate their knowledge is different. Flexible mathematics groups can include ones created for question 4 students who are asked to go deeper and demonstrate greater understanding of the material. By using fractional magnets, for example, the teacher can have higher-level students see how many different fraction combinations they can create and then reduce using the various manipulatives instead of merely grouping the various manipulatives into fraction groups.

5. **By process:** In this strategy, students are working on similar outcomes while using different processes to accomplish the goal. Here, teachers might have question 4 students compare and contrast information instead of assigning less challenging activities such as charting or ranking information. A social studies teacher might ask students who mastered content to compare and contrast the reasons for the American Civil War whereas other students might be asked to list reasons for the war.

6. **By product:** Finally, we will go deeper into this strategy later in the chapter, but teachers also tier by learning products. In this approach, teachers group students by learning preferences and styles. Because students are grouped by these preferences, they develop outcomes based on these individual styles, so some students create a musical outcome, others a video, others a paper, and so on (Heacox, 2002; Tomlinson, 2014).

Tiered lessons enable teachers to allow students to differentiate the curriculum while studying the same topic and find the zone of proximal development and challenge for all students—especially those who have mastered the content. We encourage teachers to seek professional learning opportunities to ensure strong knowledge of this strategy prior to its implementation to ensure the desired impact for students who would benefit from this approach (Richards & Omdal, 2007). Before moving on to read about the next instructional strategy, take a moment to reflect on table 3.3, which highlights how tiered assignments directly relate to each of the five personalized learning elements.

Table 3.3: Tiered Assignments and Its Connection to Personalized Learning

Personalized Learning Element	Connection to Tiered Assignments
Knowing Your Learners	When using tiered lessons, teachers must know their learners so they determine the appropriate time to implement a tiered lesson, leading to increased learning and engagement.
Allowing Voice and Choice	Voice and choice is critical when assigning tiered lessons. In many cases, students collaborate with teachers to determine modifications to the lessons.
Implementing Flexibility	Flexibility is at the heart of tiered lessons. Teachers and learners remain flexible while students learn similar content but at different levels of complexity, challenge, and process.
Using Data	Teachers use data such as those from common formative assessments when making decisions on which students should be assigned to which tier and when.
Integrating Technology	Teachers are able to integrate technology into the tiered lessons for students. Technology is helpful to create more complexity, challenge, critical thinking, and problem-solving opportunities for learners.

Product Choice

Product choices are opportunities for students who know the content to construct and apply their knowledge using the standard being studied. Students understand their learning styles, strengths, and skills and use them to develop products aligned with the standards and benchmarks that make up the unit of study. Jaime Casap, Google's chief education evangelist, explained in a keynote at the 2015 Education Elements Personalized Learning Summit that teachers should be asking students what problem they want to solve, not what they want to be when they grow up (Education Elements, 2015). He went on to say that educators should help students develop those talents and skills to accomplish their goal.

Product choice is a perfect design for those students who already know the material. In this strategy, teachers guide learners to apply their knowledge in areas of interest, solve real-world problems, and create original content. The students know their skills and preferred learning styles and employ various art forms, writing assignments, and technology, allowing teachers and students to balance deductive and inductive models of learning (Renzulli, n.d.a). Renzulli (n.d.a) explains:

> The Deductive Model is the one with which most educators are familiar and the one that has guided the overwhelming majority of what takes place in classrooms and other places where formal learning is pursued.

The Inductive Model, on the other hand, represents the kinds of learning that take place outside of formal school situations.

Renzulli's (1977) enrichment triad model identifies investigations of real-world
problems and the development of products or services for local and regional audiences as an appropriate type of enrichment for gifted students. For the purposes
of this book, we will extend this enrichment type to all question 4 students. This
model further supports the effectiveness of product choice as an instructional strategy. Renzulli (1977) explains how in this enrichment, young learners mitigate real-
world problems such as developing an Americans With Disabilities Act–approved
playground for students with disabilities. One of us authors has observed a middle
school student develop a school weather station by working with a local meteorolo-
gist and can attest to the extension and excitement for all involved in seeing students
solve problems or provide services that are needed in this way. Question 4 students
who receive such opportunities develop confidence, own their learning, and persevere
to accomplish their goals.

In addition, self-directed learning or open-ended learning opportunities with product choices allow students and teachers to collaborate on the development of what
we call a "stretch project." Teacher and student choose from a menu of projects or
design a new project that is aligned with the standard or in some cases is a completely different standard. Penny Van Deur (2004) explains that gifted students such
as question 4 students prefer self-directed learning because they use strategies such
as proofreading and project planning and improve their time-management skills.
These students also enjoy working outside the school and with mentors from the
field of study.

Students who have mastered content enjoy the opportunity to drive their own
learning by choosing the content they want to create, whether it's through an investigation or a stretch project. They develop a growth mindset from product choice
opportunities because they depend on their own skills and abilities. Before moving
on to read about the next instructional strategy, take a moment to reflect on table
3.4, which highlights how product choice directly relates to each of the five personalized learning elements.

Table 3.4: Product Choice and Its Connection to Personalized Learning

Personalized Learning Element	Connection to Product Choice
Knowing Your Learners	Teachers and students have an understanding of each student's skills, abilities, interests, and strengths.
Allowing Voice and Choice	Students are able to choose from a menu of products, investigate a problem of interest, or provide a service that is needed in the school or community.
Implementing Flexibility	Flexibility of choice of products allows students to develop a growth mindset (Dweck, 2006), take greater ownership, and feel a sense of accomplishment as they attain their goal.
Using Data	Teachers and students use various forms of data from a variety of sources to better understand student interests, examine real-world problems, and learn about people.
Integrating Technology	Using technology is an important aspect of allowing students to apply their knowledge and create original content when solving problems, and show their learning.

Multilevel Learning Stations

Learning stations tend to focus primarily on exploration and less so on knowledge acquisition, skill development, or improved understanding of a topic. In this way, learning stations are different from what Carol Ann Tomlinson (2014) calls *learning centers*, which she explains are "a classroom area that contains a collection of activities designed to teach, provide practice on, or extend a student's knowledge, skill or understanding" (p. 123).

Interestingly, however, learning stations are an approach where you see many of the strategies discussed earlier employed within the use of centers. For instance in this approach, teachers may flexibly group students, compact the curriculum or tier assignments, or ask students to produce a product.

Teachers should develop learning stations using Bloom's (1956) taxonomy with several stations focused on the lower levels of knowledge and comprehension and others at the levels of synthesis and evaluation. Students are then grouped according to their readiness to work at those levels. Further, learning stations use blended learning, an approach that integrates technology with traditional instruction, by offering activities that students complete by using an electronic device and related software. Teachers are then released to focus on students in other stations as they guide them in their learning.

Learning stations may be used with all age groups, ability levels, and content areas in a developmentally appropriate manner. A teacher needs to use imagination and have good command of the content standards along with an understanding of how to differentiate formative assessments. It is important that a teacher is willing to take risks and have an entrepreneurial spirit when developing learning stations. High-quality professional learning for teachers seeking to use this strategy is important so that student outcomes match our academic expectations.

Learning stations usually contain teacher-developed materials that promote student growth and engagement through a variety of activities on a continuum of challenge and complexity. However, we encourage teachers to incorporate student-generated materials with older and more advanced students. For instance, a student keynote presentation explaining the Declaration of Independence could be used to introduce the topic prior to discussion among the group's members.

Learning stations are designed with an academic focus at a variety of levels to allow students to work at or near their zone of proximal development. Because the classroom is so busy with a variety of activities, students are not usually aware of the differentiated assessments or activities leading to improved student performance and engagement. Before moving on to the next chapter, take a moment to reflect on table 3.5, which highlights how multilevel learning stations directly relate to each of the five personalized learning elements.

 Table 3.5: Multilevel Learning Stations and Its Connection to Personalized Learning

Personalized Learning Element	Connection to Multilevel Learning Stations
Knowing Your Learners	Teachers and students have an understanding of each student's skills, abilities, interests, and strengths and are able to assign them to the correct stations.
Allowing Voice and Choice	Voice and choice is connected through multiple assignments and product development options for students to choose from, and instructional materials that are used at the learning station.
Implementing Flexibility	Flexibility in this area is found in how groups are organized and assigned to certain stations based on challenge and complexity of the activities of a certain station.
Using Data	Teachers use formative assessments to determine the station a student or group of students is assigned to when using this approach to differentiation.
Integrating Technology	Technology is integrated during blended learning approaches where students use a device as they complete the center's activities.

Next Steps

This chapter has offered an introduction to specific instructional strategies teachers can use to extend learning for those students who already know the material. We hope that readers who were already familiar with these strategies have gained insights into ways they can modify them to more specifically fit the needs of their question 4 learners.

Before moving on to the next few chapters that will offer a detailed exploration of the five elements of personalized learning, use the reproducible "Collaborative Team Discussion: Extending Learning" (page 60) to discuss in your collaborative team ways to identify learners who have mastered the content and how to best extend their learning. Ensure you include in your discussion the idea of pretesting in students prior to each unit to understand whose learning should be extended and in what content areas. Consider how you may modify classroom activities such as through learning stations and varied projects and products, along with using open-ended questions to address the needs of your question 4 students. Having this discussion will help collaborative teams to move beyond question 3 and spend time preparing extension activities for question 4 learners.

Collaborative Team Discussion: Extending Learning

As educators, we must create environments that demonstrate our trust in our students and acknowledge them as active as opposed to passive learners. How can you design lessons that extend trust to your students while asking them to perform at high levels?

After reviewing the five instructional strategies that support question 4 students, how would you implement or modify them to extend learning and meet the needs of these learners?

How can your collaborative team move beyond question 3 to ensure that it is addressing and discussing question 4 on a consistent basis?

CHAPTER 4

Knowing Your Learners

In addition to being authors, all three of us have served in the roles of teachers, administrators, and parents. As teachers, the times when we truly make connections with our students and know who they are as learners and as people are the times we know we have done our best work. We understand that by building and nurturing relationships, we are making connections with students. As administrators, we see what happens when connections are being made between a teacher and students. We hear teacher comments to students such as, "I noticed you did great on that quiz last week," "Strong argument in the class conversation," or "You have a strong understanding of the current election." We hear similar statements from the students to the teacher as well. As parents, we know when a teacher knows our own children's strengths and motivators and how to best support them. Again, there is not a special formula telling us this is true; we feel it. Not coincidentally, our children enjoy the classes they have with these teachers and do better in them than in other classes.

Many of us feel that making these kinds of connections with students should be *a given*—something that happens in all classrooms—but the reality is that it is not. These wonderful relationships typically occur in pockets. We need to be intentional and deliberate in this work to make it more widespread. When we, as educators, take the time to know our students well, great things can happen. In this chapter, we will share information that describes what knowing your learners is, how it helps educators personalize learning, how it extends learning for students who have demonstrated proficiency, and what it looks like in action.

How Teachers Know and Build Relationships With Their Learners

Knowing your learners means being able to identify, describe, nurture, and respond to their intellectual, social, and emotional characteristics. When we know our learners, we understand what makes them excited and challenged, as well as when they are on the brink of frustration. Knowing your learners is essential to personalization. In a study defining and tracking schools that personalize instruction, all sixty-two schools cite a focus on a learner profile and knowing your learners as best practices for personalization (Pane et al., 2015). Following are four deliberate frameworks teachers use to get to know their students and build relationships with them.

Individualized Education Plans (IEPs)

You are likely familiar with individualized education plans (IEPs) for students with disabilities. When creating an IEP, educators, students, parents, and outside agencies agree on the plan that will best help a student succeed with the support of everyone in the room. These plans cover students' academic, behavioral, and social-emotional needs, and include goals, strategies, and outcomes. In many ways, those interested in personalized learning would benefit by taking a page from their special education peers by looking at a similar type of personalized learning plan.

There are a few schools and districts that have taken this idea and applied it not just to students with an IEP, but to those across all levels of achievement, including question 4 students. A district we have worked with, for example, has developed an "interactive data backpack" for students that is continually updated with student achievement results, protocols for setting goals, student interests, and student work. This data backpack—the personalized learning plan—is regularly used as a tool for communication between students and teachers, and students and parents, and parents and teachers. This type of structure supports all learners.

Extension Education Plans (EEPs)

An extension education plan (EEP) is a group plan a collaborative team creates for question 4 students. Like an IEP, an EEP should be created collaboratively; address the academic, behavioral, and social-emotional developmental needs of students; and be written with short- and long-term goals. Once a collaborative team has identified students who already know the material, it should meet to create an EEP together. See figure 4.1 for a template teams can use to create EEPs.

Extension Education Plan
Question 4 students (list names):
Academic
Using your curriculum vertical alignment, what are the upcoming skills that can be previewed now for your proficient students?
In what ways can how and why questions be utilized in extension work?

Academic short-term goal (this unit):	Academic long-term goal (ongoing):

Social Emotional	
How will the extension work develop your proficient students' self-awareness of talents, skills, and challenges?	
How will proficient students influence the design of extension work?	

Social-emotional short-term goal (this unit):	Social-emotional long-term goal (ongoing):

Figure 4.1: Template for EEP creation.   continued ➜

Behavior

Looking at your school, team, or classroom rules, which rules will be emphasized in the extension work?

Which rules might be difficult to follow in the extension work?

Behavior short-term goal (this unit):	Behavior long-term goal (ongoing):

---

*Visit **go.SolutionTree.com/PLCbooks** for a free reproducible version of this figure.*

Together, the collaborative team agrees on the plan that will best help proficient students succeed with the support needed to extend and personalize learning. EEPs are not only a great tool for building relationships with learners. They also support student voice and choice. Consequently, you will see EEPs again in chapter 5, with an example of a filled-out template (pages 105–107).

Renzulli and Reis's Schoolwide Enrichment Model (SEM)

In a book about how to work with question 4 students, we would be remiss not to discuss Renzulli and Reis's (2016) Schoolwide Enrichment Model (SEM), specifically the enrichment clusters aspect of this concept. In this model, there are three major delivery components: (1) the total talent portfolio, (2) curriculum modification techniques, and (3) enrichment learning and teaching. These three delivery components are achieved through either the regular curriculum, enrichment clusters, or a continuum of special services.

The enrichment clusters aspect of this model provides students regular authentic learning opportunities to apply their learning to real-life problems. This concept may remind readers of similar concepts they may have heard of, such as academies of inquiry and talent development, extension time, Genius Hour, or mastery hour. As Gara Field (2013) has stated, call it what you want; what is important is that students are given time to explore their passions. In schools that use enrichment clusters, a block of time is reserved for adults and students to interact with one another with the goals of developing students' talents and interests and providing a broad range of enrichment experiences. This approach provides opportunities for students to expand on interests and develop necessary skills. In districts where we have worked, enrichment cluster time is usually sixty to ninety minutes weekly for six to eight weeks each semester.

Prior to this reserved time, a group of staff members assigned to organize enrichment clusters works to best determine clusters by asking students and teachers to complete an "Interest-A-Lyzer" or similar tool to analyze their interests. This team takes the results and does its best to create clusters of individuals who have similar interests. Then, for the allotted time, like-interest teams work together toward a culminating activity to show and demonstrate their learning. Many of the experiences result in a community product or service. The interesting thing with this model is that it is not a miniseminar. It is personalized learning at its finest. Students and teachers co-create what they want to learn and how they will demonstrate it through real-world learning. Teachers and students are partners.

The impact of enrichment clusters on a school culture and climate can be outstanding. Our favorite impact is that it gives educators practice in teaching the student-directed personalized learning framework, stressing the importance of knowing your students well. A study by Sally M. Reis, Marcia Gentry, and Sunghee Park (1995) shows approximately 60 percent of teachers who took part in a SEM saw a positive impact on their classroom teaching as a result. These teachers transferred ideas and instructional strategies from the less-structured SEM environment and applied them into their traditional classroom setting. This included what Reis et al. (1995) describe as "the use of authentic 'tools' related to the topic; the use of advanced resources and reference materials; the use of advanced thinking and problem solving strategies; the integration of creative thinking and historical perspectives; and the development of presentations or performances" (p. 16).

Enrichment clusters provide complex and hands-on learning opportunities for all students and professional learning for teachers in personalization, in differentiation strategies, and in teaching extension strategies. Much like a collaborative team working in a PLC, both the students and the adults gain and learn from the experience.

Rickabaugh's Honeycomb

Rickabaugh (2016) also reminds us all learning is personal. He uses a honeycomb shape to show the type of work necessary in a personalized learning environment and how these pieces all connect. The core of the honeycomb contains the three key areas of personalized learning: (1) learner profiles (most important and positioned at the top), (2) customized learning paths, and (3) proficiency-based progress.

Rickabaugh (2016) writes about the need for four dimensions of a learner profile: (1) demographic data, (2) academic status, (3) learning-related skill set, and (4) potential learning drivers. By knowing and, more importantly, using this information, customized learning paths are possible. Without this beginning information about our learners, the rest will not happen. The honeycomb also identifies areas where an individual teacher or a collaborative team can begin the process of trying new strategies and ideas in the classroom.

Contributing Factors of an Academic Profile

Personalized learning respects the fact that each of us is a unique and complex individual. The combination of a student's intellectual, social, and emotional characteristics is his or her *academic profile*. In years past, we may have only thought of a student's academic profile as the list of test scores in a folder. Test scores and progress on common formative assessments are still important, but not as the sole source of a student profile. But we need to know more than only what this traditional information may tell us about learners. Now, we embrace a much more robust and diverse definition of an academic profile to include many factors—not just test scores. As educators, we work hard to meet our students where they are. We acknowledge that each of our proficient students is a unique and complex learner. By developing a multifaceted academic profile, we are better equipped to personalize and extend the learning for our proficient students. The following sections will examine six factors (or characteristics) that help comprise comprehensive student academic profiles: (1) strengths, (2) curiosities, (3) interests, (4) learning styles, (5) motivators, and (6) energy sources. These factors will help support educators in thinking differently about what they know about their students and how they can better know these learners. If a teacher doesn't have information about all six areas, we encourage they expand their data collection approaches to fill in the gaps. It is our belief that stretching our information known about question 4 students is beneficial for us as teachers and for the students' self-awareness as well.

Strengths

A strengths-based approach focuses on strengths and talents (instead of deficits) each student naturally brings to his or her learning each day (Liesveld & Miller, 2005). All students, including proficient students, have their top strengths that rise above the others. Strengths can be accelerators for our students, helping them achieve their personal best. This is particularly useful for proficient students as they work to excel beyond original expectations. Gallup has created a service called StrengthsExplorer to support educators in identifying and cultivating grades 5–12 students' strengths. Visit https://bit.ly/2shd0GA to learn more about this service.

INDIVIDUAL REFLECTION

Considering your proficient students, the students who have already mastered the content, make a quick note of a particular gift, talent, or strength that each of your students brings to the classroom each day. Is it easier to list a strength for some students than others? Why? Name at least one benefit that could come from focusing on each student's individual strengths.

Curiosities

What are your students curious about? Curious students dig deep into the content and don't stop at surface information. With curiosity, what starts as "I wonder . . ." spins into critical analysis of "Why, why not, what if . . ." A useful resource to measure curiosity is the Curiosity and Exploration Inventory (CEI-II; Kashdan et al., 2009). Additionally, a less formal option is to have students list all the big questions they've always wondered about but haven't yet explored the answers to. A quick skim of these student lists will open up many possibilities for pushing their learning further or for connecting a lesson to their individual curiosities. For example, Tami asked a group of middle school students the following questions.

- What is something you've always wondered about but don't know the answer to?

- If you could change one thing in your school, what would it be?

- If you could change one thing in your community, what would it be?

The students' answers showed a range of curiosities that can grow into bigger ideas with more research and divergent questioning. Some of the answers included "I wonder why hot water cleans dishes better than cold water," "I wonder why people act the way they do," and "I wish I could change the school schedule." In just these few examples, students expressed curiosities about science, behavioral psychology, and logistics planning and management services. The curriculum connections and opportunities for extension are endless and personalized to the students' curiosities.

INDIVIDUAL REFLECTION

How can you learn about your students' curiosities?

Interests

What are your students interested in? What do your students like to learn about on their own? When they have free time at home or at school, what do they like to do? Connecting curriculum and student interests will hook students into their learning and build momentum for more exploration. Interests are definitely not trite. Learning about students' interests involves more than asking a student wearing a basketball jersey who his or her favorite team is. Interests can be deep passions and guide students on their life journeys. When we can pair a student's area of passion with new content, the sky is the limit. Their engagement is contagious and learning is fun.

Many interest inventories on the internet focus on career exploration. However, for classroom purposes, we really like the comprehensive resources from the Renzulli Center for Creativity, Gifted Education, and Talent Development at the University of Connecticut's Neag School of Education (Renzulli & Reis, n.d.b). Along with many others, one example, the Interest-A-Lyzer (part of the SEM), is a simple tool appropriate for use in most grade levels to learn more about individual students. Alternatively, you can simply ask students a quick series of questions like these: What do you like to do outside of school? What is a favorite memory from school thus far? and What are you most looking forward to at school? These and other learning-focused preferences are great ways to get to know your students.

INDIVIDUAL REFLECTION

Curiosities and interests are very similar. What are you, as an adult learner, most interested in and curious about? How does this curiosity and interest drive your professional work? Name at least one potential benefit of focusing on each proficient student's individual curiosities and interests.

Learning Styles

How do your students like to access information and demonstrate their knowledge? Teachers often discover this through a learning-style inventory. Learning-style inventories are tools that offer students insight about available learning options and information about what helps and hinders their individual learning. However, you should not overinterpret inventory results. Generally, learning-style inventories are not diagnostic, but instead promote students' metacognition. When students are tuned into how they input and express information best, they start to take ownership of their learning. All of us are constantly growing and changing, so it is important for students to experience a variety of learning and teaching approaches as they are developing their individual preferences. Some resources for learning-style inventories include the VARK (visual, aural, read and write, kinesthetic) model (Fleming, 2006; VARK Learn, n.d.) and variations of Kolb's Learning Style Inventory (Peterson & Kolb, 2017).

For a simple tool, we find Bray and McClaskey's (2017) access, engage, and express questions highly effective. Bray and McClaskey (2017) describe a *personal learner profile* (PLP) as a key document that reflects how a student learns best based on what he or she is good at, where he or she struggles, what he or she is interested in, what he or she aspires to do in the future, and his or her strengths, talents, and passions. This can facilitate increased challenge or rigor for proficient students. For example, if a proficient student is very competent at listening and verbal summary of large amounts of content, the challenge might be helping that student synthesize the content in writing, thus setting the student up for success in future academic writing tasks. Knowing how proficient students access, engage, and express their learning informs how to personalize learning for these students. In addition, Bray and McClaskey (2017) suggest asking students how they like to access, engage, and express new learning. We have seen access, engage, and express questions work well with K–12 students as well as adults when learning a new concept.

INDIVIDUAL REFLECTION

Imagine you overhear a student say, "I'm not going to take notes today because I'm an auditory learner." What are the benefits of this student's insight? What are the cautions? What is the most appropriate follow-up the teacher should have with the student that same day? In the next week or month?

Motivators

How do you best motivate your students? Different activities may reveal different student motivators. That is, a student might be very competitive in a group-work setting but extremely motivated for teacher approval on an independent assignment. Like all academic profile factors, it is important for you not to overgeneralize or put a student in a box. Motivation can be tricky and is closely associated with a person's sense of success.

INDIVIDUAL REFLECTION

How do you define a successful work day as an educator? How does that professional success align with your personal motivators?

How do you think your proficient students define success in your classroom (for example, by earning a good test grade, tackling a challenging problem, or having fun with friends)? How can you influence these students' definition of success?

Our goal as educators in the classroom is to foster intrinsic motivation and grow students' ownership of their learning. Intrinsic motivation is related to authentic engagement (Saeed & Zyngier, 2012) and mastering a task according to self-set standards (Chan, Wong, & Lo, 2012; Pintrich, 2004). Students with these attributes are aware of their competencies and are willing to attain new knowledge and skills and focus on self-development (Elliott & Dweck, 1988). When we help cultivate intrinsic motivation in students, we are pinning their definition of success to things they can control: their effort toward mastery of goals. In contrast, sometimes our classrooms narrowly pair the concept of success with earning good scores on assignments and acing the test. Proficient students, then, can be receiving the message that good grades equal success and that because they get good grades they are successful, thus, aligning self-worth with an external outcome. The risk of this message is that students who consistently achieve at high levels can accidentally put their personal definition of success and self-value into test scores and positive teacher feedback. This external feedback is not sustainable in life. As adults, our supervisors do not consistently praise our actions and score our daily performance, and we don't get a good grade for paying our taxes. Instead, in our maturity, we know that success comes through personal effort, passion, and perseverance (Duckworth, 2016; Duckworth, Peterson, Matthews, & Kelly, 2007). Because engagement and intrinsic motivation feed each other (Saeed & Zyngier, 2012), it is essential that we continue to encourage grit and internal definitions of success for our proficient students.

Energy Sources

Think of the proficient students in your classroom. Does being around other people energize and strengthen these students? Or do they get a boost by being alone? Where individuals choose to spend attention and get energy defines if they lean toward introversion or extroversion. The Myers & Briggs Foundation (2018) offers the following statements as indicators of extroversion:

> I like getting my energy from active involvement in events and having a lot of different activities. I'm excited when I'm around people and I like to energize other people. I like moving into action and making things happen. I generally feel at home in the world. I often understand a problem better when I can talk out loud about it and hear what others have to say.

In contrast, introversion is a trait often found in students who identify with the following statements (The Myers & Briggs Foundation, 2018):

> I like getting my energy from dealing with the ideas, pictures, memories, and reactions that are inside my head, in my inner world. I often prefer doing things alone or with one or two people I feel comfortable with. I take time to reflect so that I have a clear idea of what I'll be doing when I decide to act. Ideas are almost solid things for me. Sometimes I like the idea of something better than the real thing.

Many quality learning and teaching techniques used today favor extroverted students (Godsey, 2015). The hustle and bustle of collaborative learning, interactive classrooms with technology to facilitate group interaction, and project-based demonstrations of learning can be energizing for extroverted students. However, from experience, we educators know that not all question 4 students are extroverts. In fact, it may be your experience that introverted question 4 students outnumber extroverted ones. Structuring activities with both extroverts and introverts in mind will help meet the needs of all of your proficient students.

INDIVIDUAL REFLECTION

Consider the proficient students in your classroom. Is each student more of an introvert, an extrovert, or a balance of both (ambivert)?

How can you encourage a variety of independent and social learning options? When is it good to challenge a student beyond his or her natural introvert or extrovert tendencies?

What are some strategies you will suggest to your team to ensure any work you do to learn about students is not ignored?

Academic Profile and Academic Identity

Teachers collect information and data to make assumptions that contribute to their perceived *academic profiles* of their students. Just as teachers have perceptions about these pieces of information for each student, students have a sense of their own strengths, curiosities, interests, learning styles, motivators, and energy sources. When students look inward, we call that *academic identity*. Both views are important.

Academic identity is an individual's perception of his or her intellectual, social, and emotional characteristics that contribute to who he or she is as a learner. An individual student interprets experiences and makes assumptions that contribute to his or her perceived academic identity. Knowing our learners helps us create robust, more accurate academic profiles of students. Helping our proficient students know themselves as learners allows them to own and develop their individual academic identities.

The benefits of proficient students owning their academic identities are huge. Remember, an academic identity has many parts. No longer is a student's sense of success narrowed to only the latest test score. As students own their academic identities, they are learning more about how they engage in discovery, what propels them to the next learning quest, and what strengths they have to persevere through challenges. Becoming more aware of the many facets of their academic identity—their strengths, curiosities, interests, learning styles, motivators, and energy sources— allows them to further shape that identity. With this self-awareness knowledge, we are empowering students to have the skills and knowledge to focus on self-development and have an internally driven definition of success that doesn't come from grades or teacher feedback. Our question 4 students deserve opportunities of authentic engagement, not just passive compliance. Connecting with the complexity of their academic identity by knowing your learners is one very compelling strategy to promote authentic engagement. Use the tool in figure 4.2 to reflect on the possible benefits to teachers of knowing each of the factors that contribute to students' academic profiles, and the benefits to students of knowing their academic identities.

If you are already deliberately doing things to get to know your students, keep up the good work. If you are thinking about things you can do better, that is good as well. Just be sure that no matter what, you do something with the academic profiles and personal characteristics information you collect. We have seen well-meaning teachers do student-interest inventories at the start of the year and then forget where they put them or just file them away for another day. As with collecting student achievement data, don't collect information you don't plan to use.

	Teacher Benefit (Academic Profile)	Student Benefit (Academic Identity)
Strengths		
Curiosities		
Interests		
Learning Styles		
Motivators		
Energy Sources		

Figure 4.2: Benefits of knowing academic profiles and identities.

*Visit **go.SolutionTree.com/PLCbooks** for a free reproducible version of this figure.*

To keep student information at the forefront of your mind, consider using methods to ensure daily reminders, such as including strength-survey information on bulletin boards that feature all students' strengths; posting student-created posters that indicate how each learns best; or keeping a recipe box on your desk with note cards containing student information. This is not an exhaustive list, but it will hopefully spur your thinking about ideas that will work for your collaborative team.

INDIVIDUAL REFLECTION

What are some strategies you will suggest to your team to make sure that any work you do to learn about students does not go ignored?

It is likely that what any of us—educators or students—name and claim as factors of our academic identities today may be different a month from now. Personal development is organic and ever changing. Who we are today is not who we must be tomorrow. New experiences, opportunities, and challenges shape us constantly. For example, a ten-year veteran teacher in a graduate-level class discovered a new love of reading after reading a challenging book for class. We are *all* growing and changing.

INDIVIDUAL REFLECTION

Thinking of the wisdom you have as an adult learner, brainstorm components of *your* successful academic identity.

Did you include characteristics such as strengths, curiosities, interests, learning styles, motivators, and energy sources? If not, add these to your academic identity description. What did you notice as you completed this reflection? You may have realized that your academic identity is complex and dynamic.

Our students' academic identities are similarly dynamic. Today, students may discover an online video clip very useful in learning a concept, but tomorrow seeing examples in a book and working with a peer could be the most useful resources to them. A student's personal inclinations and preferences toward learning, interests, and emotions all influence his or her success (Swinke, 2012).

As teachers, we are focused on the future. We know the seeds we sow today will be harvested many years from now. The lessons in our classrooms often have long-lasting impacts into the future, and we cultivate critical thinkers who direct their own learning and advocate for personal mastery in all areas. We are creating self-directed learners who will academically grow now, with the support of the school, and continue growing in the future. In that vein, students are constantly developing a sense of their academic selves. Students perceive what their strengths are in different content-area learning targets, and their ability to collaborate with others, speak publicly, think critically, persist through a tough problem, and so on. Because learning is a mix of cognitive and noncognitive factors (Farrington et al., 2012), we recognize that academic tasks and our dispositions about those tasks are both influencers of how we see ourselves as learners.

Each student's personal academic identity is multifaceted and complex. If we ignore the complexity of our students' academic identities, we are ignoring a significant part of their development and the gifts they bring to the learning experience. There are many ways to extend learning for students who already know the content. We can dip into their curiosities and interests as well as design learning experiences that leverage their strengths, motivators, and energy sources and align with their learning styles. When we extend learning past showing proficiency on the content, students are more likely to be authentically engaged in their learning.

A Look at Knowing Your Learners in Action

Maximizing learning for all question 4 students means we help find the maximum challenge for each of these learners. It is stretching and finding the connection with each proficient student in order to push individual learning beyond original limits. Challenge, in the right dose, produces efficient and meaningful learning. Learners can be challenged in many ways; when they are confused, they are on the cusp of understanding and great learning happens (Duckworth, 2017). In a personalized learning classroom, proficient students have the opportunity to persist through the ideal challenge. Use the reflection tool in figure 4.3 (page 76) to think about possibilities for how you might challenge question 4 students.

Now that you have thought about your students' profiles, consider the following exemplar approaches for challenging two students similar to your own. This scenario describes one teacher's work in a sixth-grade mathematics class for a lesson focusing on multiplying and dividing fractions. Mrs. Sanders introduces the concept of ratios and represents ratios through various forms of the fine arts. She brings an artwork print to class and measures its length and width and writes a ratio of length to width as $l{:}w$ and l/w on the board. Then, she shows an image of the same piece on the computer and uses software with a scale ratio tool on her computer to show the class how the picture gets bigger and smaller but the ratio stays the same. The teacher shows mathematical equations on the board to illustrate that scaling bigger is multiplying the length and width and scaling smaller is dividing the length and width, and repeats the demonstration again with a few more examples. This is also a great opportunity to expose students to works of art from various cultures and eras. At this point, students move into small groups the teacher has preselected based on their similar interests using previously administered inventories and her personal knowledge of the students. The small groups are each given photocopies of famous works of art, including da Vinci's *Mona Lisa*. The small groups are asked to measure

Think of two of your current students: one strong student, who consistently shows proficiency and is nearly always part of extension work, and one student just chugging along in the curriculum who shows proficiency to be part of the extension work about half the time. What are the unique talents and strengths, curiosities, interests, learning styles, motivators, and energy sources for each student?

Student 1:

Student 2:

What do you want to know more about each student? If you could uncover just one more layer of information to add to each student's academic profile, how could you use that information in your classroom?

Student 1:

Student 2:

What are your hopes and dreams for all your students' futures? In what ways are you cultivating those hopes and dreams right now in your classroom?

Figure 4.3: Knowing your learners—Two students exercise.

*Visit **go.SolutionTree.com/PLCbooks** for a free reproducible version of this figure.*

the length and width, show length to width as ratios, scale the ratios by multiplying and dividing, and outline on butcher paper the dimensions of the resulting new lengths and widths.

During the ratios lesson, the teacher checks progress with the small groups to gauge their creativity in coming up with further examples of ratios in different activities. The teacher is not surprised that some groups are struggling with this direction because it is open ended and challenging. For those groups, the teacher encourages the students to continue to find more ratios in the art provided and complete a worksheet with a set of drill questions for multiplying and dividing fractions. The drill questions also involve examples of ratios in nature and furniture design. Students can complete the worksheets independently at this point or keep working with peers.

Up until this point in the lesson, proficient students are working equally and collaboratively with their peers. Now we would like to focus on specific actions for student 1, a strong student who consistently shows proficiency and is nearly always part of extension work, and student 2, a student just chugging along in the curriculum who shows proficiency to be part of the extension work about half the time.

Through conversation and inventories, the teacher learns that student 1 (a strong student) plays piano and avoids mathematics work beyond required homework. During the small-group formative checks, the teacher asks the group, "How could we represent a music chord with ratios?" as she gives the students blank music staff paper, a picture of a violin, and a picture of a piano keyboard. Some students will not be hooked or curious with this question. However, it is likely that student 1 will be. The teacher follows up with student 1 later during independent work time, saying, "I understand that you play the piano. Could you do some more investigation on that question I asked the group about how we can represent a music chord with ratios? I wonder if there are certain chords or intervals based on specific ratios that are more pleasant to hear." This already strong student, who is able to quickly multiply and divide fractions, is now challenged with an abstract concept that is not well defined, but is in his area of interest. For those readers who are not musicians, we should note that the possible answers to this question are almost infinite. This is about expanding thinking rather than coming up with one correct answer. If you are interested in thinking this through more yourself, check out the following resources. Visit **go.SolutionTree.com/PLCbooks** for live links to these resources.

- *Pythagorean Intervals*: https://bit.ly/2jRCqWK
- *Fibonacci Sequence in Music*: https://youtu.be/2pbEarwdusc
- *Songwriting and the Golden Mean*: https://bit.ly/2FUODCi

Thinking of student 2 (a middle-of-the-road proficient student), from earlier conversations and inventories the teacher learns that this student is part of the school Dungeons & Dragons club. One question on the independent worksheet shows a table and asks students to calculate the ratio of the length to width of the table. The teacher asks student 2, "When you sit down to play Dungeons & Dragons, what makes a chair or table comfortable as you sit and play for long periods of time? What are the ratios of a comfortable chair? What about a chair that is uncomfortable?" The teacher gives student 2 a tape measure to explore this more and excuses the student from most of the drill problems on the worksheet.

Because the teacher in this scenario knew these two students, she was able to create unique challenges to take them from where they were comfortable in their learning and advance that learning. We can hook students into deeper engagement and greater challenges in their learning by using their unique interests, personal invitations, and academic connections.

Next Steps

We all have dynamic and unique talents that enhance our learning. The more we know about students' strengths, curiosities, interests, learning styles, motivators, and energy sources, the more we understand their growing academic identities. Students' complex academic identities help guide current classroom instruction and challenge students just the right amount to engage them in high-quality learning. Knowing our learners beyond test scores and class grades helps us know how each question 4 student is meeting his or her best personal academic challenge.

Now that you have explored the personalized learning element of knowing your learners, read and reflect on the following personalized learning stories that feature practical examples of teachers implementing this element. Use the reproducible "Individual Reflection: Knowing Your Learners" (page 86) to evaluate your current reality with knowing your learners. Then, use the reproducibles "Collaborative Team Discussion: Knowing Your Learners" (page 87) and "Knowing Your Learners Collaborative Team Formative Check" (page 88) to support collaborative conversation and learning in your collaborative team. Visit **go.SolutionTree.com/PLCbooks** to download these free reproducibles. We recommend your collaborative team use the reproducible "Knowing Your Learners Collaborative Team Formative Check" (page 88) at regular intervals, such as once per grading period. Review your results as a team, and support each other in progress toward an ideal rating.

Personalized Learning Stories

Following are two examples that focus on element 1: knowing your learners. In each story, note the examples of knowing your learners as you read.

Knowing Your Learners in an Elementary Classroom

Judy Long recently left her first-grade teaching position in small-town New Hampshire to become curriculum coordinator at another school district in New Hampshire. Blane spoke with Judy about her work as a first-grade teacher. This interview was different from others he conducted because she was no longer an active teacher.

Judy explained to Blane that her former school had approximately 324 students in grades preK–5, with 8 percent minority students and approximately 6 percent receiving free and reduced-price lunch. The school, at the time, was not a one-to-one learning environment (in which each student receives a device to use in class); in this case, her students shared five iPads and three desktop computers in the classroom.

Judy explained she was drawn to the idea of knowing her learners because she wanted to teach students where they were academically. She said that following the traditional scope and sequence with a standard set of expectations left students either behind or bored, and also didn't appeal to her need to engage all students in their learning. She told Blane she needed to create structures to help her understand and know her students—especially the question 4 students. She realized on some days with different students, she would extend learning, and with others, she may need to reteach the content. However, she was maximizing the learning of the question 4 students because she was pushing each one and extending learning for students ready to move forward. She was able to design activities to challenge all students because she knew her learners well.

Goldilocks's Approach to Teaching First Grade

Judy explained to Blane that at her previous school she worked very hard to understand her students and know their strengths and areas of challenge. Under the direction of principal David Cronin, the school had set up learning progressions for both English language arts and mathematics. The school staff developed rubrics that provided information to help teachers know their students in ways they had not in previous years when they taught toward the middle or the average student, with little extension of learning, leaving some students behind and unfortunately allowing question 4 students to become bored and disengaged. She also explained that she learned to use formative checks from the Responsive Classroom (2018) approach, which integrates the teaching of academic and social-emotional skills. This led her to better understand her students and their academic needs. By connecting her students' emotions with their learning, she felt she could help them grow in confidence. She felt that she was

continued →

able to meet the needs of all students and engage them when she could maximize learning for all students, especially the question 4 students.

In the first-grade collaborative team, the team members reviewed data from the learning progressions, rubrics, and social-emotional lessons and discussed how to best move students forward, allowing them to grow at their own pace. The collaborative team members devised several ways to address a variety of levels to meet the needs of their learners based on their knowledge of their learners. They used competency-based centers, benchmark assessments with a Fountas and Pinnell (2016) curriculum and assessments in a workshop approach, and the team-developed performance assessments around both content and social skills to understand their students better. Finally, the teachers used element 3— implementing flexibility (see chapter 6, page 121)—and created mixed-ability groups that engaged students with the content.

Blane asked Judy to lead him through a typical mathematics lesson for first-grade students. Judy explained that her collaborative team had reviewed formative assessments and learning progressions prior to designing the lesson. She told him that by using learning progressions, the concept of grade levels disappeared and students were grouped more like a multiage classroom, which allowed the team to extend learning for question 4 students. It used a multilevel center approach, and question 4 students were assigned to the more complex second-grade learning goal of estimating length with and without tools.

The district had adopted the Everyday Mathematics curriculum (Center for Elementary Mathematics and Science Education, n.d.), and this center-based lesson was formed around the first-grade and second-grade Everyday Mathematics content thread on length, weight, and angles. The goals the lesson focused on were "use nonstandard tools and techniques to estimate and compare weight and length; measure length with standard measuring tools" (for first grade) and "estimate length with and without tools; measure length to the nearest inch and centimeter; use standard and nonstandard tools to measure and estimate weight" (for second grade) (Center for Elementary Mathematics and Science Education, n.d.). Judy combined these grade-level goals to develop the multilevel center-based lesson and extended the learning of question 4 students by using the second-grade goal.

Judy and her colleagues determined student placement into the centers based on complexity. Judy provided brief instruction and explained classroom expectations. She organized the competency-based learning centers for students by considering their readiness as indicated by results of the learning progressions and formative assessments. She designed the centers for performance assessment where learners showed what they were learning. She told Blane that several students at one center were using body parts (like hand or arm lengths) to measure objects and they were more like beginning first graders. She asked the question 4 students in the center that used the second-grade standard to use rulers to measure the objects set out for them to measure and estimate the length of the object being measured.

Finally, students in another center were cutting straws and using them as tools to measure and construct a basket to hold the papers on Judy's desk. All students spent time in this center because, as Judy said, "I search for ways to help every child shine in my class."

After this lesson, no student felt like a failure because the center-based lesson had been designed for them to do their best work. By knowing her students well, Judy and her collaborative team developed lessons for each student, including an extended learning opportunity for question 4 students that stretched their learning. They did not teach to the middle, but instead created lessons that were neither too easy nor too hard but just right for each student in first grade—just like Goldilocks.

Lessons Learned

Blane learned by speaking with Judy why she committed to learning as much about her students as possible. She made sure every student received what he or she needed from her, and the only way to do that was to use formative assessments and rubrics to understand her students. Judy said, "I needed to know if I was to push forward and extend learning or provide a guided minilesson." He found it interesting that she incorporated social-emotional district lessons alongside the academic grade-level goals. She explained to Blane that these social-emotional lessons were adapted from the Responsive Classroom (2018) approach. She indicated that they were critical in her ability to develop a growth mindset with her students. The idea of teaching her students how to assert themselves and take responsibility for their learning even in first grade led to less student anxiety. She said, "Anxiety is taken away because there is no achievement gap whereas before students felt they fell behind or were bored waiting for other students to catch up." Now she could customize and advance learning for all students based on readiness within the standards and benchmarks.

When Blane asked her what these lessons looked like before, she reiterated the importance of knowing her students to teach her students well, but he was surprised by the rest of her answer. She focused more on her and her collaborative team's behavior than on student behavior. Previously, teaching would have been more large-group instruction toward the middle and pulling out those learners who needed assistance, but nothing to stretch the learning for the question 4 students who were meeting or had mastered the goal and needed to have their learning extended. However, as the collaborative team met and increased the trust between team members, members started looking at student work differently. From the various assessments, they began to see strengths in their students they had not seen before. Their team shared ideas, strategies, and assessments, and after reflecting, it built time in the schedule to flexibly group students to maximize their learning and extend the learning of the question 4 students who might have been bored.

Finally, Blane asked Judy how she knew this worked in her classroom. First, she mentioned the more traditional measurements like improved state and local test

continued →

results. She then explained that parents told her their children were less anxious and liked coming to school. She felt that her students were invested in their learning and that the team was setting the stage for students to take responsibility for their learning in first grade and future grades. She was most proud that the teachers were meeting their learners where they were and no longer leaving them behind or boring them. They were teaching like Goldilocks—finding the lesson that was just right for each student.

Knowing Your Learners in a Secondary Classroom

Jane Kelly is an experienced high school science teacher. She teaches in a suburban Wisconsin town where the high school's enrollment is roughly 1,800 students, with 20 percent students of color and 12 percent who qualify for free and reduced-price lunch. The school recently implemented a standards-based grading system that helps staff get to know their students in a deeper manner. It raises expectations for both students and teachers and promotes personalized learning to challenge all students. The stated purpose of the school's standards-based grading system is to clearly measure and communicate the performance of an individual student.

All of the school's science instructors teach scientific reasoning and an intentional process that guides students to extend their learning to the highest level of the standards-based grading system. The department teaches all students a process to obtain, evaluate, and communicate information throughout the year to frame their learning.

Jane builds students' capacity throughout the year since she teaches a variety of science courses for grades 10–12. She assesses the readiness of students throughout the first quarter and then prepares them for a gradual release of responsibility throughout the year.

The Path to Independence

Jane's class seemed disorganized as Blane entered the room. It did not feel like a traditional anatomy and physiology class. The class was made up of grades 10–12 students, many of whom aspired to work in the medical field. It was a chilly day in late February, and students were working alone or in small groups around learning target HS-LS1 from the Next Generation Science Standards (Achieve, 2013).

The question students were working on was, How does the digestive system resolve disruption? The NGSS crosscutting concept of stability and change was a thread that wove through all the units throughout the school year. Jane employed the instructional strategy of product choice to extend the learning. She told her learners to use any unit resources they wanted and select one of the assessment options to demonstrate their understanding of the unit. It was up to them. However, she had diverse resources that Jane knew her students would use as they created a learning product to complete the assignment.

Students were to research a teacher-assigned disruption found in the digestive system through open-ended questions found within the crosscutting concept of stability and change. Students were to explain how the system resolved the issue, or they could opt to take a more traditional multiple-choice test covering the content. There were various intentional starting lines and several different finish lines; there was no specific course route students followed other than the department's approach to a scientific study process that asked students to obtain, evaluate, and communicate information. Students used this process to independently explain their thinking to Jane. Jane mentored them and encouraged them to go deeper into the curriculum to answer the questions and stretch their learning because she knew her students' interests. She used this information to help them determine the product they might choose to demonstrate their knowledge.

At the beginning of the period, she reminded all students of several "fence posts"—or progress markers—students needed to reach to demonstrate progress toward the finish line. In this case, she focused students on the two areas: the Next Generation Science Standards (NGSS) crosscutting concept they were assessed on—stability and change (Achieve, 2013)—and the district process of obtaining, evaluating, and communicating information to explain thinking. She explained that she would be looking for both standards in the summative evaluation.

It was clear that students had freedom when it came to selecting resources needed to demonstrate progress. Based on her knowledge of each student, Jane created an assessment nook in the classroom for formative assessment checks and ensured that students made progress that fell within the fence posts before they selected one of the summative assessment product options. Jane worked in the assessment nook for ten to fifteen minutes each day. Blane noticed that she talked to several students and seemed to know they were lagging behind their peers regarding the fence posts. She was providing not reteaching necessarily but more of a minilesson on using the resources available to focus their learning on the lesson focus (the concept of disruption) as they developed a product to submit as the summative assignment. Jane made time to speak with students and gave them advice as they were individually working on their product for this unit. She used her formative assessments to maintain an understanding of each student's progress, knowing who needed help and the question 4 students were for whom she would extend learning.

She asked students if they had signed up for their assessment appointment by visiting the Google document she used to schedule these appointments. Students who opted for the traditional test as their product were told that it would be administered the following Tuesday, or day six of the unit. Those who opted for a nontraditional assessment product—usually a multimedia presentation, a writing assignment, or, interestingly, an oral examination—were given the opportunity to choose an alternate date depending on what was best for them and their schedules.

continued ➞

Next, Jane excused three senior students to the library to use a separate set of resources to create their product. It was clear that these students owned their learning and did not need to be tethered to the teacher. Clearly, she trusted them and knew what they were capable of in and out of the classroom.

Throughout the remainder of the class period, Jane moved around the room answering questions and interacting with students. Blane noticed again how she differentiated for some of her younger and less-prepared students. She told him that the rigor of this class was amped up with the shift to standards-based grading; some learners needed more guidance while other learners needed to have their learning extended. This part of personalized learning was invaluable. The students were able to become independent learners because Jane knew them well and could offer options for them to show their learning that aligned with their preferences and profiles. Her trust and knowledge of students blurred the line between element 1 (knowing your learners) and element 3 (implementing flexibility).

Lessons Learned

After the lesson, Jane and Blane sat down during her planning period. He had so many questions to ask her and things Blane wanted to learn about her classroom. She told him that her classroom evolved throughout the school year and functioned differently in February than it did in September. Earlier, many of her students were not ready to take responsibility for their own learning and would not have been successful in a personalized learning environment. Jane was very clear that during the first semester, she slowly taught specific skills (which included the science department's academic standard to obtain, evaluate, and communicate information through the lens of the content standard that focused on stability and change) in a step-by-step process for students to follow. During this time, Jane challenged student learning in a more traditional, gifted-education manner, waiting until students were ready and only using selected standards to stretch or extend learning for students.

Jane continued to work to improve this approach to better serve her students. As personalized learning becomes more prevalent in the district, she believes students will come to her with a better sense of what is expected, be better prepared to think critically, and want to go deeper into the curriculum on their own because they want to learn the information. As standards-based grading grows in the culture of the school, students will hopefully strive for the highest levels of achievement. Collaborative teams will collaborate and develop better questions to stimulate critical thinking among all students.

Jane told me that critical thinking increased during the unit. She said in previous years and even earlier that same year, students did not demonstrate a deep understanding of content. Now she saw students who applied their knowledge in new contexts because of the product options she provided to question 4 learners. Among the comments students made to her about this new way of teaching and learning were "I have to actually learn it" and "I really had to know my stuff." Jane said, "I knew almost immediately if the learner was prepared or not. I knew my students very well through this process and could easily extend their learning."

She saw more confident students after she implemented these approaches. By the end of the course, students now believed that they could learn the content because of the gradual release of responsibility she used, and now science curricula were less intimidating. She went even further and told Blane it was her goal to prepare her question 4 students and really all of her students for postsecondary education. At times, college instructors do not always cover the material in class, yet students are responsible for learning it—something her high school students did not usually realize until they enrolled in postsecondary course work. However, her students already exhibited some of those behaviors while still in high school. For example, they told her they wanted to keep working to attain advanced status as evidenced by the standards-based rubric used in the high school.

By knowing her students well, Jane laid out a learning road for students to follow that allowed them to grow more confident and take responsibility for their learning. This would not have occurred without Jane first taking the time to understand the strengths and challenges of her students.

INDIVIDUAL REFLECTION

As you reflect on the stories about knowing your learners, what are three actions you can take in the next five days to increase your knowledge about your learners?

Individual Reflection: Knowing Your Learners

On your own, rate yourself using this reflection rubric. Use this key: never is zero days, seldom is one to three days, often is four to six days, and consistently is seven to ten days.

Knowing Your Learners Definition: Teachers intentionally take steps to learn about their learners and act on what they know. Teachers identify, describe, nurture, and respond to the intellectual, social, and emotional characteristics of their students.				Today's Date:
	Never	**Seldom**	**Often**	**Consistently**
A. I conduct activities to learn about my question 4 students.				
Notes:				
B. I maintain accurate records, which provide learning information on each question 4 student.				
Notes:				
C. I use the information about my question 4 students to design instruction accordingly.				
Notes:				
D. My question 4 students are aware of their academic identity.				
Notes:				

Collaborative Team Discussion: Knowing Your Learners

This form is intended for use in a standard forty-five- to fifty-minute collaborative team meeting.

As a team, define the ideal rating (never, seldom, often, or consistently) for each of the following actions involved in knowing your learners. Is *consistently* ideal for A, B, C, and D? Is *often* the best choice? Record your collective team ideal rating for each action of knowing your learners. Use the following key: never is zero days, seldom is one to three days, often is four to six days, and consistently is seven to ten days.

Knowing Your Learners Action	Ideal Rating
A. I conduct activities to learn about my question 4 students.	
B. I maintain accurate records, which provide learning information on each question 4 student.	
C. I use the information about my question 4 students to design instruction accordingly.	
D. My question 4 students are aware of their academic identity.	

Why are these the ideal ratings for each action?

How close are each of us to that ideal rating for each action?

How can we help each other get there?

For those of you who rated your actions as *often* or *consistent* on knowing your learners, how does it feel for you, the teacher? What feedback do you hear from your students and their parents?

Knowing Your Learners Collaborative Team Formative Check

Directions: At regular intervals (such as once per grading period), collectively rate your team using the following formative check. Review your collaborative team results and support each other in progress toward an ideal rating. Use the following key: never is zero days, seldom is one to three days, often is four to six days, and consistently is seven to ten days.

Knowing Your Learners	Formative Check # _____			
Definition: Teachers intentionally take steps to learn about their learners and act on what they know. Teachers identify, describe, nurture, and respond to the intellectual, social, and emotional characteristics of students.	Date:			
	Never	**Seldom**	**Often**	**Consistently**
A. I conduct activities to learn about my question 4 students.				
Notes:				
B. I maintain accurate records, which provide learning information on each question 4 student.				
Notes:				
C. I use the information about my question 4 students to design instruction accordingly.				
Notes:				

	Never	Seldom	Often	Consistently
D. My question 4 students are aware of their academic identity.				
Notes:				

How close are each of us to that ideal rating for each action?

How can we help each other get there?

Look at your ratings over time. Is your implementation of knowing your learners the same or different over time?

How have your actions around knowing your learners changed over time?

CHAPTER 5

Allowing Voice and Choice

Whether it is picking a restaurant, selecting a workout regimen, or choosing an outfit, we all want to have voice and choice in our personal experiences. Most of us would agree that in our experiences inside and outside of school, the more choice we have, the more motivated we are, while the less choice we have, the more likely we feel something is being done *to* us and not *with* us. Even though this is something that very few people would disagree with, it doesn't always get a lot of thought in schools.

For us (the authors of this book), voice and choice is something that we never thought much about when we were students ourselves or when we were earning our undergraduate degrees, or even when beginning our teaching careers. When thinking of our formal training, we remember lots of conversations around Madeline Hunter's (2004) work that includes an emphasis on anticipatory sets, clearly stated objectives, input, modeling, checks for understanding, guided and independent practice, and a strong closure. We recall discussing Benjamin S. Bloom's (1956) taxonomy and how teachers need to deliberately challenge students to synthesize and evaluate. Later in our careers, we learned about Howard Gardner's (2011) multiple intelligences. We never once remember learning about student voice and choice.

Since we didn't experience much voice and choice as K–12 students or learn about it in undergraduate school, it stands to reason that we didn't think much about it when we first started leading classrooms, buildings, and districts. If Mary Helen Immordino-Yang's (2016) statement that "emotions are the rudder that steers our thinking" (p. 28) is true, it only makes sense to us that teachers must find strategies that go beyond rote memorization and lecture. Aha moments in our own learning came at different times and ranged from lessons learned while teaching in or leading schools implementing schoolwide enrichment for gifted education and special education IEPs. Even though we each came to our learning in different ways, we discovered a very important lesson: the more autonomy students have, the higher their intrinsic motivation levels.

From our life lessons, it has become clear to us that voice and choice is a critical element to personalized learning. In fact, we feel strongly that this element is the linchpin to personalized learning. For example, knowing your students, designing your classroom in a flexible way, and incorporating technology does not necessarily mean that personalized learning is taking place. We would argue that it is critical to learning by including voice and choice for those who have mastered the content. In fact, allowing the learner to develop additional projects or learning opportunities based on his or her interests, talents, and strengths will improve student agency and efficacy, leading to deeper and possibly more authentic learning by that student. In this chapter, we will first define voice and choice separately, highlight the role of voice and choice in popular personalized learning instructional models, and offer considerations for positioning these concepts in an equitable, meaningful, and empowering way.

How We Define Voice

Voice is sharing our words, ideas, and insights with others as well as having an audience for our expression. Voice allows us to contribute to the learning environment and social interactions. Students use voice to engage in learning with others and express their ideas and insights in social situations. Voice is a student's actual vocal expression, but also any mode in which the student expresses his or her ideas and insights with others. This can be through writing, action, art, social media, and other expressions of ideas. Voice in personalized learning is important for ensuring and nurturing each student's sharing of words, ideas, and insights with others.

INDIVIDUAL REFLECTION

Thinking of student voice as an expression of ideas and insights with others, how do you already cultivate each student's voice in your classroom? How have you been successful in seeking proficient students' voices? Are the ways you already seek voice diverse enough to meet the complexity of your proficient students' academic profiles (their strengths, curiosities, interests, learning styles, motivators, and energy sources)?

Class Discussions or Presentations

One form of student voice in the classroom is class discussions or class presentations. Typically, though, discussions and presentations are focused on content on which proficient students have already demonstrated their mastery. Class discussions and presentations that focus on the *what* of the lesson can be boring for proficient students and unintentionally set up proficient students to look like know-it-alls to their peers. In fact, to avoid peer scrutiny, proficient students may even disengage from class discussions or presentations in order to blend in (Fox & Hoffman, 2011). The opportunities for voice we offer proficient students should go beyond regurgitation of content and move toward deeper analysis and impact.

Influence

Because student voice involves expressing ideas and insights with others, having voice in learning is having influence. In your classroom, student influence with each other can become an echo chamber. What would happen if proficient student voices were positioned to influence outside of the classroom?

Remember the list of middle school curiosities from chapter 4? *I wonder why hot water cleans dishes better than cold water. I wonder why people act the way they do. I wish I could change the school schedule.* Connecting student influence outside of the classroom yields opportunities for curriculum extension that can build engagement beyond the class period and into actions that can potentially impact others and the system. We want our proficient students to take both small and big ideas outside of the classroom walls.

A small idea like water temperature and clean dishes could look like this: For example, a student could research why warmer water cleans better, possibly conduct a few experiments, and check the correctness of his or her conclusions with a science teacher. The teacher could then ask the student, "Who else should know this information and how could that be shared?" In this example, the proficient student practices taking a train of thought through inception to conclusion as well as connecting the learning by sharing, even when it is a small idea like clean dishes. Teachers can take this same line of action with question 4 students with a larger idea such as *I wonder why people act the way they do.* Who knows what the social impact could be!

For proficient students, having voice helps them think bigger than the content in front of them. Voice helps make connections outside of the classroom and extend influence beyond their peers.

INDIVIDUAL REFLECTION

What is something new that you can integrate into a lesson within the next three days that fosters student voice?

Cultivation of Voice

When students find their voice, they start to define their influence over self, others, and the environment. *Voice* is an expression of ideas and insights with others. Our academic ideas are constantly growing and developing, and so our opportunity to express our learning with others is dynamic. As we express our learning and demonstrate understanding of the curriculum with others, we are cultivating what Aspa Baroutsis et al. (2016) call *pedagogical voice*. Specifically, pedagogical voice is defined as "young people's active engagement, participation and voice in the areas of teaching, learning and the curriculum" (Baroutsis et al., 2016, p. 125). One of the most powerful, personalized actions teachers can take is to cultivate opportunities of student expression in order to extend the learning for proficient students.

INDIVIDUAL REFLECTION

When looking at the ways to integrate student voice into a lesson, who is the audience? Is it small or large? For students who crave a large audience, how could you make the audience even larger?

We've all had students who need a big stage to express their voice. These students have a natural knack for pulling people in and getting others on board with their ideas. For students who are comfortable in the spotlight, we want to foster those experiences. However, we know that influential voice can be either loud or soft, on a small stage and on a large stage. It is important that we help our proficient students learn this as well. Today, many of our classroom activities leverage students' sociable, action-oriented, and talkative characteristics. Susan Cain (2012) describes these characteristics as the *extrovert ideal* in her book *Quiet: The Power of Introverts in a World That Can't Stop Talking.* She emphasizes that influence and voice should not be limited to extroverts and big stages. For any learning extension, critical thinking and analysis is the key, not immediacy or volume. Allow space and independent time for those students who need time to think during group activities. Introverts may prefer expressions of their ideas that can be done over time such as writing or artistic expression instead of public performance or leading a crowd. Student voice can also be cultivated through digital space where proficient introverted students can discuss and question classroom content, extension, and activities.

INDIVIDUAL REFLECTION

How can the power of proficient introverted students be leveraged in your class? What opportunities can you provide to soft-spoken students so that their ideas and insights are known to others?

How We Define Choice

Like researchers Miriam Evans and Alyssa R. Boucher (2015), we like to consider both the noun and verb forms as we consider *choice. Choice* as a noun is an opportunity—the existence of choices. *Choice* as a verb is the act of choosing. In the classroom, a teacher must both provide appropriate choices and coach a student's independent act of choosing. A teacher cultivates both the choices and the choosing.

The Impact of Student Choice

Choice fosters autonomy and enhances our internal locus of control. People with a strong internal locus of control believe they can influence the events around them and take responsibility for what happens to them (Rotter, 1954). For example, if a proficient student receives an A on a test, a student with a weak internal locus of control might think, "She gave me an A." In contrast, a student with a strong internal locus of control might say, "I earned an A." As students experience control over their learning, they are more likely to take ownership of their learning and develop an internal locus of control. One of the best ways to have students control their learning is to give them choice. When question 4 students get choice in the classroom, they feel like learning is something being done *with* them, not *to* them. Students are more engaged and hooked in their learning. Choice helps alleviate boredom and hooks question 4 students into learning by involving their personal interests and other aspects of their academic identity. To state the relationship among these ideas simply, choice allows ownership and control, and ownership and control result in engagement (see figure 5.1, page 96).

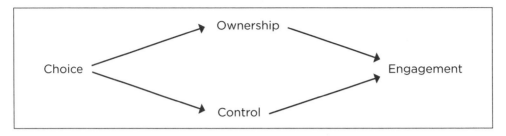

Figure 5.1: Choice flowchart.

Choice is especially important for proficient students. When students make a choice in how they access, engage, or express (Bray & McClaskey, 2017) their learning, they are leveraging elements of their academic identity and increasing their engagement in the curriculum. Like student voice beyond the classroom walls, choice invites proficient students to engage in the curriculum beyond the mastered content in front of them.

Choice Design

To guide our thinking when structuring choice in the classroom, Evans and Boucher (2015) provide five questions for teachers to ask themselves when considering choices to offer:

1. Can students adjust the learning experience to meet their needs?
2. Are the choices or curriculum I am / curricular materials are offering personally relevant to my students?
3. Have I explained the relevance of the choices?
4. Do the choices provide the right level of challenge?
5. Am I / are the curricular materials providing varying degrees of support with each choice? (p. 90)

These five questions help ensure that, as educators, we have crafted robust and quality choices for our proficient students. Specific to the needs of proficient students, we would like to offer a sixth question.

6. Do the choices also include "other"?

When we design choices for proficient students, we help ensure diversity of expression and access. Proficient students, who have already mastered the content, may also consider curriculum connections and inquiries that we, as the teachers, have not. Our system of choice must include an opportunity for proficient students' divergent thinking. We do not want to get in the way of a creative curriculum connection that is personal and unique to a student only because we didn't originally think of it. Of course, as the adults steering the learning, we have final judgment on accepting the "other" or not.

INDIVIDUAL REFLECTION

When thinking of the choices you offer in class, are some choices more engaging and robust than others? Specifically, analyze an upcoming lesson in which you offer choice. Is the academic benefit and rigor similar among the choices? If there are differences in the quality of the choices, why?

Amount of Choice

Columbia University professor Sheena S. Iyengar and Stanford University professor Mark R. Lepper (2000) use the phrase *choice overload* to suggest that too much choice can be overwhelming. When the act of choosing is too laborious, a student's sense of autonomy can decrease and thus motivation can decrease. Great Schools Partnership (http://greatschoolspartnership.org) senior associates Becky Wilusz and Ken Templeton (2017) also write that educators need to be mindful that unlimited choices are usually not helpful to students and can mask low-quality or low-challenge work under the guise of personalization.

Like choice overload, tasks that are too challenging or too easy are demotivating. Choices should include a variety of challenge levels so teachers appropriately challenge all students, resulting in the proximal area of success for each learner.

Some proficient students are self-aware of their academic strengths and are able to choose appropriate levels of challenge for extension work. Students who engage in self-regulated learning (planning, moderating, and evaluating their learning) are less likely to be overwhelmed by too many choices (Koh, 2015). As students continue to develop self-regulated learning skills, it is important for teachers to monitor and adjust the number of choices available to students within a lesson or unit.

Choosing the right level of challenge can be difficult for some students. For example, when students try to avoid failure or mistakes, they may choose activities less challenging than their ability (Elliot & McGregor, 2001). This may be common for a proficient student who is accustomed to mastering content. Proficient students who avoid failure may need additional encouragement to engage in challenging extension.

INDIVIDUAL REFLECTION

What strategies could you try to discover which of your students need more or fewer choices?

Type of Choice

We can integrate choice into many aspects of our classrooms. Coauthors Candice R. Stefanou, Kathleen C. Perencevich, Matthew DiCintio, and Julianne C. Turner (2004) analyze three types of choice: (1) organizational, (2) procedural, and (3) cognitive. In a study for the *Journal of Educational Psychology*, University of New Mexico professor Terri Flowerday and former University of Nevada, Las Vegas professor Gregory Schraw (2000) find that teachers typically offer classroom choice in non-curricular ways (for example, through seating and group arrangements or classroom procedures as well as types of assessment and project topics). The best way to integrate choice, however, is specifically through academic choice. Academic choice can involve students choosing from a menu of learning strategies (how to learn the information) or choosing assignment options (how to demonstrate their learning).

Intrinsic motivation increases when academic choices are age and culturally relevant, and align with students' lives (Rose & Meyer, 2002). What one student perceives as relevant and aligned with his or her interests, another will not. Each student's values and goals influence what choices he or she perceives as motivating (Assor, Kaplan, & Roth, 2002). Therefore, teachers need to provide a variety of choices. Curricular choice with the influence of personal interests and strengths promotes autonomy within the social context of school (Baroutsis et al., 2016).

INDIVIDUAL REFLECTION

Early in the chapter, you reflected on ways you already offer choice in your classroom. What lessons have you already created that incorporate student choice in how to learn the information? What lessons have you already created that incorporate student choice in how students demonstrate their learning? What lessons could you enhance with more choice?

Voice and Choice in Personalized Learning

The ideas of voice and choice are present in most any personalized learning example. In the following sections, we'll examine examples of voice and choice embedded in the extant models, practices, and research that resonate with us and center on personalized learning.

Rickabaugh's Honeycomb

Rickabaugh (2016) offers a honeycomb model to support school districts looking to implement personalized learning strategies. His work reminds us all learning is personal, and describes the various levels of personalized learning, using a honeycomb shape to illustrate the type of work necessary in a personalized learning environment and how these pieces all connect. This model represents three phases teams should work through (learning and teaching, relationships and roles, and structures and policies) wrapped around three core components (learner profiles, customized learning paths, and proficiency-based programs). These core components rely heavily on student voice and choice. We have seen firsthand how when learners have a say in what they learn, they have a greater investment in and commitment to their own learning.

Kallick and Zmuda's Learner Voice

Authors Bena Kallick and Allison Zmuda's (2017) work also highlights the importance of learner voice. They describe four key defining attributes of personalized learning: (1) voice, (2) co-creation, (3) social construction, and (4) self-discovery. Kallick and Zmuda (2017) write that having voice is empowering because it encourages learners to see the power in their own ideas and how these ideas evolve over time when combined with the ideas of others to then form new ideas and understandings. The fourth attribute, *self-discovery*, is a kind of by-product to providing student voice and choice. By being able to develop ideas, reflect, monitor, and ultimately demonstrate learning, students learn about themselves in the process. This kind of personalized learning not only allows teachers to know more about learners but also allows the learners themselves to learn more about who they are when directing some of their own learning. This is particularly important for proficient students because we want them to stretch, think for, and challenge themselves. Extending learning and personalized learning, in this context, are integrated and combined.

Bray and McClaskey's Learner Agency

Bray and McClaskey (2017) write about developing *learner agency* or giving learners the opportunity to shape and manage their own learning. They share that students will be ready for their future if they are developing skills to be self-directed and self-regulated on a daily basis. They have determined through their work that there are seven elements that contribute to learner agency: (1) voice, (2) choice, (3) engagement, (4) motivation, (5) ownership, (6) purpose, and (7) self-efficacy. This framework provides a continuum for educators to consider when moving from teacher-centered to learner-centered to learner-driven environments (Bray & McClaskey, 2017).

Considerations of Equity When Implementing Voice and Choice

When thinking about how to allow opportunities for voice and choice in the classroom in general or within specific lessons, equity is an important issue to consider. In schools, adults implement procedures and design the opportunities provided for students. As such, it is good for us to be reflective practitioners about equity in our actions.

Marginalized groups are those excluded from mainstream power based on a variety of contextual factors such as race, religion, political or cultural group, gender, or financial status; to be part of a marginalized group is to feel a sense of "otherness" (Given, 2008, p. 494). The consideration of marginalized students regarding question 4 is important both in ensuring access to question 4 performance and in supporting the response to question 4 for all proficient students equitably. Specifically, we should consider who our question 4 students are, our expectations for these students, and how stereotype threat can affect both of these items.

Who Your Question 4 Students Are

Who are the students who are receiving intentional instructional programming designed around PLC critical question 4? Are students from marginalized groups regularly part of the question 4 work? If not, we invite you to consider the systemic and institutional actions that may be limiting student opportunity of access and demonstration of learning. To explore this idea further, a resource we recommend is Anthony Muhammad's (2015) *Overcoming the Achievement Gap Trap: Liberating*

Mindsets to Effect Change. Muhammad's work helps the reader investigate institutional policies and mindsets that may contradict our intentions of equity.

Consider also how personal preferences for personality types or behaviors might affect where you spend your time and attention as a teacher. Sometimes teachers prefer the interaction of some students more than others (Babad, 1995). We might prefer students who are quick responders and blurt out answers, or sit quietly and wait for directions, or doodle on the corner of the lapboard while deep in thought. Likewise, we might feel less comfortable with some students and unintentionally avoid working with them or giving them the support they deserve to extend their learning. Although it doesn't feel good to admit that it can be hard to work with some students; it is important to acknowledge our adult faults and, with humility, seek to serve all students with unconditional, positive regard and optimism.

INDIVIDUAL REFLECTION

Are there students you favor who you find easier to be near than others? Are there students you avoid?

Expectations

Once students have demonstrated their proficiency, we need to be intentional about our adult actions to help ensure our programming around voice and choice is engaging and accessible for all question 4 students, especially those who may be vulnerable or who are members of marginalized groups. Many studies (Duke, 2000; Flowerday & Schraw, 2000; Wehby, Symons, & Shores, 1995) show that teachers are less likely to provide opportunities for choice to students with disabilities, low-achieving students, low-income students, and racial minority students. That is, we sometimes limit choice to the very students we should be intentionally supporting.

We all have biases (Banaji & Greenwald, 2013) and our biases impact how we interact with others, including our students. In addition to the caution of unintentionally limiting access to choice for some students, we might also unintentionally lower expectations for some students and subsequently limit their potential, contributing to an achievement gap. We aren't perfect. We have yet to meet an administrator or teacher who doesn't wish for a do-over in some way. Perhaps you, like us and many others, have justified a question 4 student's average performance with something that sounds like an excuse, such as, "Matt couldn't do his best because he had to watch his younger sibling." Or maybe you, like us and many others, have changed and lowered your expectations because of a student's perceived academic strengths, saying to yourself, "Maria doesn't write as well as she speaks. We'll just let her talk it out instead of writing." Both of these justifications are reasonable, but they can also have a lasting impact of setting different expectations for some students.

As the adults, we structure our supports for students. Matt may have shown proficiency, but his academic profile indicates he could have gone further. What can we do within the school structure to support his high-quality independent academic work? If Maria doesn't write as well as other skills, let's allow her to share the content knowledge verbally *and* support her in developing academic writing skills. Matt and Maria, two question 4 students, need to be challenged beyond their initial performance. Use the tool in figure 5.2 to begin to identify how you may be accidentally lowering standards and expectations for specific students, and how you can correct this by using what you know about these students to offer engaging and challenging choices for their learning.

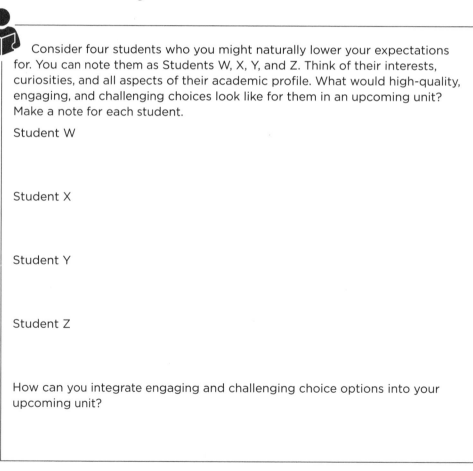

Consider four students who you might naturally lower your expectations for. You can note them as Students W, X, Y, and Z. Think of their interests, curiosities, and all aspects of their academic profile. What would high-quality, engaging, and challenging choices look like for them in an upcoming unit? Make a note for each student.

Student W

Student X

Student Y

Student Z

How can you integrate engaging and challenging choice options into your upcoming unit?

Figure 5.2: Individual reflection—Challenging four students.

*Visit **go.SolutionTree.com/PLCbooks** for a free reproducible version of this figure.*

Stereotype Threat

Another concept to be aware of when supporting proficient students from traditionally marginalized groups is *stereotype threat* (Steele, 1998). The Teaching Center at Washington University in St. Louis defines stereotype threat as "a phenomenon in which a person's concern about confirming a negative stereotype can lead that person to underperform on a challenging assessment or test" (The Teaching Center, 2016). An example of stereotype threat is a female student, aware of the negative stereotype of boys outperforming girls in mathematics, who then underperforms on a mathematics assessment despite her knowledge of the content. In this cycle, negative stereotype and negative action feed each other and result in continued gaps in performance for some students who are vulnerable to stereotype threat (Steele, 2011). Question 4 students from traditionally marginalized groups may especially be at risk. Proficient students deserve our intentional planning and emphasis of high standards with assurance of support. However, when teachers can emphasize the complexity and multifaceted academic identity of proficient students, students are less likely to identify with the singularity of one negative stereotype (Ambady, Paik, Steele, Owen-Smith, & Mitchell, 2004; Rosenthal & Crisp, 2006). That is, to mitigate stereotype threat, we can help students embrace the complexity of their talents and skills so that a single identity is less likely to define their perception of success.

As teachers, none of us wakes up thinking, "How can I limit the voices of some of my students?" But, on close reflection, we may realize that the reality in our classroom is that some students are heard while other students are unintentionally quieted. Each of us has his or her own natural tendencies in class that may accidentally lift up some voices and inhibit others. This is also true for proficient students; we may be more inclined to personalize learning for some and seek some question 4 student voices more than others.

INDIVIDUAL REFLECTION

Which proficient voices get heard in your classroom? Whose voices do you seek for opinions on an issue? Whose voices are limited within the scope of the classroom assignment? Whose voices get spoken over? Are there silenced voices in your classroom? Are these students also members of traditionally marginalized groups?

As you can see, it is morally imperative that we cultivate *all* students' voices in order to develop a sense of influence, value, and richness that comes from the diversity of ideas and personal contexts. Voice is individually empowering and creates community and connection. Voice is being heard. It is the vehicle for contributing to our environment and social interactions.

A Look at Allowing Voice and Choice in Action

Voice and choice might seem easier to implement in some settings than others. As authors, we hear from teachers that it is difficult to build voice and choice into a mathematics classroom, so we provide the following sixth-grade mathematics example to illustrate one possibility. We will continue to build on the work this sixth-grade mathematics team did in chapter 4 (page 61).

The collaborative team has begun the sixth-grade mathematics unit on ratios. Based on common assessment data, the collaborative team has identified students who know the material well (question 4 students), students who need reteaching, and students who are on track for continued reinforcement and practice. The team will use flexible grouping for the next four days to allow specific programming for each of the three groups of students (proficient, reteaching, and on-track). Mrs. Wilkens will monitor the progress of the question 4 students and provide back-up support for her colleague who will be working with the on-track students. To plan for the proficient question 4 students, the collaborative team uses the extension education plan template we presented in chapter 4 (pages 63–64). Figure 5.3 offers the team's completed template and notes.

The EEP was developed as a collaborative team. In this example, the extension was a quick four-day experience with a noteworthy product at the end. Students used the academic vocabulary of ratios and had a large audience (readers of the book). Students had the choice of personal connection and out-of-classroom ratios examples.

Voice and choice look different for each class. If you would like to publish student work as one way of sharing their voice, there are many programs available. For younger students, Tik a Tok (www.tikatok.com) and Lulu Junior (www.lulujr .com) are options. For older students consider flipsnack (www.flipsnack.com). Other options for student publishing include Studentreasures Publishing (https:// studentreasures.com) or Classroom Authors (www.classroomauthors.com). Visit **go.SolutionTree.com/PLCbooks** for live links to these sites.

Extension Education Plan
Monitored by Mrs. Wilkens from October 4–October 7

Question 4 students: *Becky, Mahit, Angel, Meg, Ben, Mateo, Shanice, and Marc*

In this unit, students will create a digital book of ratios in our daily life in which they will explain ratios, give examples, say whether there is an ideal ratio for each example, and why or why not. The book will be shared with the library feeder elementary schools and published on the sixth-grade team webpage.

With Mrs. Wilkens, students will brainstorm examples of ratios in our daily life (such as the number of minutes of a song verse compared to the number of minutes of a song refrain; the width of a desk or a window compared to the length; the number of flower petals compared to stamens; and so on). Students will self-select in similar topic groups or can work individually. The entire group will need to check in with each other in order to manage the project and determine the layout. Mrs. Wilkens will use a Google Sheet to manage the project (who does what by when). This role of project manager will be student-led in the future. With a tight four-day turnaround, students should experience quick success and the opportunity for continuous-flexible grouping (not too long on just one project).

Because we have noticed that the question 4 students here are the same group as in the last unit, we will keep track of other students who are near-proficient and possibly stretch some EEPs in the future to include near-proficient students.

Academic

Using your curriculum vertical alignment, what are the upcoming skills that can be previewed now for your proficient students?

Upcoming skills will be representing ratios on a number line and showing arithmetic (additive structure) and geometric (multiplicative structure) tables as a graph.

Note: As a team, we decided we will not use future content as the extension work for this unit. However, as we discussed extension options, we decided that for the next unit after this one, we will preview slope of line and writing equations with the additive and multiplicative tables as graphs. Keep this note for next unit! ☺

In what ways can how and why questions be utilized in extension work?

As a collaborative team, we decided this is the focus for this ratio unit extension. We will focus on the questions of: How are ratios represented in our daily life? Is there an ideal ratio for each type of example? If so, why are these ideal ratios? If not, why is there not an ideal ratio?

Figure 5.3: Completed template for EEP creation. continued ➝

Academic short-term goal (this unit):	Academic long-term goal (ongoing):
Question 4 students will be able to apply concepts of ratios to real life by identifying ratios in our daily life and classifying them as ideal or not, with justification.	— *Use academic vocabulary.* — *Capture continued how and why questions from proficient students in order to steer continued extension.* — *Communicate concepts clearly for others to understand.*

Social Emotional

How will the extension work develop your proficient students' self-awareness of talents, skills, and challenges?

Question 4 students will receive feedback on accuracy of their work including use of ratio concepts, academic vocabulary, and clarity in describing their work via the book draft. Students will be encouraged to leverage artistic design skills in determining book layout, graphics for explanation, and text features for consistency for the reader.

Question 4 students will turn in a reflection describing what was easy and why, what was difficult and why, what skills and talents they used in this project, and what skills they'd like to develop for the future.

Note: Last unit, Angel identified graphic design as a skill to develop. Reach out to Mr. Hubb (school librarian and skilled at art with visual communication) to work with Angel on designing cover of book.

How will proficient students influence the design of extension work?

In this extension, the teacher collaborative team determined the project and end goal. Students will influence the content of the book, layout of the book, and how best to communicate their findings.

Social-emotional short-term goal (this unit):	Social-emotional long-term goal (ongoing):
Question 4 students will share their voice through creating an original set of explanations of ratios in daily life. The digital artifact will last as a reference for others beyond just their time as a sixth-grade mathematics student.	— *Influence decisions about their own student learning.* — *Identify and own individual skills and talents used in this project.* — *Identify individual skills yet to develop.*

Behavior

Looking at your school, team, or classroom rules, which rules will be emphasized in the extension work?

Our sixth-grade student team rules that will be emphasized in this project are:

- *Make space and take space. (Be heard and listen.)*

- *We are better together than alone.*

- *Be respectful of each other.*

- *Be responsible for your learning, words, and actions.*

With Mrs. Wilkens's guidance, complete a reminder of what each rule means and how it will apply to this project.

Which rules might be difficult to follow in the extension work?

The collaborative team discussed areas of support for some students. The notes are listed here.

- *Mateo: Currently leads by telling others what to do—individually challenge him to lead without being in charge, subtle influence*

- *Shanice & Meg: Have excluded themselves from others in previous projects—encourage to work with new partners and seek the insight of others*

- *Marc: Has chosen to work alone the last several times—will need to be encouraged to work with a partner or in a small group*

Behavior short-term goal (this unit):	Behavior long-term goal (ongoing):
Question 4 students will work with new or different partners for the small group (or individually) and work collectively as a team to create the final project.	*Develop leadership traits of question 4 students (leadership is about influence, not the spotlight).*

Next Steps

Educators must be vigilant about ensuring equity in the classroom and its lasting impact on marginalized groups. When structuring opportunities for voice and choice, be sure you provide all students with choice in their learning and a big stage for their academic voice. These experiences will impact students' perceptions of themselves as learners and their subsequent actions not only today but also into adulthood. We may be unintentionally setting up some students for beautiful learning challenges while others are unintentionally steered to less-engaging, easier tasks. Being mindful as we design learning opportunities is key for extending learning.

Now that you have explored the personalized learning element of allowing voice and choice, read and reflect on the following personalized learning stories that feature practical examples of teachers implementing this element. Use the reproducible "Individual Reflection: Allowing Voice and Choice" (page 116) to evaluate your current reality with allowing voice and choice. Then, use the reproducibles "Collaborative Team Discussion: Allowing Voice and Choice" (page 118) and "Allowing Voice and Choice Collaborative Team Formative Check" (page 119) to support conversation and learning in your collaborative team. Visit **go.Solution Tree.com/PLCbooks** to download these free reproducibles. We recommend your collaborative team use the reproducible "Allowing Voice and Choice Collaborative Team Formative Check" (page 119) at regular intervals, such as once per grading period. Review your results as a team, and support each other in progress toward an ideal rating.

Personalized Learning Stories

Following are two examples that focus on element 2: allowing voice and choice. In each story, note the examples of allowing voice and choice as you read.

Allowing Voice and Choice in an Elementary Classroom

Belinda Knowles is a sixth-grade teacher at Elwood Elementary School in a Nebraska town. The district's grade configurations are preK–6, 7–8, and 9–12, so we include this sixth-grade example as an elementary example here. Belinda explained to Blane that Elwood is a high-achieving school of 318 students. Further, 16.6 percent of students at Elwood are eligible for free and reduced-price lunch, and 12 percent are students of color. The district is a one-to-one learning environment, which is beneficial to Belinda and her teaching partner, Jackie Simpson, as they use the collaborative time to develop ways to extend learning through voice and choice.

Belinda and Jackie are co-teachers who are innovators and student advocates. Both teachers were involved with the district's personalized learning early-adopter group where they received professional learning on this topic. In fact, they are so committed to creating a student-directed learning environment to foster student ownership and efficacy that they requested the wall be removed between their classrooms, creating a double classroom. They wanted to make it easier to collaborate with one another and to flexibly (element 3) group their students when using voice and choice to extend student learning of those who demonstrate proficiency.

Trusting Your Students

When Blane walked into a sixth-grade classroom at Elwood Elementary School, he immediately felt that it was different from other classrooms he had recently visited. This was not a typical classroom where students were neatly aligned in tidy rows listening to their teacher or working quietly on an assignment. Blane took a 360-degree view of the classroom that allowed him to see a buzz of activity. In this classroom, learners were doing most of the talking, not the teachers. It was clear that something was alive in the room, and Blane wanted to learn more.

Belinda was introducing an English language arts lesson. She told students the results of the previous day's pretest; learners were to identify several types of text organization, such as fact or opinion or compare and contrast. She explained that the standard was to demonstrate the skills to summarize the text and the organizational patterns contained in the passage.

Due to the various student results, Blane observed students working on a variety of activities, including extension activities, some with teacher direction and some directed by the students themselves. Belinda organized the class into two groups: those students who had tested out of the standard on the pretest and those who had not yet demonstrated mastery of the standard through the pretest. For the students who tested out, she created an assignment to facilitate curriculum compacting.

As a result of the pretest, the learners who tested out were emailed an assignment to extend their learning and knowledge of the standard. Belinda asked these students to write five different paragraphs using different organizational text patterns all on the same topic. They chose their topic to write about—a person, an invention—any topic of their choosing. It was clear that Belinda wanted her proficient learners to go deeper into the standard related to text organization to demonstrate their skills of applying different organizational patterns to communicate their thoughts and ideas to the reader.

As those students began their lesson on iPads (element 5: integrating technology), Belinda took the remaining nine students who had not demonstrated mastery and provided a twenty-minute large-group lesson. The lesson focused on Nebraska ELA standard LA 6.1.6.j "Apply knowledge of organizational patterns to comprehend informational text (e.g., sequence/chronological, description, cause and effect, compare/contrast, fact/opinion)" (Nebraska Department of Education, 2014). She used a PowerPoint presentation to cover the information. Interestingly, some students were using paper copies while others used their iPads to take notes with the Notability app (http://gingerlabs.com). Students had the choice to organize their notes and thoughts regarding the standard on paper or digitally.

After the twenty-minute lesson, Belinda shifted the language arts lesson from this standard to guided reading. At this point, she pulled all the learners back into small reading groups. The groups were heterogeneously grouped, creating a mix of students in each group. Students saw one another's thinking regarding

continued →

the novel they were reading. Blane observed interaction between students that extended the learning of all students to a higher level. Belinda was very careful and made sure all students contributed to the conversation and certain students did not dominate. Blane enjoyed the interaction and give-and-take between the students.

Proficient students could continue reading as much of the book as they wanted, but needed to at least be at a certain point for the small-group discussion. One student finished her assigned book on manatees, and Belinda extended her learning through a lesson in which the learner chose to develop a website about manatees. Belinda did not hold back her proficient students, but extended their learning through curriculum compacting strategies and allowed them to go at their own pace. It was great to see that Belinda was ready to extend the lesson for this student and allow the manatee project. She told Blane later, "I would never have come up with that lesson, but the student's drive and ownership led her to learn more about the topic and share that through a website."

Belinda and Jackie called all the students together as the English language arts block was ending. They provided closure to the lesson and reviewed the standard and the work completed during the block. They held a quick conversation and decided to continue with this lesson the next day because several students still needed time to show their skills and understanding of the concepts, while others would complete teacher-provided extension activities.

Lessons Learned

Belinda told Blane she knew this was working because students would tell her things like, "I feel more responsible for my work." Parents, at first worried, would later tell her things like, "This is the best year of my child's elementary experience." Additionally, this sixth-grade class has more students enrolled in seventh-grade accelerated mathematics than previous sixth-grade classes taught with a different, more teacher-centered approach. The state test results were also much better than in previous years.

Through this work, Belinda reflected on her previously held beliefs about teaching and learning and found she connected with the elements of personalized learning, especially voice and choice. She found they assisted her in extending the learning of those students who demonstrated proficiency in the various content areas. She was aware her teaching mindset had also shifted from a teacher-directed environment to a student-directed one, and she intentionally relinquished some of her classroom control to her students.

For instance, her feelings on pacing were challenged. Her lesson planning was now very different than it was prior to using a more student-centered personalized learning approach. Today, students directed where to go with the lesson, not her. Her planning was in real time as she and Jackie made learning decisions all day based on their students' needs, which allowed them to extend learning for different groups of students who demonstrated mastery. She and her teaching partner felt that curriculum compacting strategies outlined by Reis,

Burns, and Renzulli (1992) along with those activities outlined on the district's gifted website provided many opportunities for students to choose from when extending learning.

The assessment of students also changed in this classroom, as Belinda used the pretest as the summative test. If a student passed the pretest, he or she did not take the summative assessment but extended his or her learning through these various strategies and activities (with Belinda's help). It was hard for Belinda to release some of her learners from the large-group lesson, but she realized that these students already knew the information and it made no sense to have them sit through the information or take the test again. She was able to infuse voice and choice into her lessons and differentiated her various groups based on class results. Interestingly, different students passed different pretests throughout the year, rather than the same students always passing the unit pretests. This allowed Belinda to extend learning for all students based on their mastery, knowledge, and interests within the various standards and benchmarks. In fact, her students told Belinda things like, "I like that I am not always in the same learning group and can be with other kids."

However, there were some challenges with voice and choice and implementing question 4 plans and activities. It took a lot of time to manage learning extensions for multiple proficient students. The up-front preparation took more time than a traditional teaching approach, but completion of the unit was made easier for the teacher because students had made many of the learning decisions. Student learning was much deeper, and engagement grew among students. Belinda heard from her middle school colleagues who saw a difference in her students since they now owned their learning, took initiative, and seemed to organize themselves better than students from other elementary schools. Belinda was now helping those colleagues and others make question 4 a part of the collaborative team conversation, along with the five personalized learning elements, to better serve students throughout the district.

Allowing Voice and Choice in a Secondary Classroom

Arnie Evans is a ninth-grade English teacher at a large Nebraska high school of about two thousand ninth- through twelfth-grade students. The school has about a third of its students eligible for free and reduced-price lunch and 40 percent students of color. It is a high-achieving school with an average ACT score of 23.8.

Edutainment

As students filed into the classroom, Arnie told Blane the students were given a project proposal form, which served as a contract between the teacher and his students. Students were required to choose a "main dish" and two "side dishes." The main dish was an assessment required of all students. After they completed and showed mastery with their main and side dishes, students participated in various class discussions where each learner was asked to choose one poem from the class poetry collection that truly resonated with him or her to go deeper

continued →

into Nebraska ELA standards LA 10.1.6.p "Analyze multiple interpretations of a story, drama, or poem (e.g., recorded or live production of a play or recorded novel or poetry), evaluating how each version interprets the source text" and LA 10.1.6.c "Analyze the function and critique the effects of the author's use of literary devices (e.g., simile, metaphor, personification, idiom, oxymoron, hyperbole, alliteration, onomatopoeia, analogy, dialect, tone, mood)" (Nebraska Department of Education, 2014).

If there was a poem not in the collection that the student wanted to use, he or she was given permission to request its use. Arnie explained that at the beginning of the unit, he had pretested his students to understand their prior knowledge (element 1) with these standards and benchmarks. Students were informed on the pretest that if they missed multiple questions for any benchmark or concept, they would attend a minilesson on that benchmark.

In addition, Arnie maintained a chart with information from past lessons at his students' disposal, so they monitored whether they met a specific standard or benchmark from the unit. He differentiated his lessons through tiered activities and varied tests that extended learning in a personalized manner. His minilessons were often accompanied by video lessons that students could access later. All students were allowed to participate in the minilessons. Some were required to do so based on their pretest scores; some who had demonstrated proficiency were politely nudged to attend the sessions because Arnie felt they needed an extra session. Otherwise, students were asked to extend their learning beyond the benchmark and use their voice and their choice to go deeper into the content based on their interests and talents.

When Blane walked into the classroom, the first thing he noticed was that the room was set up much differently from other English classrooms. The room was divided into four areas: one was reserved for students who were working quietly on their own while they watched a premade video; another was where students worked in groups of two to three and engaged in conversation; a third area was where a large group of students were working on a project together; and the fourth area was set aside for the teacher to conduct minilessons with students who needed help and who needed to demonstrate mastery. It was clear that differentiated instruction based on student needs and student voice and choice was occurring in the classroom and that each station was developed for the varying needs of the students in the room.

The classroom observation was on day seventeen of a twenty-two-day unit. Arnie and the English 9 team used district standards regarding poetry, specifically analyzing the function and effects of the author's use of literary devices. Students were given a set of goals they were required to meet. Some goals took more time than others; some required working alone, some required working with a team of two, and still others required working in a large group. Those learners who exhibited proficiency had a great deal of voice and choice in how they used class time to extend their learning in the poetry unit. Additionally, those who needed more direction or specific interventions received this support. The teacher used his *time to check on how the students were meeting their goals, providing feedback, and conducting minilessons.*

Blane gravitated to a long table where students worked quietly with headphones. When Blane looked over their shoulders, the students were watching a five-minute video of their teacher. Later, when Blane asked if he could watch the clip, he could see why the students were so amused and laughed at what they were watching. The teacher had previously filmed himself providing a comic description of symbolism. Later, Arnie called these types of videos edutainment. When students are engaged and sharing a laugh, you would be amazed at the level of enthusiasm for learning that can ensue.

The next group Blane visited were students in the smaller-group setting engaged in very deep dialogue about poetic devices, textual evidence, and themes. In this setting, the students worked on their "main dish." Learners were asked to write a PEEL (point, evidence, explanation, and link) paragraph that identified and described the poem's speaker and tone by using textual evidence from the poem. Another component included using the same PEEL method to identify at least two poetic devices and include the specific terms and examples. Finally, students selected a poem and identified the poem's theme including evidence of how a poet developed a poem. A few students selected the same poem because of the teacher-provided voice and choice. All these students participated in a prewriting activity where they could try out their ideas with partners before committing to a final draft. A group of four students worked in a small group with Arnie, where he provided extra support and examples to assist in this writing. The natural flow of conversation and respect for one another seemed beyond what one would expect from typical freshmen.

As Blane looked around the room, he noticed the variety of activities. One student was working on a computer program that looked like a Super Mario Brothers game, another was painting, and yet another was developing a photo story on her laptop. When Blane asked the students what they were working on, they told him it was the "side dish" requirement. A student told him that the "side dish" component was a set of twelve options where students chose tasks that best fit their strengths and allowed for learning extensions based on students' interests and progress. Choices included writing their own poem, writing a retort to an existing poem, reciting a poem on video, researching a poet, writing a tribute to a poem or poet, converting a song into a poem, writing a poem inspired by a quote or artwork, choreographing an interpretive dance from a poem, or creating an animation from a poem. These are excellent examples of tiered assignments and multilevel learning stations.

Blane read the teacher-provided rubrics given to students ahead of time. He could see many students referred to these rubrics as they worked. With further inspection, he saw the rubrics were expertly written in a way that the instructor could use the same rubric regardless of the students' selected choice. In addition, like any good personalized learning teacher would do, a choice of "other"

continued →

was used on the "side dish" choices. As Arnie said, "I use 'other' to extend learning for those students who are ready to go deeper into the content and just in case a student comes up with the best idea in the world that maybe I would have never considered." Over the course of the unit, the choice of "other" occurred more than once, pushing students to extend their own learning, cultivate efficacy, and develop a growth mindset. Students were actually extending their learning without the teacher's help because it was important to them.

Arnie asked students to finish their final thought as the class period was ending. Blane was amazed at how quickly the forty minutes went and how much was accomplished by the ninth-grade English class.

Lessons Learned

Blane went back later to visit Arnie, and he shared his students' work on the "main dishes," and their final products astounded Blane. The best examples included one student who developed a Super Mario Brothers–type video game (element 5: integrating technology), where the action of Mario matched the voice-over narration of the poem "Diving into the Wreck" by Adrienne Rich. Another brave student videotaped herself performing an interpretive dance to a poem she had written for a different "side dish."

Arnie told Blane that in past years he did not extend learning opportunities; for the most part, all students completed the same assignments. The activities aligned with these lessons have included sharing a keynote presentation (lecture) where the teachers presented two key terms to the class, shared some classic poems that use the terms, and then gave students assignment options based on these poems. Assignments ranged from completing worksheets to whole-class discussions. Terms such as simile, metaphor, onomatopoeia, alliteration, hyperbole, theme, imagery, and others were taught in this traditional format for about three weeks: learn the terms, read the poems, and then complete the class activity. The unit culminated in a final summative assessment; students were given a multiple-choice test and asked to identify the poetic device in the sample poems. With the use of voice and choice and several differentiated lessons, he was able to extend and stretch learning to engage many more learners. He expanded students' thinking by offering a choice of projects that allowed them to demonstrate their knowledge of the standard. It was very different than Arnie's traditional classroom.

Due to Arnie's desire to extend and personalize learning, the new unit on poetry looked very different this school year than it had in past years. Blane was most curious to see how these students performed compared to past students who participated in more traditional activities. Arnie proudly shared that these students did just as well, if not better. Students demonstrated their mastery of the standards in ways that also showed they could transfer knowledge from the classroom to other learning situations. It was a sign they understood the content much more deeply than in past years.

In addition, student levels of engagement were nothing like the prior year. Arnie shared what one student jokingly said: "Usually assignments are the most boring thing in the world. But I enjoyed the freedom and ability to create, and I am excited to do homework." The student went on to say (tongue in cheek) that she must be confused about life if she has grown to enjoy doing homework. Additionally, with regard to more traditional outcomes, students' final grades on this unit were somewhat better than in past years. Additionally, proficient students' learning was extended, and they showed they can think deeply, apply what they have learned, be in control of their own learning through more voice and choice opportunities, and improve their results. The case to attend to question 4 is a compelling one.

INDIVIDUAL REFLECTION

Looking at your notes on the stories about allowing voice and choice, what are three actions you can take in the next five days to allow voice and choice for your learners?

Individual Reflection:
Allowing Voice and Choice

On your own, rate yourself using the following reflection rubric. Use the following key: never is zero days, seldom is one to three days, often is four to six days, and consistently is seven to ten days.

Allowing Voice and Choice Definition: In *voice*, teachers invite, respect, and consider the perspectives, opinions, and preferences of learners. In *choice*, teachers give learners options for ways they engage in learning.	Today's Date:			
	Never	**Seldom**	**Often**	**Consistently**
A. I demonstrate a mastery of the content, which enables me to encourage individual question 4 students to take risks.				
Notes:				
B. I facilitate opportunities for question 4 students to alter assignments that make learning more relevant to them.				
Notes:				
C. I design lesson plans that reflect opportunities for question 4 students to have voice and choice.				
Notes:				

	Never	Seldom	Often	Consistently
D. I analyze strategies to support diverse student representation in my question 4 student group.				
Notes:				

Collaborative Team Discussion: Allowing Voice and Choice

The following is intended for use in a standard forty-five- to fifty-minute collaborative team meeting.

As a team, define the ideal rating (never, seldom, often, or consistently) for each of the following actions in allowing voice and choice. Is *consistently* ideal for A, B, C, and D? Is *often* the best choice? Record your collective team ideal rating for each action of allowing voice and choice. Use the following key: never is zero days, seldom is one to three days, often is four to six days, and consistently is seven to ten days.

Allowing Voice and Choice Action	Ideal Rating
A. I demonstrate a mastery of the content, which enables me to encourage individual question 4 students to take risks.	
B. I facilitate opportunities for question 4 students to alter assignments that make learning more relevant to them.	
C. I design lesson plans that reflect opportunities for question 4 students to have voice and choice.	
D. I analyze strategies to support diverse student representation in my question 4 student group.	

Why are these the ideal ratings for each action?

How close are each of us to that ideal rating for each action?

How can we help each other get there?

For those of you who rated your actions as *often* or *consistent* on allowing voice and choice, how does it feel for you, the teacher? What feedback do you hear from your students and their parents?

Allowing Voice and Choice
Collaborative Team Formative Check

Directions: At regular intervals (such as once a grading period), collectively rate your team using the following formative check. Review your collaborative team results and support each other's progress toward an ideal rating. Use the following key: never is zero days, seldom is one to three days, often is four to six days, and consistently is seven to ten days.

Voice and Choice Definition: In *voice*, teachers invite, respect, and consider the perspectives, opinions, and preferences of learners. In *choice*, teachers give learners options for ways they engage in learning.	Formative Check # _____ Date:			
	Never	**Seldom**	**Often**	**Consistently**
A. I demonstrate a mastery of the content, which enables me to encourage individual question 4 students to take risks.				
Notes:				
B. I facilitate opportunities for question 4 students to alter assignments that make learning more relevant to them.				
Notes:				
C. I design lesson plans that reflect opportunities for question 4 students to have voice and choice.				
Notes:				

page 1 of 2

	Never	Seldom	Often	Consistently
D. I analyze strategies to support diverse student representation in my question 4 student group.				
Notes:				

How close are each of us to that ideal rating for each action?

How can we help each other get there?

Look at your ratings over time. Is your implementation of voice and choice the same over time? Different?

How have your actions around voice and choice changed over time?

CHAPTER 6

Implementing Flexibility

If we know our students and their individual needs and preferences, and we give them voice and choice to experience learning and display it in the ways that allow them to best reflect what they know, it follows that we must integrate flexibility into our classrooms. Flexibility is necessary to allow students a variety of physical environments in which to learn and to allow teachers to differentiate instructional approaches to meet student learning needs. The traditional, static classrooms where all learners are in lockstep with one another is a dated look. It is important for classrooms to shift and evolve throughout the day and have the flexibility to flow from large to small groups and back again, and to provide spaces for students to create and be innovative. Intelligence and learning are not static, so our classrooms shouldn't be either. As we work to meet the needs of our proficient students, we might need to consider our current mindset and educational structures differently, thus, flexibility.

Flexibility, for the purposes of this book, is far too broad to cover in great detail in just one chapter. In fact, entire books cover specific aspects of flexibility. We will limit our focus to the aspects that we find most relevant to personalized learning. In this chapter, we offer our definition of flexibility and explore possible forms of flexibility in the classroom.

How We Define Flexibility

Picture two classrooms: in one, everything is flexible, and in the other, every-thing is standardized. Neither is ideal. The first might be chaotic, loud, and dis-organized, with students only doing work they choose. The second might be stale and highly structured, with quiet students obediently taking notes while sitting at desks arranged in rows. Our definition of *flexibility* is actually in the middle of these two scenarios. Some elements of our classroom are important to standardize, such as routines, teacher feedback, and continuous formative assessment (France, 2017). These standardizations can help improve efficiency and comfort for both the students and the teacher. At the same time, implementing flexibility in curriculum structure, physical space, and student grouping can help teachers meet the needs of learners in a very personalized way. *Flexibility* is the balancing of control by teachers and students.

Balance

Teachers set the environment and make curriculum decisions that determine how much control they will relinquish to students and how much control they will keep. Teaching is a constant balance of that control and freedom. In any given situa-tion, one may outweigh the other. Heavy teacher control is paired with less student freedom. When teachers are strongly in control, students have little freedom. Less teacher control is paired with heavy student freedom. When teachers have little control in the learning, students have a lot of freedom. Neither of these extremes are great. A balance of control and freedom is ideal. Consider chapter 5 (page 91) on voice and choice; proficient students can extend their learning through increased voice and choice in the classroom. The opportunities, however, of voice and choice are guided by the teacher. Students have influence in their learning (heavier student freedom), but under the guidance of the teacher (heavier teacher control). Ideally, the pulley weights should be oscillating in the middle between teacher control and student freedom to keep a balance, and not lopsided with one over the other. See figure 6.1.

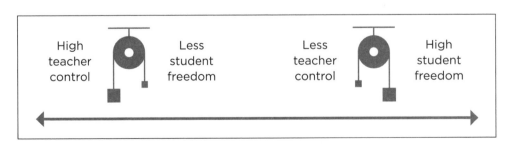

Figure 6.1: Balancing control.

INDIVIDUAL REFLECTION

Think of a successful lesson where your students engaged in their learning and grew in their ability to think deeply, and you were having a great time. In this lesson, did your classroom display more teacher control or more student freedom?

Our ideas of what success looks like often carry the bias of our own natural tendencies. For example, if a teacher enjoys organized, quiet learning, he or she may teach in an organized and quiet way. If a teacher enjoys peer collaboration, he or she may design lessons with collaboration. Further, because many teachers have implemented quality lessons that have shown success for the majority of students, it can be hard to find motivation to try teaching a different way. When considering the element of flexibility, we invite you to look inward about your current practices and consider how those practices enhance personalized learning.

Gradual Release of Responsibility

Strong teacher control is OK at some points in learning, and high student control is appropriate at other times. The scale continues to tip in both directions throughout the learning process. Authors Douglas Fisher and Nancy Frey's (2014) gradual release of responsibility (GRR) model explains this well. The GRR continuum starts with direct instruction (teachers do it), to guided instruction (both teachers and students do it), and then to independent practice (students do it). If we think about this in terms of our pulley weights, when teachers do it, there is heavy teacher control; during guided instruction, there is balance between the teacher and student weights; and during independent practice, there is heavy student action. Take a moment and consider the extension work you may be designing for proficient students. Does it have all of the components of GRR? Often, extension work can look like individual students researching an idea on their own while the rest of the class is receiving direct instruction on the content. However, what would extension work look like with GRR design? First, the learning objective of the extension work needs to be identified. The learning objective might be a deeper dive into the current curriculum topic through critical thinking and analysis or a tangential topic which requires new information. Once the learning objective is identified, proficient students should be provided direct instruction (heavy teacher control), guided instruction (balance between the two), and independent practice (heavy student action). Like other classmates, proficient students, too, should be receiving high-quality direct and guided instruction.

Forms of Flexibility in the Classroom

Flexibility plays out in a variety of ways in a classroom. As we've examined in the preceding section, the most important part of flexibility is sharing control in the classroom. Other forms of flexibility include a flexible mindset, competency-based curriculum structure, continuous-flexible grouping, and flexible use of classroom space.

Flexible Mindset

Dweck (2006) argues that *intelligence* is a malleable quality developed over time, as opposed to being set and fixed at birth. She uses the term *growth mindset* to refer to students' belief that they can develop their intelligence (as opposed to it being "fixed" or an inborn trait). She writes that we all start with certain talents, but how we view ourselves makes a tremendous difference. For this reason, ensuring students' flexible (growth) mindsets is essential to their growth and success. When proficient students hear, "You're so smart," it reinforces a fixed mindset that "smart" is a status that you either have or don't. Students who are consistently proficient in their academic content are at risk of avoiding possible failure with difficult work. Their first failure can leave them questioning their ability and if they no longer have the "smart" status. We want our students to strive for new challenges and find reward in the productive struggle. In Tami's home, this is called *produggle*.

Various studies find those who believe working hard is the key to results are the ones who perform the best (Dweck, 2007, 2015; Haimovitz & Dweck, 2017), and those who believe working hard reflects an absence of talent or giftedness didn't perform as well (Rattan, Savani, Chugh, & Dweck, 2015). In a personalized learning environment, we believe it is critical for teachers and learners to use a growth mindset and look at each day as an opportunity to learn something new. Specifically, Dweck's (2006) idea of adding the word *yet* to phrases helps define a path for greater persistence and leaving the possibility of solving still in the future. Consider our proficient students who are working on an extension project. As the teacher checks in on the progress, she notices that the content is incorrect, and the logic of thinking is not supported. The informal formative check provides the opportunities to redirect the students and reinforce that they just hit a bump along the learning process; they are not there *yet*. In *The Gift of Failure* (2015), Jessica Lahey explains that failure helps foster independent thinking and doing. With failure, students can persist through both tough and easy times. Also keep in mind that teachers modeling a growth mindset can help students persevere through failure. When we model a value of progress over perfection in difficult tasks, we are more likely to be able to support our students in the same. For a more detailed analysis of flexible mindsets, see Dweck (2006).

Competency-Based Curriculum Structure

Each teacher operates within the boundaries and parameters of the district-approved curriculum and assessment requirements. For many, grade-level expectations define the educational setting. A student's age aligns with his or her grade level; each grade level defines the learning targets for each subject. In contrast to this design is a fluid model of *competency-based curriculum*. In this fluid setting, a student progresses through vertically aligned learning targets at his or her pace. When a student demonstrates mastery or more, he or she moves along the curriculum progression. When a student needs more support, he or she digs into that learning concept in a variety of ways until he or she achieves mastery.

Curriculum design is essential for this to work. For proficient students, in competency-based curriculum, a clear vertical progression of concepts is needed. That is, in competency-based curriculum structure, the curriculum is outlined from one concept to the next in such a way that an individual student can progress through the continuum well beyond a traditional grade level.

INDIVIDUAL REFLECTION

Is your educational setting a series of grade-level progressions or a fluid progression of competency-based learning targets? If not competency-based, how might you introduce elements of competency-based learning within your required structure?

Fluid progression of competency-based learning targets allows for the most flexibility in the classroom. In this structure, students can be at a variety of learning progression points and interacting with the curriculum at their optimal level of challenge. However, the most common educational structure is grade-level progressions.

Within your class, you likely have students who have not yet mastered the learning targets from the previous grade level, as well as students who have mastered the targets in the current grade or beyond.

Even in a fixed grade-level progression, a student can experience ongoing responsive flexible programming to meet his or her personal challenges and learning needs (Prain et al., 2013). The most common way to increase rigor for a curriculum standard is to increase the level of critical thinking and critical questioning with that topic. We recommend the tools found at The Foundation for Critical Thinking (www.criticalthinking.org) to support extension work at any level in any subject. Another way to increase rigor for individual students is identifying the curriculum standard at future grade levels and teaching the new content indicator to students— that is, truly moving students beyond the content of your pacing guide and exposing them early to the next content. Additionally, teachers can increase rigor by extending learning on the current grade-level curriculum by investigating related, but not exact, topics of the curriculum. For example, if a student is already proficient at geometry proofs, he or she can explore content on inductive and deductive reasoning as applied to mathematics and other content areas like philosophy.

Students, parents, and other stakeholders should all have access to the full learning progressions to achieve greater understanding and optimal results. In order to best facilitate this flexible programming, consider the following guidelines for teacher, student, and adult stakeholder knowledge of learning progressions.

Teacher Knowledge of Learning Progressions

Vertical curriculum alignment occurs when grade-level teams find the learning progressions (or scope and sequence) of their grade-level expectations *and* the grades before and after. These before-and-after documents guide teams on how to best challenge and support students at different levels of understanding. As described previously, access to future learning standards and indicators is one way to extend learning. It also helps teachers guide extension work if choosing to go deeper into current content. For example, sixth-grade mathematics indicators are to determine the perimeter of a triangle, rectangle, and square while the seventh-grade indicator is to identify congruent shapes. In sixth grade, then, as an extension of perimeter, the teacher would expose students to the meaning of *congruent* and what role or limitations perimeter can play in determining congruency.

INDIVIDUAL REFLECTION

Before your next collaborative team meeting, do the following:

- Identify the essential standards and learning targets for your grade level. Essential standards are the non-negotiables of your curriculum, and learning targets are the definitions of mastery.

- Review the learning progressions for the grades before and after yours. What do you notice about the vertical curriculum alignment? Is any content stand-alone for just for your grade level?

COLLABORATIVE TEAM REFLECTION

At your next collaborative team meeting, compare your interpretations of the essential standards, learning targets, and learning progressions. Establishing a shared understanding of curriculum expectations is essential to facilitate conversation about student progress.

Student Knowledge of Learning Progressions

Seeing the big picture of curriculum helps students know where they are in their learning continuum and have a sense for what is ahead. In a personalized learning setting, it is important for students to understand their learning targets and articulate their progress along the learning continuum. Self-awareness of learning strengths and support strategies help foster a strong sense of one's academic identity.

INDIVIDUAL REFLECTION

As a teacher, you have a big-picture understanding of what you teach and what students learn each day. How can you help each student have a big-picture view of the class plan? How can this broader understanding contribute to a student's academic identity?

Adult Knowledge of Learning Progressions

Parents and other adult stakeholders are excellent partners in student learning, but school can be intimidating. Transparent learning progressions, written in plain words without educational jargon, can help parents know how best to hook into their child's learning. Because parents and guardians are the primary caregivers for their children, they have unique insights on the out-of-class connections and interests that can be connected to the classroom. Transparency also builds trust with parents. Knowing the learning progressions provides insight and invites collaboration.

Conversations at home can be robust—even beyond homework assignments and personal reading time. Parents enjoy knowing what their child is learning and supporting learning extension.

INDIVIDUAL REFLECTION

How do you communicate with parents and other adult stakeholders? How can you use these communication channels to share curriculum content? How can you use these communication channels to invite conversation about curriculum connections?

Continuous-Flexible Grouping

Grouping students for learning is not new in education (Oakes, 1986; Slavin, 1987). Before discussing strategies we recommend, we briefly want to outline a few we believe are counterproductive and caution you against them. You may be familiar with some of the following strategies.

- **Fixed- or static-ability groups** are student groups the teacher determines only a few times a year. Once a student is in a group, significant time passes before the group changes. Traditionally, beginning-of-the-year benchmark tests or previous performance recommendations define static-ability groups. As we note in chapter 3 (page 47), the ability group the teacher assigns a student to impacts the student's academic identity as well as choice. External definitions of academic potential can become self-fulfilling for students, and students can become vulnerable to negative perceptions of their own abilities and capacity for learning. Static-ability groups reinforce a fixed mindset. A student who is assigned an advanced static group based on beginning-of-the year assessments can internalize his or her sense of pride and self-worth with being part of the "in" group of "clever and smart people." Similarly, a student who has previously been part of extension work before but fails to earn the advanced static group may see this as a personal failure with little chance of demonstrating proficiency to earn opportunities of extension in the future.

- **Faux flexible–ability groups** are student groups that end up having the same students in them unintentionally. How can this happen? Surprisingly easily. As a teacher, you might switch up groups based on student interests and ability levels. After three iterations of group work, you notice that in groups of three students, you actually have the same pairs of two often. The only variable changing is one student. This also happens when students choose their own groups. Students get in patterns of working with each other and naturally start to seek out the same peers for collaborative work. For proficient students, this can limit who they work with and thus limit the opportunity of diverse perspectives.

- **Independent study groups** are student groups participating in talented and gifted (TAG) or high-ability learning (HAL) programs clustered together for a series of independent study units. Students who are proficient in the content may very well also be part of TAG or HAL programming. Unfortunately, teachers often give independent study units limited support and minimal feedback on their challenging work. The result is a group of HAL or TAG students not receiving support in their learning.

- **Peer teaching groups** are student groups with members who have and have not mastered the learning objective. Those who have achieved mastery teach their peers who are working toward mastery. To be clear, student collaboration in learning is a good thing. However, collaboration is distinctly different than student-to-student (or peer) teaching. In peer teaching, the students who have mastered the content are derailed from their continued personal learning in order to teach a peer. Students who are learning the content from a peer may be exposed to frustration and novice teaching approaches. Additionally, knowledge influences one's perception of power. Students should not be forced into a situation with an imbalance of power. Students should not be taught by peers because it influences a power dynamic that causes struggling students to place negative value judgments on themselves, and high-achieving students to incorrectly regard themselves as holding a position of power over other students. We understand that some advocates of personalized learning support peer-to-peer instruction. However, because of the potential detriment to the proficient student forced to teach content without support and to the receiving student forced to consume instruction from a peer instead of a teacher, we are not in support of peer-to-peer teaching.

INDIVIDUAL REFLECTION

Reflect on the following questions and prompts:

- Recall the definition of *academic identity* in chapter 4 (page 72). What impact could static-ability grouping or faux flexible–ability grouping have on a student's academic identity?

- If you currently have independent study groups or peer teaching groups, what are some alternative delivery models for curriculum?

Static-ability grouping, faux flexible–ability grouping, independent study grouping, and peer teaching result in inequitable distribution of learning opportunities and limit the access to challenge for all students. Therefore, we strongly recommend *continuous-flexible grouping* in your personalized learning classroom.

Continuous-flexible grouping specifically meets each learner's individual challenge goals and does not have the boundaries of fixed labeling of learner capacities. Continuous-flexible grouping goes hand in hand with continuous formative assessment (see chapter 7, page 151), as well as other dynamic characteristics of knowing your learners (see chapter 4, page 61). Students can ebb and flow from learning groups as their interests and mastery organically change. Continuous-flexible grouping provides diverse student perspectives in groups, including the groups who are proficient in the content. There are many ways to leverage the diversity within the proficient group such as student characteristics, interests, talents in expression, and so on. Additionally, proficient students can sometimes benefit from working in groups of near-proficient students as well. Both proficient and near-proficient students can dig into content more deeply together through critical thinking analysis. The near-proficient students will also be engaged in continued content practice that proficient students may not need.

Teachers should leverage their collaborative teaching teams to share student grouping. Marcia Gentry's (2014) work *Total School Cluster Grouping and Differentiation* provides a wonderful background on the different types of student groupings and provides specific detail on the approach known as *cluster grouping* (Gentry, 2014), and we recommend readers refer to this resource to support their grouping work and learn more about cluster grouping. By adopting a version of Total School Cluster Grouping (Gentry, 2014), teachers can rotate between student mastery groups so both students and teachers can have new opportunities for social interactions and benefit from the variety of teaching and learning approaches. In order to best facilitate continuous-flexible grouping, consider the following guidelines.

- **Call on collaborative team expertise.** Your collaborative team represents a network of diverse expertise for mutual benefit (Prain et al., 2013). Together, your shared goal of personalizing learning becomes easier with the help of your peers. Collaborative teams can work together to create fluid student groups and share the responsibility of including just the right amount of challenge for each group.

- **Make medium- or short-term groupings.** Student groups should not be long-term commitments. Teachers should refresh student groups at least every month. Teachers may form groups based on interest as well as level of mastery. All students deserve the opportunity to see themselves as high achievers capable of mastery learning. Relationships with many students foster a flexible vision of a student's academic identity and do not limit how students see themselves in the future. Proficient students may come and go from the group. With a robust sense of academic identity, students are less likely to be disappointed and less likely to see not participating in the proficient group as a failure. Conversely, proficient students who are consistently in the proficient group benefit from new peers engaging in extension work with them because this helps them develop new relationships and perspectives. Because of the frequency and curriculum alignment, short-cycle formative assessment results are helpful in determining fluid groups.

- **Allow student choice.** Student choice allows ownership of academic engagement. Student groups can naturally form when teachers give them a choice in learning approach and options in accomplishing an extended learning goal or deeper analysis together.

- **Avoid groups becoming faux flexible.** Keep track of your student groupings. It is very easy to lose track of the details of who works with whom and when. This can lead to faux-flexible grouping. Faux-flexible groups occur when teachers rearrange groups but the same students keep working with each other. Conversely, continuous-flexible grouping allows students to work with different peers throughout the year.

INDIVIDUAL REFLECTION

How can you use your knowledge of the robust composite of a student's academic profile (see chapter 4, page 61) to ensure diverse, changing, and flexible grouping in your classroom?

For a more detailed description of flexible grouping, we would be remiss if we did not direct you to Tomlinson's (2001) seminal work. With the profound connections between differentiation and personalization, it only makes sense that we refer back to Tomlinson's (2001) expert work on flexible grouping. She writes, "Flexible grouping is a central part of respect for all learners, honoring differences, collaboration, teaching for success, and collaboration in a differentiated classroom" (Tomlinson, 2001, p. 26).

Flexible Use of Classroom Space

Large-group instruction is still acceptable in a personalized learning classroom. Sitting in rows is still appropriate at key points for some learning experiences. Gone, however, are the continuous days of students taking silent, feverish notes in order to consume the sage on the stage's ever-powerful knowledge. Most classroom furniture is now designed to move easily into creative configurations, providing the flexible space needed for changing student groups in the classroom. In order to best facilitate this flexible use of classroom space, consider the following guidelines.

- **Create standardized routines.** Direct instruction regarding classroom routines to facilitate efficient movement of desks or tables will help ensure the integrity of instructional time. Work stations or other typical configurations are most efficient when students know the logistics and expectations for each space (Tucker, 2017).

- **Make space for student groups.** Collaborative student extension work groups require space. The group size will change depending on the type of grouping strategy as well as the learning task. Be sure to keep all students in your line of sight, for supervision as well as for dynamic responses to support them academically.

- **Make space for individuals.** Some proficient students work best alone or with limited stimuli. Additionally, some students accomplish learning tasks better independently. Learning with or near others can feel competitive. Some students might perceive others are judging them in their learning experience. Creating private space in a classroom for some students allows them the safety of learning as fast or slow as they need without the pressure of those nearby. For proficient students who are working on a challenging problem, the safety of slow processing in private helps protect their dignity and encourages continued risk taking.

Use the tool in figure 6.2 to review your classroom configurations and brainstorm additional configurations that may be helpful.

Look over your classroom. Sketch at least four classroom designs, at least one for each of the following configurations.

Whole-group instruction (Everyone learns the same content at the same time.)	All in work groups (The teacher places the entire class in student work groups.)
All individual student space (Every student has a dedicated, individual work space.)	Mix (The classroom combines individual work space and student work groups.)

What routines do teachers need to establish to move students efficiently between configurations?

Figure 6.2: Classroom configurations activity.

*Visit **go.SolutionTree.com/PLCbooks** for a free reproducible version of this figure.*

To dig deeper into flexible classroom spaces, we recommend Scott Doorley and Scott Witthoft's (2012) *Make Space: How to Set the Stage for Creative Collaboration*, and professional development opportunities offered through Learning Environments for Tomorrow (LEFT): Next Practices for Educators and Architects, a program from the Harvard Graduate School of Education (see https://bit.ly/2J9HOiq). While some changes like a classroom renovation or new building require architects and bond issues, we have seen individual teachers do wonderful things in their traditional classroom to create more flexibility with little budget. As researchers Prema Nedungadi and Raghu Raman (2012) note, flexibility is the essence of implementing innovation.

A Look at Implementing Flexibility in Action

To further illustrate flexibility, let's return to the collaborative sixth-grade mathematics team we've discussed in preceding chapters. The team had a goal of increasing rigor for each student with hopes of seeing individual growth on the annual state mathematics test, not just maintained performance levels. It was focused on all students improving their individual score, including students in the top proficiency category.

To start the semester, the team first identified the required curriculum must-haves and traditions. For example, traditionally, this team ended the year with a preview of geometry ideas to generate buzz and excitement for future mathematics concepts. Teachers would perform proofs, rotations, and dilations, all with a bit of pizzazz and sense of "mathemagic." An aha moment came when the team planned a visual representation of multiplying and dividing fractions concepts. Could the proficient students preview geometry concepts early as a way to stretch students' learning of multiplying and dividing fractions? Absolutely! The lesson they tried follows. Notice the intentional direct and guided instruction provided for the proficient students, not just independent practice.

Students who had already demonstrated proficiency are given two cutouts of similar triangles, rulers, and two problems on the board.

1. Find the factor relating the length of the sides of the two triangles.

2. These two triangles are similar triangles. What do you guess are the minimum rules needed to call two triangles similar?

Students can choose to work independently or in partners. All of the triangles in the classroom are similar to each other, so the more triangles they work with, the more examples of similar triangles and dilation factors they get. Some triangles have more complicated ratios than others. The teacher distributes the triangles according to students' appropriate challenge levels. For students working independently, the teacher casually drops off more triangles to feed their exploration. The teacher delivers increasingly more difficult triangle ratios to keep raising the skill challenge. The teacher notes who is working with whom or independently on her classroom chart. Students note who they are working with (or if alone) in their mathematics notebooks. All students are working on the first problem for skill competency in multiplying and dividing fractions. The second problem stretches students' thinking about the concept of multiplying and dividing fractions and previews geometry concepts.

All students in this proficient group are invited to explore the second problem. About halfway through the class period, the teacher posts a third problem.

3. How does multiplying and dividing fractions help us make triangles bigger and smaller? (See figure 6.3.)

For the third problem, students are previewing dilations while reinforcing the content of multiplying and dividing fractions.

Near the end of the class period, the teacher displays the geometry symbols for congruent angles of two triangles (see figure 6.3). She distributes a half-sheet of paper with independent exercises of multiplying and dividing fractions, including making triangles bigger and smaller. The most prominent question on this page, though, is, "These two triangles are similar triangles. What do you guess are the minimum rules needed to call two triangles similar?"

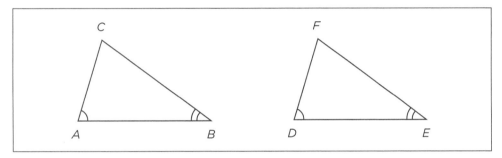

Figure 6.3: Two similar triangles.

The next day, the lesson starts with a big unveiling of angle-angle similarity—ta-da! The teacher also just teased the geometry fun ahead and related it back to the current content.

How is this flexible, and how does this stretch the learning for proficient students? First, the mathematics team had to think flexibly about the curriculum order and approach to teaching multiplying and dividing fractions. The team relinquished its traditional end-of-year geometry preview and gave the excitement of previewing geometry proofs and symbols to the students earlier in the year. Second, the teachers knew what and how to preview because of their knowledge of learning progressions. Lastly, students became aware of the current skill focus (multiplying and dividing fractions) and a skill they will learn in the future (proving similar triangles), helping them understand their learning progressions. This allows students to see the relevance of what they were learning by applying it to a new concept, heightening their engagement with the content. Teachers give students the flexibility to choose a group or partner, or to work independently within a flexible classroom structure that allows for these configurations. The teacher was aware of whether student self-selection of partners and groups created a faux-flexible grouping, ensuring students tried new working relationships rather than gravitating to the same friends each time.

Next Steps

Teachers can demonstrate flexibility for question 4 students in a variety of ways. Flexible control, flexible mindsets, a competency-based curriculum structure, continuous-flexible grouping, and flexible use of classroom space all influence the degree of personalized learning for question 4 students. What should flexibility look like in a classroom? The answer is *variable*. There is no one correct answer for a perfect, flexible plan for question 4 students. By definition, a flexible classroom is fluid. The actions in the plan for question 4 students will demonstrate high teacher control at some points and high student freedom at others. Some days, question 4 students will be independently challenged to the brink of frustration, and other days, teachers will provide them with direct instruction on a specific, in-depth skill. One week, question 4 students may rotate through work stations, and the next week, question 4 students may be in one large group learning the same content. However, one aspect of flexibility is the same: teachers in a personalized learning classroom are aware of the balance of control and freedom for each question 4 student. Variety and flexibility are critical in creating meaningful and memorable learning opportunities for these students.

Now that you have explored the personalized learning element of implementing flexibility, read and reflect on the following personalized learning stories that feature practical examples of teachers implementing this element. Use the reproducible "Individual Reflection: Implementing Flexibility" (page 144) to evaluate your current reality with implementing flexibility. Then, use the reproducibles "Collaborative Team Discussion: Implementing Flexibility" (page 146) and "Implementing Flexibility Collaborative Team Formative Check" (page 148) to support collaborative conversation and learning in your collaborative team. Visit **go.SolutionTree.com/PLCbooks** to download these free reproducibles. We recommend your collaborative team use the reproducible "Implementing Flexibility Collaborative Team Formative Check" (page 148) at regular intervals, such as once per grading period. Review your results as a team, and support each other in progress toward an ideal rating.

Personalized Learning Stories

Following are two examples that focus on element 3: implementing flexibility. In each story, note the examples of implementing flexibility as you read.

Implementing Flexibility in an Elementary Classroom

Terri Taylor is a former first-grade teacher in a large urban district with extreme poverty in California. The school has approximately 70 percent students living in poverty and an equal number enrolled in English learner (EL) programs. The school's espoused values include personalized learning approaches. Further, the California Department of Education (2017) supports flexible grouping specifically in the middle grades, rather than using permanent groups that tend to marginalize certain student populations. In addition the department encourages flexible spaces for learning to take place, including multiage classrooms, open areas for learning, and flexible furniture for both teachers and students to create learning spaces that support rigor and constructivist learning theories (California Department of Education, 2017). The district's guiding documents encourage teachers to explore and innovate with these types of teaching strategies. It is very clear that flexibility is an important classroom expectation for all teachers in the district.

No Place Like Home

Terri and a special education teacher had two classrooms and forty-eight students; thirty students were considered general education and eighteen were students with individualized education plans (IEPs). Upon entering Terri's classroom, Blane was immediately drawn to the layout, which was unique compared to others he observed. The first classroom was where large-group instruction took place. Most of the desks had the legs removed so students were sitting on the floor, which seemed like it would be uncomfortable, but the first-grade students looked very much at home. In addition, there were six traditional student desks and chairs in a corner of the room and two kidney-shaped tables with chairs in another corner. Students were sitting in each of the three reserved areas based on where they were the most comfortable. The second room, which was adjoined by a door to the first room, was just a big open classroom with floor space and bookshelves full of reading materials. This was where the students moved when learning was student directed and where they would advance their learning at their own pace. Terri and her teaching partner reviewed student data to create flexible learning spaces that fostered flexible student groups based on student need.

The ambience of both rooms felt different from any room Blane had previously visited. Terri shared with him that many of her students did not have nice homes to go home to at night; therefore she made every effort to make the classrooms feel homey. Blue sheers covered the fluorescent lights, lamps and pillows were in

continued →

every nook and cranny, and cozy curtains covered the windows. These additions truly made the rooms feel like someone's living room.

Shortly after Blane arrived, students began the daily ninety-minute language arts block. On this day, Terri and her co-teacher began by asking students to take their places as a large group in the room designed for such instruction, either on the floor, at a traditional desk, or at the kidney-shaped tables. At that time, Terri began her minilesson about narrative writing. Terri and her teaching partner took turns reading short stories and talked about what it means to be a narrative writer. Terri read Salt Hands by Jane Chelsea Aragon, followed by Joshua's Night Whispers by Angela Johnson.

After reading these stories, Terri talked about what they have in common, which included how the authors had expertly added feeling and emotion to their stories. Then, she made the connection for her students that the writers of these stories did the same things students would do during the lesson. To further illustrate what she wanted students to do, Terri shared some of her own narrative writing examples. One personal story included how she felt scared when falling off a horse and another about how she was excited when she first learned how to read. With each story, Blane could see that the students were enthralled with what she was sharing.

Next, Terri asked her first-grade students to close their eyes and think of a time when something happened to them that caused an emotion. After a few moments, she asked the students to turn and talk with a partner about their example. When the students started talking on cue, the two teachers sat down on the floor and crawled their way around, meeting with the partnered pairs. Students were 100 percent on task and shared stories about their sports accomplishments, new pets, and eating at their favorite restaurants. One student, with bright eyes and excitement, shared with another student how he watched a big football game with his dad the previous weekend.

As students began to move to the second room, Terri explained to Blane that every unit had my time and your time. My time was when the lesson was teacher directed, and your time was when the students directed their own learning. The second room was reserved for your time. In this setting, she expertly arranged students in flexible groups that ranged from one student to as many as five. She grouped students based on their readiness to write their personal experiences and to provide feedback to one another. She used the concept of a gradual release of responsibility based on students' readiness and needs. She also shared with Blane that, in many schools, educators were forced to take the joy out of teaching and followed a lockstep curriculum and high-stakes testing regimen. Consequently, these educators did not provide flexible groups and learning pathways for students. She shared that her young students regularly blew her away by outperforming what even she thought they could do. She provided opportunities for students to move at their own pace developing ownership for their learning and allowing question 4 students to extend and learn at their skill levels.

She told Blane that she was very intentional when she released responsibility to her question 4 learners. They moved at their own pace and made learning decisions not usually made by first-grade students. Terri said, "My time does not take that long but is a way to bring the class together and introduce a topic. Your time is when I get students working on their personal projects."

The two teachers made their way to each of the students and made sure one teacher always remained in one of the rooms. For some students, writing was very new. Terri challenged one student to stretch her few sentences about time spent with a relative into a story. It was interesting to see teachers stretch and extend the learning of each student, regardless of level.

Over the next hour, students worked while the teacher gathered groups of students at the kidney-shaped tables in classroom one. At one point, she worked with a small group of about six students (what she called a strategy group) on some basic punctuation. Interestingly, these six students were flexibly grouped and ranged from some of the highest- to the lowest-performing members of the class. Then she worked with question 4 students on descriptive word choice, as these students had proven through previous writing work to be proficient in the punctuation learning targets. Every day, Terri specifically created groups of students who were competent in the district-identified benchmark being taught as well as flexible groups for those students who had not yet demonstrated mastery to focus them on the appropriate content or extend their learning with a comparable but more complex benchmark for the next grade level.

At this point, it was nearing the end of the English language arts block of time and students didn't want to stop working. Terri asked the students to return from their flexible areas of learning where they were ready to do so. They stretched and then made their way back to the large group space. Terri provided closure to the lesson and shared some of the themes that emerged from her observations with the students and praised them for being writers, just like the professionals. The ebb and flow of large-group time, personal work time, and the turn and talk made Blane feel as if the students were around the kitchen table at home discussing, reflecting, thinking, and communicating with each other.

Lessons Learned

It was clear the teachers designed this classroom with flexibility grouping in mind. The space provided a variety of learning areas for students. The spaces lent themselves to flexible grouping the teachers utilized to bring out the best in their students. The students, especially question 4 students, were gradually given more responsibility and demonstrated more ownership of their learning, resulting in deeper learning for many students. Question 4 students were given an opportunity to work together and have their learning extended. It was clear that students were engaged and striving to do their best work.

When asked if she thought this flexible approach worked for her students, Terri explained that there were two unique measurements she cared about when

continued ➜

determining if this worked. First, she shared that she was engaged and excited to teach because she thought about the art of teaching and helped all students learn at their own pace, while also engaging and extending learning for question 4 students. Another way she measured its effectiveness was how students responded when the lesson ended. When time was up for a block of time, did students say, "Yay, it is over," or did they say, "What? I want to keep working!" Many wanted to keep working on their projects or learning activities.

Finally, Terri wove flexibility into her instructional approach to the district specifications. At times, this required whole-group instruction. However, within this common structure, many students were given free rein to explore their own ideas and think while working with a teacher who mentored and extended their learning. As Blane left the classroom, he realized this flexible approach of my time and your time is a perfect example of how to structure time in a personalized environment. It offered a nice balance between teacher- and student-directed learning.

Implementing Flexibility in a Secondary Classroom

Kathy McWilliams is an eighth-grade U.S. history teacher in a central Ohio school district. This typical suburban middle school has about one thousand students. The school's diversity is slightly higher than the state average with 28 percent minority students (primarily Asian) and 12 percent of students are eligible for free and reduced-price lunch. Kathy co-teaches with a partner, so they can personalize and extend learning in their classrooms. Kathy explained to Blane that her collaborative team was working on using element 3, implementing flexibility, by using multilevel lessons and a learning station–based approach in her eighth-grade classroom.

Failure Is Not an Option

The bell rang and students filed into the classroom. The two teachers greeted students, and Kathy then provided students with a printout describing how well they did on the pretest the day before. The teacher used this assessment to determine her students' next steps (element 1: knowing your learners). As students reviewed the results of the common assessment, Kathy explained to Blane that for the past fifteen days, students had been learning about push and pull factors for immigrants and refugees to the United States. The lesson reflected the district's curriculum content map for grade 8, with a focus on colonization and economic decision making and skills, and the Ohio Department of Education's (2010) social studies standard topic area of human systems, which states:

> Human Systems represent the settlement and structures created by people on Earth's surface. The growth, distribution, and movements of people are driving forces behind human and physical events. Geographers study patterns in culture and the changes that result from human processes, migrations, and the diffusion of new cultural traits. (p. 11)

Blane quickly saw a flexible classroom design centered on student learning. There was an open wall between the two classrooms, essentially creating one large classroom that accommodated the two eighth-grade classes. With such a large classroom, the teachers altered the traditional classroom setup of rows of desks and took advantage of multilevel learning stations based on various students' needs.

In one corner of the room were two circular tables with five chairs around each. Blane also saw ten traditional desks set up with five desks in two rows; however, in this room they faced each other, making it easy to share with a partner. On the opposite side of the room from the traditional desks was an area of fifteen desks set up around a computer cart equipped with a set of Google Chromebooks. The middle of the room was unchanged, with the remaining twenty-five to thirty desks in rows for large-group instruction.

Throughout the large room were seven large poster boards showing the learning targets for the upcoming test on factors influencing immigration and refugee migration prior to and during the early colonization of North America. Kathy told Blane that at the end of the fifteen-day unit, the co-teachers would administer a pretest prior to the unit test to see how well students had learned the material and to ensure students would be prepared for the unit test. In this unit, she explained the six learning targets she developed from both the district's curriculum and the Ohio Department of Education (2010) standards.

1. *I can describe the leading theory (land bridge theory) behind the first migration of people to North America.*

2. *I can define push and pull factors and identify and describe the factors that led to European colonization in the Americas.*

3. *I know that all Native American tribes had distinct cultures based on geographical environmental factors. When given the information, I can determine the general region in which the tribe lived.*

4. *I can explain the motivations (push and pull factors) and experiences of the people who traveled to Roanoke, Jamestown, Plymouth, and other colonies. I can also explain why each colony was successful or unsuccessful.*

5. *I can explain early representative governments and democratic practices.*

6. *I can explain how religion played a role in colonial life.*

When students looked at their individual pretest score reports, they saw an overall grade, but more importantly, they saw a specific percentage tied to each standard. Students knew from day one that their entrance ticket to the unit test was an 80 percent proficiency on every learning target. When a student scored less than 80 percent, the teacher assigned him or her to a specific station to work individually or in small groups to improve on a deficient target. Students prepared for a successful test by demonstrating proficiency on each teacher-

continued ➔

developed target. Students were expected to master the content in Kathy's classroom. Failure was not an option.

The individual stations were set up to provide students a great deal of voice and choice (element 2), and each required that students demonstrate proficiency. For this unit, students chose between a video and accompanying activity and a game that required the participation of three other classmates. Other students viewed images and placed them on an interactive map. Several other students were given the choice of completing comic strips or reading a current event article related to modern-day push and pull factors of immigration or refugee resettlement.

Interestingly, question 4 students, who had 80 percent or greater proficiency on all the standards, were still actively engaged in the work. Blane observed those students hurrying to an area to push themselves to continue learning so they could improve their scores and explore more topics within the standard. One question 4 student who had mastered the standard in each area found the station that asked students to propose a tweet to send (element 5: integrating technology) to a current political figure about immigration. He was visibly laughing and sharing his findings with others as he shared posts that had previously been sent by real politicians. Blane found it very interesting how Kathy extended learning while blurring the historical context with current events and increased the relevance for her learners. He was amazed by the critical thinking of question 4 students as they participated in the various opportunities to maximize their learning.

While all students worked, the co-teachers continued making rounds and checking on them. At the Chromebooks station, they checked the students' work and provided suggested edits to their final products. The teachers called each other over and shared students' exemplary work. One student beamed with pride when, after several tries, he finished his interactive map correctly and one of the teachers shared it with the other students working at that station. The teachers then asked students to come to the large-group area and closed the lesson. They prepared learners for the next day by explaining who would be taking the exam and who would need to continue earning the 80 percent proficient mark in certain standards before completing the last steps of the unit.

Lessons Learned

Blane returned to the classroom after school to follow up with Kathy and her teaching partner. The co-teachers shared with him that, four years ago, their classroom looked very different. They were very traditional and had a kind of predictable pattern to their units. They ended a unit with an assessment, which included a homework assignment consisting of a vocabulary assignment for the next unit. They taught their units through lecture, worksheets, and the occasional hands-on activity one of the two teachers developed. When students took the test at the end of the unit, sometimes they did well; other times they did not. The co-teachers never had time for question 4 students to explore the *standard through various learning opportunities that resulted in critical thinking and deep learning.*

In a collaborative team meeting, the members had an open dialogue and asked the question, "Why are we giving them the test if they aren't ready for it?" With that, the eighth-grade collaborative team members discussed different alternatives and options to challenge students' learning, especially the question 4 students who had mastered the teacher-developed targets. Kathy and her co-teacher suggested multilevel learning centers. They provided students of all skill levels specific feedback on their current progress and allowed them more time to understand the concepts. It was clear the teachers were more open to flexible deadlines, spaces, and assessments, but they were also using other elements, such as voice and choice and using data, so students could exhibit proficiency on the standards.

Subsequently, students grew in confidence and developed a growth mindset through their perseverance. Because the teachers knew the students' needs and areas of strength and challenge, they created an environment for each student's success. Question 4 students worked at their own pace, expanded the boundaries of their own learning, and were able to perform complex tasks related to the teacher-developed learning targets.

Blane asked the co-teachers what they heard from parents. They told him parents loved the practice. For students just coming from elementary school, parents shared they felt this sense of relief when it came to the history class. They knew these teachers would know their children (element 1) and that students would perform well and earn the grades they deserved. It was clear that students would keep working until they performed at a satisfactory level. More important, parents of question 4 students knew their children would have their learning extended in this classroom. Learning was paramount for these teachers.

Blane left this school thinking this was how he wished he had taught many years ago. The focus was on student success, and teachers used a flexible approach for each student based on his or her strengths, challenges, or needs in a personal manner to ensure each student understood, mastered, and could actually apply the content knowledge.

INDIVIDUAL REFLECTION

Looking at your notes on the stories about implementing flexibility, what are three actions you can take in the next five days to increase flexibility for your learners?

Individual Reflection: Implementing Flexibility

Rate yourself using the following reflection rubric. Use the following key: never is zero days, seldom is one to three days, often is four to six days, and consistently is seven to ten days.

Implementing Flexibility Definition: Teachers are flexible with how they think about grouping and classroom space.	Today's Date:			
	Never	**Seldom**	**Often**	**Consistently**
A. Question 4 students experience continuous-flexible grouping.				
Notes:				
B. I provide opportunities of both teacher control and student freedom in my lessons for question 4 students.				
Notes:				
C. I reflect on the learning progressions of the content, including targets that come before and after the current lesson objective.				
Notes:				

	Never	Seldom	Often	Consistently
D. Question 4 students reflect on the learning progressions of the content, including what they've already learned and what is coming up.				
Notes:				
E. My classroom has space for both group and individual work for question 4 students.				
Notes:				

Collaborative Team Discussion: Implementing Flexibility

The following is for use in a standard forty-five- to fifty-minute collaborative team meeting.

As a team, define the ideal rating (never, seldom, often, or consistently) for each of the following actions involved in implementing flexibility. Is *consistently* ideal for A, B, C, D, and E? Is *often* the best choice? Record your collective team ideal rating for each action of implementing flexibility. Use the following key: never is zero days, seldom is one to three days, often is four to six days, and consistently is seven to ten days.

Implementing Flexibility Action	Ideal Rating
A. Question 4 students experience continuous-flexible grouping.	
B. I provide opportunities of both teacher control and student freedom in my lessons for question 4 students.	
C. I reflect on the learning progressions of my content, including before and after the current lesson objective.	
D. Question 4 students reflect on the learning progressions of the content, including what they've already learned and what is coming up.	
E. My classroom has space for both group and individual work for question 4 students.	

Why are these the ideal ratings for each action?

How close are each of us to that ideal rating for each action?

How can we help each other get there?

For those of you who rated your actions as *often* or *consistent* on implementing flexibility, how does it feel for you, the teacher? What feedback do you hear from your students and their parents?

Implementing Flexibility
Collaborative Team Formative Check

Directions: At regular intervals (such as once a grading period) collectively rate your team using the following formative check. Review your collaborative team results and support each other in progress toward an ideal rating. Use the following key: never is zero days, seldom is one to three days, often is four to six days, and consistently is seven to ten days.

Flexibility Definition: Teachers are flexible with how they think about grouping and classroom space.	Formative Check # _____ Date:			
	Never	**Seldom**	**Often**	**Consistently**
A. Question 4 students experience continuous-flexible grouping.				
Notes:				
B. I provide opportunities of both teacher control and student freedom in my lessons for question 4 students.				
Notes:				
C. I reflect on the learning progressions of my content, including before and after the current lesson objective.				
Notes:				

	Never	Seldom	Often	Consistently
D. Question 4 students reflect on the learning progressions of the content, including what they've already learned and what is coming up.				
Notes:				
E. My classroom has space for both group and individual work for question 4 students.				
Notes:				

How close are each of us to that ideal rating for each action?

How can we help each other get there?

Look at your ratings over time. Is your implementation of flexibility the same over time? Different?

How have your actions around flexibility changed over time?

CHAPTER 7

Using Data

I n the introduction to this book (page 1), we provided a brief orientation to the three big ideas and four critical questions in a professional learning community. The third big idea, being results oriented, implies that collaborative teams are regularly assessing their work with students to determine how they can grow as professionals and what needs to happen next for learners. Richard DuFour, Rebecca DuFour, Robert Eaker, and Gayle Karhanek (2010) describe common formative assessments as the linchpin to the PLC at Work process as a means by which to collect data. Without data, teams will stall out and not be able to grow together. When looking at this element of personalized learning that specifically addresses using data, it is clear that there is a direct link and interconnection between these two models. Just like a PLC needs data to move forward, so does a collaborative team planning for instruction that guides question 4 students.

In any occupation, including educator, data inform us to make better future decisions. In collaborative teams, members work together to determine goals and methods they will use to evaluate progress. In the PLC at Work process, there is a great deal of attention on teams developing SMART goals. These are specific, measurable, attainable, results-oriented, and time-bound goals that serve as the collective output for the team's collective efforts (O'Neill & Conzemius, 2006). In this team goal setting, the data context comes from common assessments that teachers co-create or that the district or state provides. After collecting the data, the team works to better support students and make informed instructional decisions.

What comes to your mind when you read the word *data*? Is it growth on a trend line of benchmark scores from a state test for an individual student? Is it a group's average composite score on a national test? Is it the results of your collaborative team's previously developed assessment? Or, are data the record you and your team members complete to determine the amount of time students have voice and choice in the classroom? To us, *data* can mean all of these things. They are a valuable tool to inform your classroom decisions and your collaborative team's actions. In this chapter, we will address a broader and richer definition of *data-informed decision making* by examining the various sources of data teachers can use to personalize learning extensions for proficient students. We will also highlight some pitfalls to avoid to ensure data-informed practices extend learning.

Sources of Data

The term *data informed* has replaced *data driven* in our educational lexicon. The distinction between *driven* and *informed* acknowledges that the teachers in the classroom are the decision makers. We are not simply implementing a series of if-then decision switches. As data-informed educators, we seek a variety of data and do not limit our data profile to only achievement scores. In chapter 4 (page 61), we discussed the many facets of a student's academic profile. This section will expand on those ideas and specifically consider academic data, learning profile data, interpersonal data, and demographic data.

Academic Data

Academic data are data that typically sit in our learning management systems, student information databases, gradebooks, and sometimes a variety of assessment portals such as data dashboards associated with specific programs like Exact Path (www.edmentum.com/products/exact-path) and aimsweb (www.aimsweb.com). Many districts have automated processes to collect this information from a variety of databases so all data are kept in one location. This single location is sometimes visualized in a district-created data dashboard using products like Tableau (www.tableau .com/products/desktop) or Naviance (www.naviance.com). It is important to recognize the different data formats (scale scores, percentiles, growth points, and so on) so educators correctly interpret the results. Examples of academic data include but are not limited to curriculum-based measures; fall, winter, or spring benchmarks; Lexile measures; and assessment scores from the HMH Math Inventory, HMH Reading Inventory, Dynamic Indicators of Basic Early Literacy Skills (DIBELS), aimsweb, Terra Nova, Iowa Assessments, ACT Aspire, PreACT, ACT, PSAT, SAT, and SAT-10. Classroom assessment results are also academic data that can come from collaborative team–created summative and formative assessments, unit or learning-objective assessment tools from purchased curriculum resources, pre- and postassessment results from, for example, Lucy Calkins's *Units of Study for Teaching Writing* series (www.unitsofstudy.com/k5writing), progress toward observed learning targets, and classroom grades.

Learning Profile Data

These data are a combination of learning preferences, learning perceptions, and unique gifts that can enhance a student's learning. Examples of this type of data include talents, interests (Renzulli, 1997), learning disabilities, results of learning-style inventories, English language fluency and exposure, in-school and out-of-school activity participation, and Developmental Assets Profile (DAP) results. Data about students' perceptions of their classes are also valuable, using tools such as My Class Activities (Gentry & Gable, 2001) and Student Perceptions of Classroom Quality (Gentry & Owen, 2004).

In particular, teacher knowledge about proficient student perceptions of interest, challenge, choice, and enjoyment in their classroom helps bring to light opportunities of connection beyond the traditional curriculum. As discussed in chapter 4 (page 61), information beyond test scores helps adults gain a robust academic profile of students and helps students gain a well-rounded academic identity, beyond only test scores.

Interpersonal Data

Interpersonal data provide insight on interaction preferences and experiences. Because learning is social, it is important to foster a comfortable learning space for students to stretch and grow in new ways. Interpersonal data may include communication-style preferences and strengths, fluid observations of introversion or extroversion tendencies, and, for older students, inventories on social justice and values like the Social Issues Advocacy Scale (Nilsson, Marszalek, Linnemeyer, Bahner, & Misialek, 2011) and the Activism Orientation Scale (Corning & Myers, 2002). Teachers may also want to consider information about successful or unsuccessful peer interactions. Motivation and engagement can be measured by tools such as the Patterns of Adaptive Learning Survey (PALS; Midgley et al., 2000), the Student Engagement Instrument (SEI; University of Minnesota, 2018) and the Motivation and Engagement Scale (MES; Liem & Martin, 2012). While proficient students are not at risk academically, they are not exempt from social and emotional challenges.

The more information adults and the students themselves know about their interpersonal strengths and challenges, the more successful personalized lesson development will be.

Demographic Data

Districts may use a student information system like PowerSchool or Infinite Campus, or a learning management system like Schoology or Canvas, to store and track demographic data that teachers can access. Demographic data may include information such as mobility trends, support networks of parents and other advocates, age, race, and gender. While academic data, learning profile data, and interpersonal data are used to predict performance or guide programming specifically for the needs of the proficient students, demographic data are not used for these purposes. Rather, demographic data are helpful for identifying trends in who is receiving extension programming as proficient students. If it is always the same students or same types of students by demographic who are part of the extension work, we recommend collaborative teams take some time to reflect on how proficiency is demonstrated and determine if the processes in place are available for all students to demonstrate their learning.

The complexity of these academic, learning profile, interpersonal, and demographic data together helps enhance a robust composite for each student's academic profile. As a reminder, be sure to follow district protocols for storing data and information about students. Use the tool in figure 7.1 to reflect individually on the types of data you keep and can easily access.

Assessment Strategies to Support Using Data

High-performing PLCs (and collaborative teams that work within them) effectively use data that focus on results. In collaborative teams, there is a concentrated effort to have clarity about the strengths and weaknesses of each student in mastering standards and outcomes, which occurs through an ongoing, collective analysis of student learning evidence. We see this as an excellent connection to personalized learning. Many leading authors of personalized learning focus on this same component and would agree that educators need to meet students where they are (Bray & McClaskey, 2017; Rickabaugh, 2016). When students demonstrate they know the material and are ready to be challenged with extension, this is the appropriate next

Consider the student data you currently track. With one hour of notice, what academic data could you pull together for each of your students?

Consider the student data you currently track. With one hour of notice, what learning profile data could you pull together for each of your students?

Consider the student data you currently track. With one hour of notice, what interpersonal data could you pull together for each of your students?

Consider the student data you currently track. With one hour of notice, what demographic data could you pull together for each of your students?

After skimming the list of possible data sources (academic, learning profile, interpersonal, and demographic), is there additional information you desire about your students? Is it possible to gather those data?

Figure 7.1: Individual reflection—Student data.

*Visit **go.SolutionTree.com/PLCbooks** for a free reproducible version of this figure.*

step. If a student is struggling with the material or is right on target, a different set of activities will ensue. Teachers who know where their students are in the learning process and react accordingly based on data are going to be successful.

In order to know where learners are, educators need to use data to make decisions that lead to personalization. This is yet another example where the key components of personalized learning and PLCs intersect. There are many different types of data collaborative teams could use to help inform them about their learners. In this section, we provide a quick glimpse at various assessment strategies and how teachers can use them in a personalized learning environment to extend learning for students who have demonstrated proficiency.

Informal Formative Assessment

Formative assessment is any low-stakes process in which teachers gather information about student understanding to inform the next bit of instruction and learning. Formative assessment can be a quiz, test, check for understanding, thumbs up or down, marker board responses, exit tickets, and so on. Formative assessment has a positive effect on student academic achievement (Klute, Apthorp, Harlacher, & Reale, 2017). In a personalized learning environment, formative assessments provide teachers with a quick check on what students know or are able to do without causing students to see the activity in terms of in or out, pass or fail, or win or lose.

Through formative assessments, both students and teachers are aware of short-term progress and challenges. Sometimes our proficient students are given independent work and do not get the same quick feedback that others in the classroom do. However, for our proficient students, formative assessments provide reinforcement that they are on the right track of their learning. All students, including proficient students, benefit from informal checks on progress. Teachers gain student learning information in real time and can respond immediately to guide the next level of challenge.

Informal formative checks are also designed to be low-stakes. That is, they do not influence the final grade on a project for a student or result in long-term group placement. Because proficient students may be cautious to take risks in learning for fear of failing, informal formative checks provide necessary feedback for them without the label of failure or risk of consequence for showing a weakness or asking questions. Informal formative checks remind Tami of her son's middle school basketball team. Each game carries pretty low stakes; no one goes to a state championship based on one middle school game. But in each weekly game there are missed baskets. The players, in the moment, need to take information about the missed shot, note what needs to be done in the future, and have a short memory of failure to keep hustling continuously in the play. Our proficient students move quickly through their learning. They need quick course corrections along the way and a short memory of their mistakes so as to not get discouraged and to keep moving in their academic challenge in front of them.

Common Assessment

One of the many strengths of PLCs is the opportunity to review student progress based on common assessments. As a team, with common assessments, you are able to compare student performance on a curriculum concept without interference of individual teacher interpretation of student understanding. As authors, we have been involved in conversations with teachers and administrators about the difference between common formative assessments versus common summative assessment. Formative assessment is the process used to "recognize and respond to student learning to enhance that learning during the learning" (Bell & Cowie, 2001, p. 536). Summative assessments are large milestones of learning and involve a compilation of learning objectives. But really, all assessment informs learning and helps the teacher to recognize and respond to student learning needs. To help clear the noise, we offer the terms *short-cycle formative assessment* and *long-cycle formative assessment*. The distinguishing factor is the amount of time that passes in between assessments.

Short-cycle formative assessment is a focused type of formative assessment that occurs frequently (National Council of Teachers of Mathematics, n.d.). Short-cycle assessment may feel almost continuous, as it should occur at a minimum of no less than four weeks apart. Short-cycle formative assessment is exceptionally useful in a responsive and personalized classroom because it creates data flow teachers use to inform continuous-flexible grouping (discussed in chapter 6, page 121). This type of formative assessment is more formal than exit tickets or thumbs up or down. Short-cycle formative assessment is tied to specific essential standards and learning targets. The teacher's careful alignment of assessment questions helps drive instructional decisions. For proficient students, short-cycle formative assessment helps ensure regular feedback and low-stakes checks of accuracy for learning.

Similarly, *long-cycle formative assessment* is an assessment that informs instruction which is administered four weeks or more after the previous assessment. Long-cycle formative assessments and summative assessments both cover multiple learning objectives. The information gleaned from these longer assessments provides information to adjust curriculum (Brookhart, 2014).

Having a strong collection of common assessments in your team's toolbox is critically important. This is an interesting consideration for your team as school leaders have heard many convincing arguments for not having common assessments. The most frequent is that the district office has not provided any. While some district assessments provide stability and points of comparison, we would argue that you do not want an overabundance of them. Some of the best assessments you will use in your classroom are ones that you and your team develop together. As collaborative teams work on common assessments, they should consider the sources and quality of those assessments and how their teams review the data they collect.

Sources of Common Assessments

Strong common assessments are the backbone of collaborative teams in a PLC. By having common curriculum and tools to assess results, teams flourish. While district assessments can be helpful, the more powerful assessments are those the teams determine or create. Note that teams do not have to develop assessments from scratch. We have seen many strong collaborative teams use one of the following four strategies to quickly develop a common assessment.

1. **Materials from textbooks:** Most curriculum packages come with supplemental materials such as short checks for understanding and other quick tools. Review the quality, sufficiency, and alignment before use. The collaborative team members are the experts, not a book.

2. **Existing tests:** It is not uncommon for same-subject teachers in the same building to be unfamiliar with one another's assessments. A team can quickly have a common assessment by asking team members to share what they have used in the past and either choosing one or the best parts of each.

3. **Collaborative creation:** Most importantly, your school-based collaborative team is a great resource when creating a common formative assessment (Bailey & Jakicic, 2012). Collaborative teams are ideal social learning networks; individual members collaboratively challenge and support each other while sharing in the creative development of formative assessments.

4. **Online communities:** Your district may subscribe to an online community, so be sure to check what is available to you at no

cost. Also, open-source sharing sites like Share My Lesson (https://sharemylesson.com), Teacher's Notebook (https://teachersnotebook.com), and TeachHUB (www.teachhub.com) can be great resources. Be sure you know your district's protocol or policy regarding sharing lessons, assessments, and other materials. Some districts limit what teachers can share with different audiences.

Quality of Common Assessments

As the experts on learning and teaching, the classroom teachers should use their expertise to evaluate assessments they may consider using. Assessments from textbooks, online communities, or even your files should be reviewed for quality. We recommend collaborative teams consider the following items to ensure they are using quality common assessments.

- **Align with learning targets:** Formative data should align with curriculum standards and indicators, and only include a few learning targets at a time. Questions should clearly measure the indicator. Aligned assessments allow the teacher to use results to inform instruction and place students on learning continua. Using common formative assessments to measure if students have learned the skill (looking backward) yields information about mastery and student progress. Using common formative assessments to measure upcoming learning targets (looking forward) helps inform plans and curriculum connections. This is especially important for proficient students because teachers may discover the student already has some knowledge about what is coming up in future lessons. Therefore, teachers can design extension work to either align with the upcoming learning objectives or dig deep around the current learning objectives.

- **Determine sufficiency:** Teachers should determine the minimum information necessary to inform them of students' progress. For a low-stakes formative assessment, a collaborative team can discuss a simple quality check like "If a student gets this correct, does that mean he or she understands the information?" to help determine if the check is sufficient. If the answer is *yes*, there is sufficient evidence and the formative assessment is complete. If the answer is *no*, teachers should keep asking for more information in the formative assessment. In creating long-cycle formative or summative assessments, teams need to consider the variety of ways students can show proficiency on the learning objectives, including possible distractors. For high-stakes assessments such as graduation tests or more substantive assessments like end-of-unit exams, more review for validity and reliability is necessary. For more information on validity, reliability, and sufficiency of assessment items, we support Craig Mertler's (2017) recommendations of the following sources.

- *Criteria for High-Quality Assessment* (Darling-Hammond et al., 2013; https://bit.ly/2HYGYZV)

- *Standards for Teacher Competence in Educational Assessment of Students* (https://bit.ly/2lJhiSc)

- *The Code of Fair Testing Practices in Education* (https://bit .ly/2I3k03S)

■ **Review for action:** One major function of a collaborative team is the consistent review of common formative data and action to support students as a result of that data review (Bailey & Jakicic, 2012; DuFour et al., 2016). Often our data review focuses on the students who have not yet learned the content. It is just as important that we take action to support proficient students based on the results of a data review. PLCs provide a great resource for determining collective opportunities for question 4 students. Data inform personalized learning. Students who have mastered a concept need the opportunity to move on through either enrichment or acceleration. Collaborative team review of common assessments also helps facilitate the conversation of flexible grouping between and in teachers' classrooms as discussed in chapter 6 (page 121). Proficient students benefit from moving between teachers for different learning opportunities and experiences and gaining multiple perspectives of challenge and insights.

INDIVIDUAL REFLECTION

How would you integrate the use of multiple sources of information (academic, learning profile, interpersonal, and demographic data) about a student into your collaborative team conversations and actions?

Review of Data

When reviewing data as a team, consider the following sequenced guidelines, adapted from Public Profit's (n.d.) guide *Dabbling in the Data*. We recommend taking the following steps as a collaborative team.

1. **Understand your data:** Use descriptive statistics to put results in context. Distributions and variance help the collaborative team observe performance trends and nuances.

2. **Use time series data:** When available, graph your assessment results (*y*-axis) over time (*x*-axis). Seeing trends over time helps ensure you are not over- or under-correcting limited data. Additionally, be sure you know what meaningful differences each data type can make. Your technical assistance manuals for assessments and inventories often highlight these differences. Not every change is a meaningful change.

3. **Align with milestones:** Align your trend data with educational environment milestones. This alignment can help collaborative team members hypothesize on program elements or assist with school-led impacts and changes related to the broader picture. Nothing happens in a vacuum, including test results. A review of milestones allows you to determine the other school-life aspects that helped frame the results. Looking back over time, you may be able to unpack possible influences leading to test results and hypothesize about causation as well.

4. **Ensure sense making:** Create a shared understanding of the data interpretation. This may result from sorting and grouping data thematically. A problem is most successfully solved not by identifying the deficit and trying to fill it, but by observing the relationships that resulted in the data. This step must be done together in your collaborative teams. The purpose is to create a shared understanding. When lining up milestones and data themes, what narrative emerges? Restate that narrative in a variety of ways to ensure everyone agrees on the conclusion.

5. **Review for action:** Once a team agrees on what the data results mean, it must decide on the actions to take. This step encourages teams to look past the first answer. For example, if reviewing a long-cycle formative assessment shows a student weakness in subtracting fractions, the first answer is to teach students more about subtracting fractions.

A less obvious action might be to consider what skills are related to subtracting fractions. If the team sees a weakness in a related skill, *that* skill is the skill it should work to correct, not the narrow skill of subtracting fractions. What is most important is that all team members agree on the shared action. Don't forget to communicate your action plan to stakeholders. Communicating the results to others leads to deeper understanding for all.

INDIVIDUAL REFLECTION

What processes, routines, or norms do you currently have in place to review common assessment data so you can make informed instructional decisions? Using the recommendations outlined in the preceding text, how can you increase your assessment quality or review of data as a collaborative team?

Incorrect Narratives

Teachers must be mindful about how they think about data in their own practice and the ways they quantify and display data when working with students. It is easy for students to compare their achievement to others' and feel competitive when exposed to class achievement data—even when a teacher removes identifiers. Definition of success and failure by data can be especially pronounced for proficient students. Our teacher actions around test scores can accidentally reinforce a false equivalency between strong test scores and personal success. In the following section we'll explore these relationships and modes of thinking.

Data and Definitions of Success

All kinds of data feed into students' academic profiles and their internalized academic identities. Teachers must shepherd data use to enhance the complexity of a student's identity, not diminish it. Students are constantly defining their individual academic identities (Kolano, 2016). Many factors, including external feedback, internal standards, peer comparisons, personal motivations, and a host of environmental influences of successes, failures, and continued persistence, influence academic identity (Elliot & Dweck, 2005). Peak performance in many different fields of study shows that hard work and consistent effort are the key variables to success (Csikszentmihalyi, 2008). Therefore, it is important that our talented students pair effort with achievement, not just an external source deeming them successful based on a test score. Proficient students benefit from hearing praise about hard work and consistent effort. Through reinforcement of effort, a minor failure becomes part of learning and not a definition of personal quality.

INDIVIDUAL REFLECTION

Teachers influence academic identity development. How do you foster your students' academic identities? How are data part of those academic identities?

Consider this scenario: A third grader came home and said, "Did you know that I'm above average?" Being unsure what this meant, the parent paused and waited. "Yeah, I mean I'm on the right side of the curve. Really clever, you know." That day the class had reviewed their reading-level results from the Fountas and Pinnell (2016) benchmark assessment system. On the board, the teacher displayed a graphical representation of students' reading-level distribution as an example of a bell curve and normal distribution. However unintentional, everyone wanted to know who the top dot was and who the lonely dot on the far left was. Placing personal performance against the class performance reinforced this student's idea of personal sense of success, or being clever as being tied to the location on the curve. This third grader paired pride with comparison over others. She was proud of how far right her dot was on the curve. What began as a discussion of the results as a class unfortunately turned into a list of implied winners and losers based on the benchmark assessment.

INDIVIDUAL REFLECTION

Thinking of your proficient students, what are the benefits of students knowing their personal performance data? When could it be appropriate or inappropriate to position those data among a larger data set?

As a result of this incident, the parent of this third grader became concerned with helping the third grader construct a personal definition of success. External markers such as being a dot on the far right of a curve communicate a clear message: "You're a winner, you're a success, you're on top!" But, fragile definitions of success built mostly on accolades (such as earning a top reading level or a solid test score performance) can build a frail sense of self.

Just like our data composite of students should be diverse and from multiple sources (academic, learning profile, interpersonal, and demographic data), so, too, should be a teacher's and student's composites of what creates their academic identities. An identity focused too much on benchmark and test scores can skew a student's sense of self and create an identity over-reliant on others' external feedback for personal success. Our students are wonderfully complex individuals. Accidentally narrowing a sense of value, definition, or worth to a number or dot on a trend line can have unintentional consequences.

In our classrooms, we can foster a personal definition of success for our proficient students. While the programming we structure is focused on content standards, our extension can focus on the depth of the content, the effort of the proficient student, the level of critical thinking and analysis of the content, and so on. Teachers should steer away from phrases like "You're so smart" or "You are really clever" and replace them with comments such as "I like how you keep working to find the best answer, not the first answer" or "Your persistence in this subject is admirable" to help tie hard work and consistent effort with personal success.

INDIVIDUAL REFLECTION

Consider the robust and complex data available to you. How can you leverage this information to help a student create a broadly defined academic identity?

Mind Traps

Teachers should be not only cautious in the ways they use data with students but also cognizant of their own thought processes when making data-informed decisions. When reviewing data, we can accidentally make mistakes and reinforce generalized mind narratives, which we call *mind traps*. *Mind traps* are automatic, quick thinking which results in wrong or incomplete results. Quick thinking can be good for many things, but can be detrimental in reviewing data. One tempting way to consider question 4 students is to go by the district's list of identified gifted students. This would show how students did on certain IQ and content-area assessments. We believe that it would be far more beneficial to all students in the classroom to think bigger. While the focus of this book is for the students who are question 4 students when they walk in the door, we would like to pause to make a case for thinking about this in a larger context. We challenge teams to determine strategies where all students get to be a part of these wonderful personalized learning ideas at least some of the time. The research is clear that if you are a certain race or income level, your chances of being formally involved in gifted education reduce greatly (Yaluma & Tyner, 2018).

How can teachers and collaborative teams be a part of something bigger, and work to identify students who are not just high achievers but also those who are of high potential? The history books are well lined with examples that demonstrate really smart, talented, accomplished, and admired adults who were not considered to be exceptional in school. We contend that personalized learning and the strategies listed in this book are even more beneficial to students who have been a part of marginalized communities and is a tool for reducing the achievement gap. Therefore, be careful of falling into the mind trap of viewing data in a way that causes you to exclude students who might most benefit from being considered to have high potential.

Mind traps can limit our thinking and change expectations. Unexamined mind traps can be dangerous and self-fulfilling (Thompson, 2004). Gaps of achievement, discipline, and other aspects of school life are still as wide today as they have ever been. Incorrect mind narratives can influence our actions in ways that unintentionally limit student success.

A Look at Using Data in Action

Let's revisit the sixth-grade mathematics team again. As a collaborative team, the team members noticed a dip in the winter mathematics benchmark scores. This dip caused concern from students and parents, who felt like they were losing ground in the academic year. On further review, the team noticed that the winter benchmark assessment items were not aligned with the sixth-grade curriculum progression. In fact, the benchmark tool the district had purchased was not aligned with the sixth-, seventh-, or eighth-grade midyear mathematics curriculum sequence. So, as proficient students were scoring well on the benchmark, it was really measuring the possible exposure of mathematics topics instead of a deep dive into the actual mathematics curriculum. Unlike a reading benchmark that can progress up with reading comprehension and speed, the mathematics benchmark this school district uses is very much skill concept–based. Because the collaborative team did an analysis of the scores for all students, including proficient students, it was able to uncover the assessment-curriculum mismatch.

So, the team had a decision to make. It could align the curriculum with the purchased benchmark test, recommend no longer implementing the winter benchmark to district curriculum because of misalignment, or continue on the same course and keep explaining the winter score dip. All three options have pros and cons.

Leveraging teachers' professional insight will help keep the decision making close to the classroom.

In this case, the team decided to not administer the winter benchmark and instead use short- and long-cycle formative assessment data to drive teaching decisions and mark student progress. The team recorded this decision in its sixth-grade mathematics data book so the rationale wasn't forgotten in the future. This is an example of a milestone the teachers would align data with as the team analyzes trend data in the future. The context of eliminating the winter benchmark data and replacing it with formative data will enhance future conversations.

Next Steps

Using data means that teachers seek and use data to inform classroom practices. Many types of data combine to create students' academic profiles. In collaborative teams, members review short-cycle common formative assessments for quick-response progress. Additionally, it is important for teams to review time-sequence trends of long-cycle formative and summative assessments. It is important for teachers to collect data from multiple sources and use that information to help create flexible student groups. When working with numbers, teachers may fall into mind traps that result in inaccurate student expectations. We can rely on collaborative team feedback as well as personal, intellectual awareness and reflection to mitigate mind traps.

Now that you have explored the personalized learning element of using data, read and reflect on the following personalized learning stories that feature practical examples of teachers implementing this element. Use the reproducible "Individual Reflection: Using Data" (page 175) to evaluate your current reality with using data. Then, use the reproducibles "Collaborative Team Discussion: Using Data" (page 176) and "Using Data Collaborative Team Formative Check" (page 177) to support collaborative conversation and learning in your collaborative team. Visit **go.SolutionTree .com/PLCbooks** to download these free reproducibles. We recommend your collaborative team use the reproducible "Using Data Collaborative Team Formative Check" (page 177) at regular intervals (such as once per grading period). Review your results as a team, and support each other in progress toward an ideal rating.

Personalized Learning Stories

Following are two examples that focus on element 4: using data. In each story, note the examples of using data as you read.

Using Data in an Elementary Classroom

Chrissy Pike is an experienced teacher in her twelfth year with a large urban-suburban district in North Carolina. She is in her second year of implementing personalized learning strategies in her classroom in a preK–5 school of approximately six hundred students. Chrissy's school was selected in the first wave of schools to implement personalized learning approaches.

She explained that her class size is twenty to twenty-two students, but she and another teacher exchanged classes for mathematics. One group was heterogeneously grouped while the other group was a "high block" of question 4 students who already demonstrated proficiency on the standard she was teaching. The district's personalized learning approach is based around these four district-identified cornerstones of personalized learning: (1) the whole child; (2) student ownership; (3) paces, playlists, and pathways; and (4) mastery learning, which is what Chrissy used to personalize and extend learning for her question 4 students. While she initially said that this was new to her, she quickly realized that she always taught in this manner. Consequently, these changes were not necessarily hard for her to incorporate into her teaching.

All Hands on Deck

Blane arrived at Chrissy's classroom to interview and observe her a few minutes before class, and they spoke briefly. They sat down and she explained the district's four cornerstones of personalized learning, noting she made excellent use of the district's paces, playlists, and pathways cornerstone. She clarified for Blane that the district defined the paces aspect as "I control the speed of my learning: when to accelerate or slow down," playlists as "I control the direction of my learning what I need to focus on based on my performance," and pathways as "I develop my aspirations by actively exploring career and college opportunities." Chrissy used these to gather data about her students. For example, she took standard 5.NF.B.7.C from the Common Core State Standards (CCSS; National Governors Association Center for Best Practices & Council of Chief State School Officers [NGA & CCSSO], 2010b) involving fractions divided by the whole. Students were asked to select two of the three playlists to show mastery of the standard. Chrissy used product choice, requiring students to pick a project that was either a visual assignment, a writing assignment, or a creative pathway such as a multimedia presentation, which were tied to the standard. She expected a more complex product choice for those students who were proficient.

Chrissy emphasized the importance of developing a growth mindset in all students. She did this by helping students see that they should own their learning.

continued →

Student ownership was one of the district's four cornerstones of personalized learning. Her students said things like "I can't do it yet" and "Mistakes make me better." These statements were evidence that students were shifting their thinking from a defeated attitude to a can-do attitude in mathematics. Chrissy created an environment where students could find consistent success because knowing her learners (element 1) enabled her to create lessons along with the playlists that maintained a level of challenge for each question 4 student.

Chrissy required students to reflect on their learning daily and asked them why they are where they are in mastering the standard. Students identified themselves as a novice (know nothing), an apprentice (need coaching), a practitioner (need practice), or an expert (can teach the standard). Learners read and completed the reflection log and completed an exit ticket each day. Students knew that Chrissy read their exit tickets, provided feedback, and knew her students (element 1) well. In fact, question 4 students could request a conference with her to review their work, get coaching, or develop an independent assignment with the teacher to extend their learning.

Chrissy went on to point out that struggling students did better in this environment. Because she knew her students well, Chrissy differentiated the student reflection sheet, and struggling students were required to tell her how they used the assigned independent time. The heterogeneous group received additional large-group instruction, and Chrissy motivated these students by showing them their progress in mastering the standard. She felt she challenged question 4 students and that they worked that much harder in class, extending their learning themselves through the more personalized mathematics curriculum.

Student work adorned the classroom walls, and Chrissy began class by explaining the day's lesson. The lesson was adding and subtracting unlike denominators or asking students to find the common denominator, aligned with the CCSS fifth-grade mathematics standard of understanding the common denominator or finding the common denominator (5.NF.B.3; NGA & CCSSO, 2010b).

The class was very active, but quickly settled down as Chrissy distributed the pretest. The pretest identified students who did not currently understand the Common Core standard being taught (to add and subtract unlike denominators; 5.NF.A.1) in a story text (NGA & CCSSO, 2010b). In this instance, the learners were asked to examine a story problem that showed two types of apples: ³/₈ red apples and ³/₄ green apples. Blane observed Chrissy incorporating the fourth-grade standards into the fifth-grade lesson that spiraled up concepts previously taught. Her focus was to ensure students fully understood previous standards and mastered current standards at their own pace and with voice and choice (element 2) regarding their assessments.

She created flexible groups (element 3) of students based on the pretest results. Novices and apprentices (identified on the pretest) were in a group Chrissy taught the standard to again. She provided a minilesson to help them add and subtract unlike denominators. Learners who demonstrated they understood how to find a common denominator extended their learning by selecting a pathway and began work on designing their assessment to share with their teacher. Practitioners and experts (question 4 students) extended their learning through individual projects (product choice) and opportunities to learn beyond the fifth-grade standards.

Again, Blane saw students make product choices and select pathways where they created a video or a visual representation of what they had learned. Other students were thinking about a written assignment that explained how they understood the information. Several students were working on their individual projects using devices to create content around the fractions standard. They were using various visuals and applications to show how they found a common denominator. By completing individual projects, students moved their learning forward, and Chrissy knew they had a better understanding of the standards and benchmark.

In fact, two students held a conference with Chrissy, and she helped each student choose assessments. She told all students she would be checking their pathways in two days. Chrissy reminded students they could sign up for a conference if they wanted to check in with her before the assignment was due. As Blane observed Chrissy, he could tell that she loved teaching and seeing her students develop a growth mindset. Her enthusiasm for her students was certainly contagious and Blane was soon talking to students and providing advice. Chrissy had an all-hands-on-deck approach, and Blane went to work helping students with their work. With five minutes until class ended, Chrissy reminded students to complete their reflection exit tickets explaining what they had learned that day. Chrissy was constantly collecting data to assist her with learning decisions with her students. They answered the following questions.

- Did you accomplish what you intended today?
- What did the lesson cover today and what did you learn?
- How many problems did you complete?
- How did you feel about the standard you studied?
- What did you learn in mathematics or science today?

Students handed the reflection exit tickets to their teacher on the way out of class.

Lessons Learned

Chrissy's students went to their art class, and Blane stayed in the classroom so they could continue their conversation on her approach to teaching. She told him that even though this approach was relatively new to the district, she had always taught by collecting data and understanding her learners. She felt the four district-developed cornerstones were very helpful to personalizing and maximizing learning for all students, and extending learning for question 4 learners. She especially liked the playlists and pathways because information was in place to successfully advance every student's learning based on his or her interests and

continued →

passions. The district made it easy for Chrissy to develop ownership for learning among her students.

In fact, this is the biggest difference Chrissy now sees in her students. Because she develops student agency with her learners, Chrissy sees a growth mindset developing. Her students now believe they can accomplish their goals and tend to work harder when they do not understand. She told Blane, "They badger me to help and push their learning because they want to learn the information."

She also finds that the playlists and pathways are opportunities to extend learning because the activities are also leveled and developmentally appropriate for all levels of students. It sends a message to question 4 students that they can find more challenging activities that take them deeper into the standard and benchmark. In many cases, students are able to transfer their knowledge into another concept or standard.

Finally, Chrissy said she feels much more comfortable teaching in this environment and is glad her school was in the first wave of personalized learning schools. It fits her natural style and she feels supported by the district and its professional learning opportunities. She told Blane that she knew this approach worked for several reasons. It changed her own mindset about her students because she knows they can accomplish their goals. She sees all students making progress, but especially the struggling students. In addition, she feels that question 4 students are engaged and working at high levels, which allows her to extend or push students to meet their potential through the playlists and pathways.

Blane left the room excited about the progress all Chrissy's students were making, no matter their levels. She did believe that her students could all be successful, but it took an all-hands-on-deck mentality to accomplish.

Using Data in a Secondary Classroom

Rachel Russell is an eighth-grade English language arts teacher in a small suburban Wisconsin community. The district committed to implement personalized learning beginning in 2013. It became a one-to-one learning environment in 2010 and will switch devices in 2018 to Google Chromebooks. Rachel has taught for more than ten years as a middle school teacher.

The English language arts department developed a writing cycle that included students beginning with individual experiences, and then moving through the following steps: (1) reflection, (2) reference, (3) additional reflection, and (4) individual reaction prior to writing.

First, students were asked to use their own experiences to determine topics for their writing assignments. Rachel did not direct these assignments, which she told Blane later was hard for her. She shared, "I've let go of traditional ideas over the years. Ten years ago, I would be assigning a string of five-paragraph literary analysis essays. But that teacher-determined pathway isn't necessary for students to improve and extend their skills and is not what is in the best interest of students as writers." She used data and developed lessons based on her students' needs, interests, and skills.

Transformational Teaching and Learning

Blane arrived at Rachel's classroom as it was beginning. He found her room to be warm and welcoming, with various motivational posters and books lining the walls. Rachel immediately excused one of her question 4 students who went to the library and worked independently on a project. She reminded him to watch the clock and be back at 11:50 a.m.

The class began with sustained silent reading (SSR) and each student read a book of his or her choice. Students were engaged in their reading and some drew in their notebooks as they made connections with what they read. Rachel began a writing conference with a student. She used a very calm demeanor that helped the student relax. Blane observed that other students used their independent choices for SSR and developed writing pieces for their writing assignments. They applied the various Wisconsin state standards (Wisconsin Department of Public Instruction, 2011b) to the assignment.

What Blane found interesting was how well she knew the student she was conferencing with. He clearly was a student with strong writing skills. She treated him as an individual and met his needs. As he observed, Rachel explained to the student his strengths and challenges with this writing assignment. She reviewed her high expectations for him, and he determined the purpose, audience, and format of the writing piece. This student seemed to have trouble determining both the audience and the format. Rachel coached him on both and told him he might be able to save this piece for an informative essay rather than the assigned persuasive essay. She also did not have a firm deadline for this student, knowing that he needed more time to complete the essay. She was more concerned that he use his strong skills and engage in the writing cycle and benchmarks in more complex ways than hand in the assignment on a certain date.

The student was very thankful because he knew that what he had completed thus far was not his best work and knew he could do better. He wanted the additional time to turn in his best work, not to slack off. Rachel's knowledge of the student's (element 1) needs was outstanding as she provided coaching throughout this session. The conference allowed her to extend this student's learning and expand his thinking. This was instrumental in keeping the student moving forward to master the Wisconsin Foundations of English Language Arts (Wisconsin Department of Public Instruction, 2011a) on writing a persuasive essay. If she had not used the data from previous assignments and tests, she would not have been able to coach this student and advance his writing, building on his abilities.

Following SSR time, Rachel explained to her students they were continuing to learn about theme, defined as a unifying idea or thought. Further, students analyzed the theme from a text by brainstorming and finding evidence supporting the theme.

continued →

The actual reading standard, which the state borrowed from the Common Core State Standards, was "Determine a theme or central idea of a text and analyze its development over the course of the text" (RL.8.2; NGA & CCSSO, 2010a). Rachel asked students to brainstorm themes in small groups. She carefully defined theme versus genre since some students thought genres such as romance or sci-fi were themes. Rachel explained that those brainstormed ideas were not themes; themes were topics such as motivation, courage, or leadership. Students then brainstormed what possible themes might emerge from the video they were to watch next.

At that point in the lesson, students watched the video Unbroken (Mateusz M, 2014), a motivational video on YouTube. This was an excellent choice for the standard since students could identify many possible themes from the video.

Following the video, students discussed theme first in small groups and then as a whole class. Students used words such as fear, growth, passion, and courage as examples of theme that resonated with them from the video. Students then began to find evidence of the themes they identified in the video. They used visual evidence (such as a video or picture) and used a variety of words as evidence to demonstrate the themes they identified in this exercise. Rachel walked throughout the room, checked student progress, and ensured students were on the right track with the lesson. She was unable to see every student's progress, but told each student she would do a quick check at the beginning of the next class.

The student who had left the class earlier returned on time and heard the teacher provide closure to the lesson. Rachel told her students she was pleased they understood the concept of theme and could brainstorm possible themes in the video. She told them they would pick up with the concept of finding evidence in the next class period, but they should continue to look for evidence outside of class. She also reminded students about their writing assignments and to sign up for a writing conference when they thought they were ready to share their work with her. The bell rang, and students filed out of class excited and talked about the video and the themes they identified. These eighth-grade learners were engaged because Rachel had used her previous knowledge of them to design a lesson that would engage this age group.

As students exited, Rachel told Blane she enjoyed the district's support to implement personalized learning opportunities that motivated and extended the learning of her students, especially the ones from whom she needed to answer PLC critical question 4. She agreed that being part of this transformation changed her teaching and mental models about teaching and learning.

Lessons Learned

Rachel and Blane continued their discussion in the media center. She gave him a quick tour and explained that she spent part of her day in the center, where she worked with students who needed help or extension of their thinking and learning based on class and other content-area data.

Blane asked what this lesson might have looked like prior to the district's initiative to personalize learning. Rachel laughed and said, "That's easy; it would have been a five-paragraph essay from a story that I chose." She went on to say, "The previous lesson would have had no practice, no exploring, no opportunity to take a risk or really to think critically." She would never have extended question 4 students' learning because she did not collect data to inform her of their interests, passions, and abilities. She and her team never previously answered question 4 but concentrated their collaborative time on those students who struggled.

Rachel indicated she learned so much about her students from previous assignments and treated them as individuals. She either extended learning for those who needed more complex assignments that asked them to analyze or synthesize or provided help to struggling students depending on what the data told her about individual students. Rachel felt by using data with students, they took more ownership of their learning, grew in confidence, and wanted to share their best work with her regardless of their abilities. Blane saw a flexible mindset developing in these students. Moving learners from a fixed mindset to a growth mindset is another critical element of personalized learning, but is impossible without using data about your students.

Rachel told Blane she saw more student interaction with the content, rather than simple compliance, using her current teaching approach. She felt she knew her students better and that they were learning for themselves because they saw it was important to learn the assigned content. Previously, she said, "I never knew if they thought they mastered the standard since they turned in the lesson at the summative stage; they made the deadline or they did not." Since Rachel and her team now include question 4 in their collaborative team time, she is able to push question 4 students deeper into the standard and benchmark because she uses data to inform her learning decisions.

Over the past several years, Rachel has learned a great deal about her own teaching with her shift from a teacher-directed to a student-directed environment. Not only did she see more joy and engagement in the classroom, which is important to her, but she found that she now encourages creativity from her students, not compliance for her sake. For example, many students drew during class and created a visual representation of their work, but more importantly, they visualized their learning in ways not previously possible in Rachel's classroom. She now aligned the standard being taught with the learning needs of her students, which allowed her to extend the learning for question 4 students, and challenge each beyond simple compliance. She told Blane, "The standards are critical to a guaranteed and viable curriculum." She and her colleagues discussed this evolution with their students, which made it easy to create lessons that brought out the best in them.

continued ➜

The teacher's development and transformation of learning was not finished and in many ways was in the beginning stages. Rachel and her colleagues will continue this journey to transform learning and to instill a joy of learning in all their students.

INDIVIDUAL REFLECTION

Looking at your notes on the stories about using data, what are three actions you can take in the next five days to increase your knowledge of data about your learners?

Individual Reflection: Using Data

On your own, rate yourself using the following reflection rubric. Use the following key: never is zero days, seldom is one to three days, often is four to six days, and consistently is seven to ten days.

Using Data Definition: Teachers use student learning information to make specific decisions about learner growth related to an instructional standard.	Today's Date:			
	Never	**Seldom**	**Often**	**Consistently**
A. I use ongoing methods to assess question 4 students' skill levels and design instruction accordingly.				
Notes:				
B. Our collaborative team reviews the quality of common assessments.				
Notes:				
C. Our collaborative team uses data to inform question 4 student programming.				
Notes:				

Collaborative Team Discussion: Using Data

The following is intended for use in a standard forty-five- to fifty-minute collaborative team meeting.

As a team, define the ideal rating (never, seldom, often, or consistently) for each of the following actions involved in using data. Is *consistently* ideal for A, B, and C? Is *often* the best choice? Record your collective team ideal rating for each action of using data. Use the following key: never is zero days, seldom is one to three days, often is four to six days, and consistently is seven to ten days.

Using Data Action	Ideal Rating
A. We use ongoing methods to assess question 4 students' skill levels and design instruction accordingly.	
B. Our collaborative team reviews the quality of common assessments.	
C. Our collaborative team uses data to inform question 4 student programming.	

Why are these the ideal ratings for each action?

How close are each of us to that ideal rating for each action?

How can we help each other get there?

For those of you who rated your actions as *often* or *consistent* on using data, how does it feel for you, the teacher? What feedback do you hear from your students and their parents?

Using Data Collaborative Team Formative Check

Directions: At regular intervals (such as once a grading period), collectively rate your team using the following formative check. Review your collaborative team results and support each other in progress toward an ideal rating. Use the following key: never is zero days, seldom is one to three days, often is four to six days, and consistently is seven to ten days.

Using Data Definition: Teachers use student learning information to make specific decisions about learner growth related to an instructional standard.	Formative Check # _____ Date:			
	Never	**Seldom**	**Often**	**Consistently**
A. I use ongoing methods to assess question 4 students' skill levels and design instruction accordingly.				
Notes:				
B. Our collaborative team reviews the quality of common assessments.				
Notes:				
C. Our collaborative team uses data to inform question 4 student programming.				
Notes:				

How close are each of us to that ideal rating for each action?

How can we help each other get there?

Look at your ratings over time. Is your implementation of using data the same over time? Different?

How have your actions around using data changed over time?

CHAPTER 8

Integrating Technology

Hattie (2009) says technology itself does not lead to gains in learning. We believe he is absolutely correct, and recall an experience one of our authors, Mark, had when visiting a school outside his district that had become a one-to-one learning school. This school had given every student a laptop. After making the rounds in several classrooms and observing the day's events, it became clear that technology was not positively impacting student learning in any way. In fact, by noon, Mark shared that it would have been nice to collect all the laptops and put them in a corner so teachers could interact with students again. Time and time again, classroom teachers were sitting at their desks, providing students an assignment on the board, and then observing while students worked through reading and answering questions on their laptops until the bell rang. If any conversation between students or off-task behavior occurred, the teacher would get those students back on task, which meant redirecting them to work on their computers. Classrooms truly became study halls with work time. Students who would be considered proficient generally just completed their tasks as quickly as they could to get to down time on their phones. The one classroom without computers was the most effective of the day. This teacher provided riddles for students to solve in groups that connected the history of their community to what was being learned in class. Each riddle had a different difficulty level that ranged from one to ten. Students could choose the riddles based on their own interest level and desire to be pushed. Student engagement and enthusiasm was off the charts, and not a computer was being used. While we have seen amazing things when teachers integrate technology correctly with personalized learning, it is more important to consider how it is being used.

Rickabaugh (2016) describes the divergence between traditional school practices and personalized learning approaches: "Technology plays a key role in personalized learning, particularly as we work to scale the approach across groups and learning contexts" (p. 7). To Rickabaugh and to us, Benjamin S. Bloom offers seminal research on the concept of personalized learning.

Bloom (1984) cites two University of Chicago doctoral students' (Anania, 1982, 1983; Burke, 1984) research on student learning to posit what he calls the *2 sigma problem*. Joanne Anania (1982, 1983) and A. J. Burke (1984) present a strong case for what we call *personalized learning*, determining that strategies such as having students learn material in small groups (followed up with formative tests), reteaching based on a student's level of understanding, and then retesting are highly effective. These highly personalized strategies have a difference of two standard deviations from the control group, which received conventional instruction. For those rolling your eyes at the mention of statistics, note that two standard deviations are really, really good. These two standard deviations are the subject of Bloom's (1984) 2 sigma problem. One might ask why it would be a problem, then, to be two standard deviations from the control group. The reason is that they had this great research, but no recommendations or feasible way for how to implement personalized strategies to an entire classroom. To follow this model would have taken too much time and manpower to accomplish. Bloom wondered whether researchers and teachers could devise conditions that resembled this model with the tools and resources available. While still a challenge, our observations tell us that technology plays a key role in providing educators with resources that Bloom did not have available in the mid-1980s. Using technology to transform classroom learning in ways that challenge students to think, adapted to their own paces and levels, moves us much closer to solving the 2 sigma problem. Consider, especially, the students in your classroom who already know the content. Technology is an engaging tool that can personalize their extension work in order to reach a level of challenge suited just for them.

In this chapter, we explore possibilities for integrating technology into our teaching approaches now and in the future, consider the role of technology in instruction, reflect on the impact adaptive technology can have for question 4 students, review considerations teachers should keep in mind when choosing technology, and examine three skills that can be amplified through technology.

Possibilities for Integrating Technology

Integrating technology happens when we leverage digital tools in as many ways as possible. For our purposes, *technology* and *digital tools* refer to forms of technology including gadgets, software, and hardware. The rapid pace of technological innovation allows us to approach education very differently than its more traditional forms (Christensen, Horn, & Johnson, 2008).

Learning and communication now occur in a variety of formats such as online and hybrid through products like Zoom (www.zoom.us) for video collaboration, Google's G Suite for Education tools (https://edu.google.com/k-12-solutions/g-suite), learning management systems like Canvas (www.canvaslms.com) and Schoology (www.schoology.com), and digital portfolio software like Seesaw for Schools (https://web.seesaw.me/seesaw-for-schools). School-controlled collaboration tools, like those mentioned here, are a safe and monitored environment in which students can post and share their ideas and final products. Other monitored social networking sites include Twiducate (www.livelingua.com/twiducate), The Wonderment (https://thewonderment.com), and Youth Voices (www.youthvoices.live). Older students can also share their voice to larger platforms like YouTube (www.youtube.com/education) and Twitter (https://twitter.com).

Virtual labs, virtual field trips, and other virtual "hands-on" experiences can make most any classroom a lab or field trip zone. Do you want an online STEM lab? Try SmartScience (www.smartsciencelearning.com). How about a tour? Trusted partners like the National Park Service (https://bit.ly/2IoboUA), National Geographic (https://on.natgeo.com/2uSVdln), and Discovery Education (https://bit.ly/2cXuEqd) all have virtual field trips that are available to you and your students. The examples listed here are engaging, take the learning experience out of the classroom, and allow students to dig deep into concepts. Sometimes, technology programs focus on repetition of skill-based work such as solving mathematics facts and identifying letter sounds. This is not necessarily needed for students who already know the content. So, instead, technology should focus on discovery and creating. For our students who already know the content, technology is not a remediation or tutoring tool. Technology is an open door to new experiences and challenges.

Additionally, we know that students' prior knowledge and intellectual curiosity, as well as a host of other complex factors such as sense of efficacy, academic voice ownership, dispositions, and habits of mind, influence their readiness to learn. Thus, readiness to learn is not static (Powell & Kusuma-Powell, 2011). We grow in readiness to learn through experiences in and out of the classroom. With technology, we can provide opportunities to pique intellectual curiosity and provide virtual experiences for students, regardless of resources or distance.

The Role of Technology

If you felt overwhelmed reflecting on the list of educational technology tools, you are not alone. We sometimes hear, "I am a 20th century person in a 21st century world." We understand. At the time of writing this book, 56 percent of K–12 public school teachers are over the age of 40 (National Center for Education Statistics, n.d.). This means many of us grew up equating a computer with a filing cabinet. The capabilities of computers and subsequent technology have changed drastically since then, opening a plethora of possibilities for how we approach teaching. Not everything always needs to change; innovation and status quo can coexist. Teachers should keep what works and move on from what is ineffective. Like any profession, educators must disrupt ineffective practices and polish effective practices. Teachers' natural gifts in the classroom should be amplified, not abandoned, and integrating technology can help them achieve this.

We already use technology in our classrooms. Sometimes technology substitutes previous analog ways of doing quality activities. The essence of the activity is the same, but the tool is different. Other times, technology enhances teaching practices, allowing us to abandon ineffective practices and replace them with more effective ones. In fact, with the benefits of technology and personal devices, the 2 sigma problem is decreased. All students can have a personal tutor in their hands and extend their learning at the challenge level they need. Use the tool in figure 8.1 to reflect on your use of technology, the effective practices you could sustain or enhance with technology, and the ineffective practices you could disrupt and improve with technology.

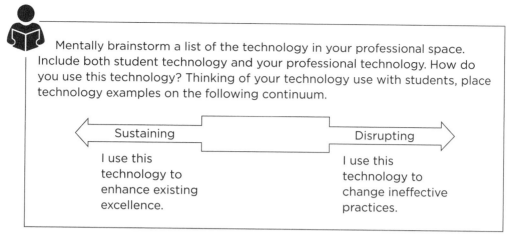

Mentally brainstorm a list of the technology in your professional space. Include both student technology and your professional technology. How do you use this technology? Thinking of your technology use with students, place technology examples on the following continuum.

Sustaining → ← Disrupting

I use this technology to enhance existing excellence.

I use this technology to change ineffective practices.

Figure 8.1: Individual reflection—Sustaining and disrupting technology.

Visit **go.SolutionTree.com/PLCbooks** *for a free reproducible version of this figure.*

For some teachers, technology is an invitation, but for others it might feel like a barrier. Integrated technology, like each of the five elements of personalized learning, may be a natural fit for some, but for others it will require more flexible thinking. Integrating technology with classroom activities is an invitation for teachers to practice flexible thinking. Integrating technology when appropriate helps teachers personalize and enhance targeted and engaging learning opportunities for students.

INDIVIDUAL REFLECTION

Dream a little. If you could create a type of technology to help personalize student learning, what would it be?

Whatever you dreamed may actually become reality sooner than we think. On the horizon in technology (which is dated as soon as we type this) is small, packaged, immersive technology like virtual-reality headsets that do not require external parts to provide augmented reality experiences. Can you imagine a student "visiting" the Colosseum in Rome, Italy, through the eyes of different spectators in order to compare and contrast the different societal roles in early Rome—without lines, heat, or plane tickets during just one class period? In a classroom, that virtual-travel experience is available to all students, regardless of financial resources. This type of experience may even pique a student's interest in exploring additional cross-cultural experiences, both throughout history and in modern times. This personalized learning experience with integrated technology is just one among millions of possibilities.

Adaptive Technology

Skilled teachers meet students where they are—both in *what* they need to learn and *how* they best learn it. In addition to engagement and worldview, integrated technology allows teachers to leverage dynamic decisions and personalize learning for each student. This is called *adaptive technology*. Adaptive technology uses information in real time to inform the next action. This enables question 4 students to demonstrate their learning and move on to more challenging work. In the following sections, we discuss two types of adaptive technology, adaptive content and adaptive assessment. The use of adaptive assessment and adaptive content has significantly changed how we can personalize instruction for our students.

Adaptive Content

Adaptive learning technology is organized around units of learning called *learning objects*. Adaptive technology authors create multiple learning objects and possible paths of accomplishing a learning objective (Karampiperis, Lin, & Sampson, 2006). The technology program monitors a student's pace and performance within the adaptive learning experience to determine his or her best path to accomplish a learning objective. The multiple learning objects and learning sequences to accomplish a final learning goal yield varying learning experiences that cater to the unique content and pace needs of each learner. Products like Exact Path (www.edmentum.com/products /exact-path) and UpSmart (www.edgenuity.com/test-readiness/#UpSmart) provide these individualized learning paths aligned to curriculum standards. As students demonstrate proficiency on set standards, they are directed to either new content or a deeper dive into the proficient content.

Adaptive Assessment

Teachers construct adaptive assessments in a similar manner. Assessment learning progressions define the various challenge levels of student assessment questions. The assessment levels go up or down depending on the students' answers to previous questions. Most adaptive assessments also have decision structures to detect student disengagement and guessing. Examples include MAP Growth tests (www.nwea.org /map-growth) and Math Inventory (https://bit.ly/2I3oK9G). Adaptive assessments provide individual student data regarding achievement of standards, making them a meaningful enhancement to other data collaborative teams use to monitor student progress and track who has demonstrated learning of specific curriculum standards.

Another consideration when using data from adaptive assessment is the rich meta-data the program captures. Adaptive technology uses algorithms and ongoing individual student data (including adaptive assessment results, progress toward learning targets, and user data such as pace and persistence) to establish dynamic learning paths for each student. Not all proficient students will progress through a module at the same pace. Efficiency in learning new material, paired with assessment results, helps teachers determine the best way to challenge and support proficient students' continued growth. Tracking the number of logins, persistence through a task, and knowing the type of and need for feedback in the learning process are all very important (Swinke, 2012). Researcher Tillman Swinke (2012) refers to these details as the *behavior dimension of the learner profile.* Many online learning systems provide student user data to help teachers review the process of how a student interacted with the online learning, such as the length of time a student persisted through a module. So, although adaptive technology monitors and uses all this metadata, we recommend teachers regularly review it as well in order to support academic learning and challenge for the students who have demonstrated proficiency on the target curriculum already.

INDIVIDUAL REFLECTION

What adaptive technology for students do you use in your professional space? Is it adaptive in content and pace? Is it based on information about learning such as cognitive styles and other learning differences? Once students demonstrate proficiency on a standard, can they "level up" to new or challenging content?

Considerations for Choosing Technology

Like any tool, it is up to the teacher to determine the quality of technology tools before implementing them in the classroom. Additionally, when designing extension work, the classroom teacher may be the main point of contact for determining what new technology tools to use in extension. For this reason, teachers should keep the following considerations in mind when determining what technology to use for extension.

- **Alignment:** Review the order in which learning objects and content standards are addressed in the technology tool. Does it align with your curriculum? Once a student demonstrates proficiency, does the module or assessment go deeper in the learning, go to the next standards, or rely on nontechnological enrichment?

- **Information:** What data are collected from the student's experience during the module or assessment? Is the teacher able to review data about sustained student effort in addition to mastery of content? Teacher knowledge about proficient student persistence and efficiency can help determine how best to challenge and engage proficient students in their extension work. This information can also help determine if an area of skill reinforcement is needed during the extension work experience.

- **Regulations:** The Children's Online Privacy Protection Act (COPPA, 1998) outlines the legal regulations of collection, use, and disclosure of personal information from and about children on the internet. Privacy policies, terms of service, and end user license agreements are all easy to overlook. Many social media tools have a user age requirement (for example, Twitter requires users to be at least thirteen years old) or limits to the number of licenses. Know your district's student and teacher social media and technology use protocols and policies. Ask your administrator if you have any questions. Most district protocols require students to get parent or guardian permission to use social media at school or other technology not in the district's domain.

- **Ownership:** Check who owns the data that are collected through the use of technology. Free resources are not always free. Sometimes the fine print includes the company's ability to collect data from the tool or website as part of its ongoing product and service research. Consider who owns the data associated with the resources. Also, if the website or tool requires each student to create a profile, consider who has access to that profile information. Check with your district about data uploads of student information to ensure you follow security and privacy protocols.

- **School versions:** School versions of apps, software, and online accounts are different than public versions. Interactive media tools like Google's G Suite, Microsoft Office 365, and others offer versions of their products specifically for student use in an educational setting. Typically, a product's education version is set up differently under the district's domain and management, which provides additional security protection for students. Just because you use a specific program at home, do not assume it is ready to transfer to the classroom.

School districts have teams and resources to help teachers navigate these considerations. It is important to open a regular and honest dialogue with your district technology support team to ensure you and your students successfully follow federal, state, and local laws and policies.

It is also important to consider who is driving technology use in schools. Technology advancements in education are sometimes driven by noneducators (Nelson, Fien, Doabler, & Clarke, 2016). Would you like to change that? Educators can amplify quality educational practices through technology if we begin to think differently about how technology can be leveraged and grown to best influence high academic learning in our classroom. To help educators think differently about leveraging technology in classrooms, we suggest Kevin Kelly's (2016) book *The Inevitable: Understanding the 12 Technological Forces That Will Shape Our Future* as a resource, which challenges readers to consider even more changes in the way we work, learn, and communicate. Use the tool in figure 8.2 to reflect individually on Kelly's list of twelve.

Choose at least three technological forces (Kelly, 2016) to think more deeply about. For those three, answer these questions: When considering this technological force, what comes to mind about the way you currently approach education? How could this force influence education in the future? How could you use this force in your classroom today to extend learning for question 4 students?

Technological Force	Reflection Response
Becoming: Moving from fixed products to always upgrading services and subscriptions	
Cognifying: Making everything much smarter using cheap, powerful, artificial intelligence	
Flowing: Depending on real-time unstoppable streams for everything	
Screening: Providing more than words on paper, but rather depth through page layout, color, and interaction	
Accessing: Placing more importance on having access to items or a content library rather than on owning them	

Figure 8.2: Individual reflection—Twelve technological forces. continued →

Technological Force	Reflection Response
Sharing: Replacing ownership with open-source and peer-production items, especially items used for only a brief amount of time	
Filtering: Harnessing intense personalization to anticipate desires	
Remixing: Unbundling existing products into their most primitive parts and then recombining them in all possible ways	
Interacting: Using devices to mimic more senses and become more humanlike	
Tracking: Allowing each student to discover an individual baseline and monitor his or her progress by reflecting on activities' details the student records with technology	
Questioning: Promoting good questions that are far more valuable than good answers	
Beginning: Starting the digital transformation that allows teachers to act and react to changing data	

Source: Kelly, 2016.

Visit go.SolutionTree.com/PLCbooks for a free reproducible version of this figure.

Consider sharing your reflections from figure 8.2 with your collaborative team. Each team member likely focused on different aspects of education's future. Some lists may be gadget heavy, while others may have thought about the educational system as a whole. Sharing these ideas will likely spark a new innovation for your professional space.

Three Big Skills

The technology described thus far (virtual field trips, STEM labs, and adaptive technology) has been content-area specific. In this next section we will discuss three big skills that are content neutral and that can be applied for students who already know the content and enhanced through technology. These three big skills are critical reading, critical thinking, and project management. Technology is an excellent way to amplify these three big skills for proficient students.

Critical Reading

Critical reading is the analysis and interpretation of a text's meaning. This is an essential skill for high-achieving students as they continue their exploration of new content and further research. These students need to be able to consume and analyze digital information with a critical eye.

Some skills of critical reading are the same for both paper and digital works, such as annotating in the margins, underlining key terms, color highlighting, determining key ideas, and summarizing in the white space of the page. Read&Write (www .texthelp.com/en-us/products/read-write), Kami (www.kamihq.com), and Diigo (www.diigo.com) are products that allow students to highlight web articles, pdfs, and online texts. Group annotation can be facilitated with Hypothes.is (https://web .hypothes.is/education). Proficient students need opportunities to practice their critical reading skills with the guidance of teacher feedback and support. By learning these digital skills early, proficient students will be able to efficiently apply these skills in group and independent extension work.

Critical Thinking

With extension work, students are sometimes working under the technology shell of the district and other times working more independently with collaborators outside of the school. As students interact digitally, they are creating a brand for themselves—a *digital identity* (Orehek & Human, 2016), which is a representation and expression of self in the digital world. It is our responsibility to help our students create a positive, academic representation of themselves. Like learning, technology is social. We are always *on*—or connected and linked through digital platforms—and we know students are always learning through these platforms, in and out of the classroom. Digital collaboration and social media are where students are connecting with peers locally and globally and where students work through questions and seek answers. Therefore, we want to equip our students to critically discern the difference between fact and opinion and to contribute to the digital information in a productive way. The best way to do so is to pair critical thinking skills with digital interactions.

Web content and social media can perpetuate misleading, nonsensical statements instead of facts; attacks on a person instead of arguments against a position; and irrelevancies instead of supported counterstatements. We want our classrooms to elevate our social media interactions and intentionally model how to be thoughtful and analytical in these interactions. We acknowledge that critical thinking and careful response are important on paper as well as on Twitter. However, we pair critical thinking with social media because we know the power of social media and we want to be intentional about elevating our students' digital footprints.

As students poise their thumbs ready to fire back a digital comment, a strategy to slow down their thinking and raise the level of intellectual interaction is helpful. Critical thinking scholars Richard Paul and Linda Elder (2006) highlight eight elements of thought as part of their critical thinking framework.

1. Purpose

2. Question at issue

3. Information

4. Interpretation and inference

5. Concepts

6. Assumptions

7. Implications and consequences

8. Point of view

Considering these elements can help students analyze their own thinking so that it is less biased, less distorted, and more informed. It can be useful for teachers to summarize and share these elements with students to encourage them to evaluate their social media postings and challenge them to think critically about their contribution before posting new noise in the shared digital sphere. Visit the Foundation for Critical Thinking webpage at www.criticalthinking.org/ctmodel/logic-model1 .htm to learn more about each element of thought. Table 8.1 includes some scripted questions based on elements of thought to support students' analysis. Teachers can integrate these questions into classroom and out-of-classroom social media learning.

As students become skilled and insightful thinkers, their out-of-school digital interactions will mirror their in-school academic digital interactions. Increasing critical thinking skills in digital social interactions cultivates a positive student digital identity congruent to the high standards of academic work we expect of high-achieving students.

Table 8.1: Critical Thinking for Social Media Use

	Scripted Questions	Benefit
Clarify the Question or Statement	What is the question I am trying to answer? What do you mean by . . . ? Can you put that another way? What kind of question is this? (For example, historical, scientific, ethical, political, economic, and so on.) What do we have to do to answer this question?	This helps get to the heart of the issue and accelerates focused attention instead of distracted and incomplete logic.
Check Your Assumptions	What is this policy, strategy, or explanation assuming? What could we assume instead? How can you verify or disprove that assumption?	This helps expose the complexity of ideas and typically fosters common ground of opposing ideas.
Understand Your Point of View	How am I looking at this situation? Should I consider another way of looking at it? Is my view the only reasonable view? What does my point of view ignore? Do I study or seek out viewpoints that challenge my personal beliefs?	This helps develop intellectual humility.

Project Management

Some of the extension work for question 4 students will occur in groups. Tami remembers a time when group work seemed to always start with assigning roles of recorder, reporter, timekeeper, and so on to group members. However, in the age of digital collaboration, these roles look different. For example, instead of a timekeeper, an extension group may have a project manager. The group can discuss the scope of the work (what is required and when) and benchmark due dates, and assign responsibility for completing different tasks. With agreed-on mutual accountability among team members, the project manager checks in with group members regarding action on tasks. Teams can use G Suite collaboration tools to manage projects (see https:// bit.ly/2jEYAes). Depending on the length and complexity of the project, older students could also use specific project management tools like Teamwork (www.team work.com) and Redbooth (www.redbooth.com). Helping students leverage efficiency and accountability through technology is an excellent lifelong skill for students, especially students who grasp content quickly and will take their creative ideas outside of the typical classroom lesson.

A Look at Integrating Technology in Action

We are once again visiting our sixth-grade mathematics team's work on ratios. In this example, the students who have already demonstrated proficiency with ratios will complete an extension activity together. The teacher gathers this group and delivers a lesson on population density. She explains, "Teacher-to-student ratio impacts us in this room. Can you imagine if we had seventy-five students in this room? It would be very different. What if we only had six students? The number of students in a particular space is the *density of the population*."

The teacher then displays the Census Explorer on the U.S. Census Bureau website (https://census.gov/censusexplorer/censusexplorer.html). The teacher chooses Census Tract from the Show by drop-down menu, and says, "This is a heat map. It displays the density of community characteristics. It can show us the density of populations, density of those age 65 and older, density of high school graduates, and more. The darker the color on the heat map, the higher percentage of what is measured. Darker means more dense or more of it."

The teacher demonstrates the website by hovering over one of the tracts on the map and noting what is being measured. For example, census tract 71.01 is shaded a medium tone and displays a population of 3,161 people, 527 of them sixty-five years of age or older, or 16.7 percent. The teacher draws the connection between online heat maps and the density of student-to-teacher ratio in their school. The teacher demonstrates zooming in on the street where the school is located on the census tract and facilitates a conversation about the drop-down menu items for a particular area. She invites students to use their own devices to zoom in on their neighborhoods or areas of town they'd like to know more about. The teacher then tells students to use the drop-down menus to explore what kinds of information are available for their areas, such as total population, age, education level, and so on.

At this point, the teacher asks students to choose five characteristics they would like to focus on. Students hover over their areas on the heat map and record the information about five characteristics displayed on their screens. Students next display the information as raw data and percentages. The teacher asks students to convert these data and percentages into fractions and ratios (*x*:*y*). Students finish their independent class work and, with any remaining time, continue exploring the website for more interesting observations.

When the teacher brings the whole group back, she displays a school floor plan. The teacher then asks, "If we created a heat map to show teacher-to-student ratios of the rooms in our building, which classrooms would have more intense colors? Which would have very light colors?" Students use class roster data from throughout the school to record teacher-student ratios on the floor plan. The students also create data tables with this information and use an open-source program like Tableau Public (https://public.tableau.com/en-us/s) to create a digital heat map. This lesson challenges students to determine credible online data and create local data to display digitally. The concept of population density is an appropriate example of ratios, and the challenge of technology helps raise the rigor of work with the ratios.

Next Steps

What is next for integrating technology to bring the real world into the classroom, especially for extension work? At the time of writing this book, cell phone companies are preparing for built-in augmented reality (AR) apps that will provide AR production access to the mass public (Hollander, 2018). Personal creation of AR experiences has the potential to explode. Soon we will access detailed 3-D maps of the entire world. What started as a fun animal face on your selfie will grow to unexpected AR interactions. Integrating technology levels student learning and provides organic out-of-classroom connections and engagement. When we consider maximizing the learning for proficient students, new discoveries like AR field trips and labs will be among the many ways to extend learning.

Now that you have explored the personalized learning element of integrating technology, read and reflect on the following personalized learning stories that feature practical examples of teachers implementing this element. Use the reproducible "Individual Reflection: Integrating Technology" (page 200) to evaluate your current reality with integrating technology. Then, use the reproducibles "Collaborative Team Discussion: Integrating Technology" (page 202) and "Integrating Technology Collaborative Team Formative Check" (page 204) to support collaborative conversation and learning in your collaborative team. Visit **go.SolutionTree.com/PLCbooks** to download these free reproducibles. We recommend your collaborative team use the reproducible "Integrating Technology Collaborative Team Formative Check" (page 204) at regular intervals, such as once per grading period. Review your results as a team, and support each other in progress toward an ideal rating.

Personalized Learning Stories

Following are two examples that focus on element 5: integrating technology. In each story, note the examples of integrating technology as you read.

Integrating Technology in an Elementary Classroom

Kara Skinner is a third-grade teacher in a growing suburb of Kansas City, Missouri. Kara has taught third grade for two years, and previously taught first grade for ten years. The school's enrollment is approximately 450 students, and Kara averages around 25 students each year. The school is diverse, with a variety of special education classes. The school serves students on the autism spectrum and medically fragile students who are in regular classroom settings when appropriate.

Since Kara began teaching in the district, it has moved to a one-to-one learning environment using Google Chromebooks. When Kara first began teaching in the district, each school was provided a set of computers for the primary classrooms and a second set for the intermediate classrooms to share. Eventually, the district purchased a set of computers for each grade level. Then, in the 2015–2016 school year, the district went to a one-to-one learning environment and provided each student a device for his or her use in the classroom.

Setting the Pace

Blane arrived at the school around 9:30 a.m. for his meeting with Kara. After introductions, he took a seat in the back of the classroom. He noticed motivational posters in the room to encourage students to work hard. In addition, Blane saw several special education students (along with their assistants) included in the regular classroom. Kara opened the mathematics workshop lesson using a six-question pretest covering the essential standards on equivalent fractions to the entire class. She created a Google classroom assignment titled "Equivalent Fractions: Have Your Cake and Eat It Too!" The objective of the assignment was to master the following mathematics indicators: I can divide shapes into parts with equal areas; I can describe the area of each part as a unit fraction of the whole; and I can use models to show and to explain equivalent fractions. Kara taught a sixty-minute mathematics block for students to complete five tasks related to the standard.

Students opened their devices and went to the Google Classroom (https://class room.google.com) to begin the assignment's first task: Mom is mixing a cake to eat for dessert. As the cake is baking, she asks you if you would rather have $\frac{1}{3}$ of the cake or $\frac{1}{6}$ of the cake. Since this is your favorite cake, you want the most cake possible. Which will you choose and why?

Students went to work on the question, and Kara and Blane stole a few minutes to discuss the lesson. She said each additional task (there were five tasks or questions) went deeper into the standard, extending the learning of question 4 students who had demonstrated mastery of that standard and benchmark and challenging them to think deeply and push themselves to learn more. She used technology for these deeper questions because it allowed students to work at their own pace and to track their progress through Google applications. Kara then hurried off to help a few students who Blane noticed were watching a video. These particular students performed well on the pretest, which Kara had administered to better know her students (element 1). These question 4 students then answered six teacher-generated questions. These questions pushed the question 4 students deeper into the standards the lesson focused on. Kara wanted to ensure these students had the opportunity to learn and apply the content in different ways and transfer their knowledge to new applications of the standard. Kara integrated the available technology to transform the learning environment, and in her classroom she used open-ended questions such as, "If the family had only eaten one-half of the cake, how many ways can you show how much is left?" that allowed her question 4 students to direct their own learning and come up with various models to show how much cake was left.

Throughout the class, as question 4 students answered the teacher-generated open-ended questions designed for the lesson, Blane observed them demonstrate an understanding of the standard by applying their learning to the new situations Kara designed. Some moved quickly and others at a slower pace, but all were using their device to complete the tasks. Kara moved about the room and mentored all students through the different tasks. Blane noticed she encouraged students to work at their own pace and not give up. He found her focus on implementing a flexible or growth mindset (element 3) important to her students as they used their devices and completed their work.

At the end of the class, Kara reviewed the standards covered in the lesson to provide some closure to the activity. Students were asked to clean up and begin the transition to lunch. Blane walked with Kara and her students to the lunchroom. They then sat down for lunch, and he asked questions about the lesson as they ate.

Lessons Learned

After observing the class, Blane followed up with Kara, asking what these lessons would have looked like prior to the district's one-to-one learning initiative. She said the lessons would have been more teacher directed, with her lecturing at the students. Question 4 students would not have explored fractions as deeply or worked at their own pace through open-ended questions that stretched their learning. She felt that, because of the digital tools now available in her classroom, she could differentiate and extend learning for all of her third-grade students.

Kara felt the district's adoption of a one-to-one learning initiative had been critical to her ability to personalize learning for students. Ruben Puentedura's (2014) Substitution Augmentation Modification Redefinition (SAMR) model was key in her development and ability to integrate digital tools to enhance learning in her classroom. This model prompted Kara not only to substitute and modify her

continued →

lessons but also to augment and redefine learning for her students. She used the SAMR model and met her students' individual needs using Chromebooks and G Suite for Education applications. She asked her question 4 students to go deeper into the benchmark by applying content or using an appropriate app such as Google Slides.

Kara felt her students now worked harder and did not give up as easily as they did in previous years. She attributed this to the immediate feedback the students received directly from her or from the software she used in the classroom. She explained that she used digital tools from G Suite to enhance her teaching and her students' learning. All of her learners seemed more engaged and motivated to work through the harder lessons because of the technology. They enjoyed using technology, wanted to learn more, and consequently maximized their learning. She also told Blane, "Some days are technology-free days to remember what it was like before technology."

The next question Blane asked was, "How do you know this approach works?" She reiterated that students are more motivated and explained, "Nobody slides by today." She went on to say, "They know it, and I know they know it." Further, she developed learning plans for question 4 students around the third-grade learning targets so these students would go deeper into the standard and be able to apply the standard in different ways and explain their understanding by answering open-ended questions with a written explanation or by creating a keynote or a mathematics model that shows their mastery of equivalent fractions. This resulted in extending learning for question 4 students, and for some, it meant reteaching the standard and benchmark, but these personalized learning plans ensured all students' learning was stretched beyond what they would have learned through lectures alone.

As an aside, Kara noted that she expected her students would show growth on the state test, but because she now employed more formative assessments she depended less on a state test analysis to inform her teaching. "I know my students much better today than in previous years," she explained. Consequently, Kara created more student-directed lessons and searched for student-directed software to meet her students' individual needs. Kara and her collaborative team now provided challenges for question 4 learners and for all students because they knew their students well, their classrooms were less teacher directed, and they integrated technology into the classroom. Students were able to set their own learning pace and were motivated to keep moving forward.

Kara and her colleagues understood the power of personalized learning to engage students and extend learning for their advanced students. The collaborative team members observed that their students want to learn because learning is important, not because the teacher wants them to work harder. This student mindset helped Kara extend learning, and all students perform at higher levels. Kara understood technology provided an opportunity for her to extend learning and differentiate her teaching. She was energized by her success and *continues her own professional learning with her collaborative team to ensure every student masters the third-grade content.*

Integrating Technology in a Secondary Classroom

Peter Davis is an English and media teacher at a private school in Ontario, Canada. This school is an all-boys one-to-one learning school for grades 3–12. The school has an enrollment of 440 young men and was founded in 1964 with a constructivist approach to learning (Brooks & Brooks, 1993), where students and teachers alike transfer knowledge by applying what they are learning to authentic real-world situations.

The Learning Game

Peter met Blane at the school office, and they quickly became acquainted. They sat in the conference room since they had time before the next class. Peter explained that the class Blane would observe was a social studies class he developed with a colleague. His colleague wanted to learn how to extend the learning of the advanced placement world history class and thought if he could integrate technology and use game theory, his learners would be more motivated and engaged. However, he was uncomfortable with technology. Peter agreed to help him try new teaching methods. Blane understood that he was about to see a multidisciplinary AP class where English and world history came together.

Peter told Blane he would be watching a nontraditional classroom where the students led the learning and the teacher facilitated the learning. Students would be playing the video game Total War: Rome II. Peter wanted Blane to truly understand the purpose of this advanced class and how the previous class activities and preparation led to the video game's integration in the classroom. Peter and his colleague researched and used a variety of media to develop a lesson for this class, where learners demonstrated critical thinking skills and applied and transferred knowledge to new learning situations. The purpose of this history class was to study various points of view since history cannot be reproduced. Students then discussed and determined what most likely occurred during the Roman Empire. Peter and his colleague designed a lesson that took multilevel learning stations to a deeper level for this group of question 4 students.

In the classes leading up to the one Blane observed, Peter asked his students to read two to three chapters of Julius Caesar's The Gallic Wars, written from Caesar's perspective, as they prepared to integrate game theory into the classroom. The book did not delve into the political turmoil in Rome under Caesar's leadership. Caesar wrote that the wars were necessary for the protection of Rome since the Gauls had attacked the city previously. He said Rome needed a natural border, the Rhine River, for protection. However, the book ignored the political boost this military campaign gave to Caesar's career. Caesar did not include the massive debts incurred during his earlier political campaigns. It's clear

continued →

that Peter's students were beginning to understand different perspectives and historical contexts.

In the next class, the students watched a documentary film developed from a historian's perspective that discussed the political issues facing Caesar at the time of the Gallic Wars. Peter explained that his teaching partner felt that the film, when compared to the book, brought completely different perspectives. The documentary told a different story than Caesar's book. It highlighted the political connections of his family and how the Gallic Wars advanced his political career. The documentary explained that Caesar had incurred a great deal of debt in his early political career and these wars were financially beneficial to him. Peter explained that Caesar's book neglected to mention these reasons for the Gallic Wars. He then explained that students would need to reconcile these differences.

Following this, the class visited the Royal Ontario Museum where they viewed Roman artifacts in the Eaton Gallery of Rome, then the largest collection of Roman artifacts in Canada. Here, students interacted with real Roman artifacts and saw how they compared to what students had read about or had seen in the documentary. It was clear students felt the museum was a great resource because when Blane came to observe the classroom, he heard them comparing artifacts to the film, book, and video game (which several students had already played outside of school and had actually suggested to Peter's colleague that he consider using it in class).

On the day of Blane's observation, Peter planned for the students to play Total War: Rome II. The students were excited as they set up their devices in their flexible groups. The students' excitement bubbled up because they had advocated to their teacher to play the game as a part of the unit. This was the final learning center for the unit and the first of two classes where students would play the video game. Both teachers seemed a bit nervous, one because he lacked familiarity with the technology and the game, and Peter because he was incorporating a video game into the lesson for the first time and just did not know what to expect.

The teachers explained the purpose of the game: to improve their ability to think critically and to authentically build a Roman army and lead those legions into battle in northern Europe. Peter asked the students to compare the game with their previous reading, the documentary film they watched in class, and the artifacts they examined at the Eaton Gallery. As small roundtables of students played the game, Peter asked the students to discuss the building and leading of an army in contrast to the other media they used in learning about the Gallic Wars.

Blane observed small groups taking different pathways as they made different game decisions in an authentic environment. The inquiry-based learning assignment was designed to integrate technology. Further, the assignment also included other media that brought in different perspectives and added to the roundtable discussions. Peter asked the students an open-ended question: "How *does the game depart from the book, documentary, or museum?" Additionally, he asked questions about if the game was true to the historic collections and writings. Were uniforms accurate? Was the historical information consistent across all media? What was life like during this period of history? How would a person determine what was true and what had been embellished?*

Blane observed students stop for fact checking while they played the game. Students reviewed facts and perspectives for accuracy and discussed such topics as a general's name, the type of weapons used in the game, or the clothing worn by game characters. Peter reminded the AP students of the purpose of the lesson: that history cannot be reproduced, so students were looking for multiple points of view to determine how those points of view converged to tell an accurate story of historical events. Students left the classroom talking about the game and seemed to look forward to continuing the roundtable discussions the next day. It was clear all students' learning was maximized as they collaborated to examine and discuss the Roman culture from multiple perspectives.

Lessons Learned

Peter noted that the one-to-one learning environment that gave each student his or her own device was key to his ability to challenge this group of students' learning by personalizing the content. Yet, these teachers did not rely solely on the technology. Blane loved how they designed multilevel learning stations with technology and other media to force critical thinking while engaging students with the Roman Empire and Julius Caesar content. Peter told Blane he hoped that students might go deeper into the book or watch the full documentary based on their interest and how they directed their own learning after being exposed to the content. Finally, in the tradition of the school, he and his teaching partner said they would continue to have these students apply these skills in other units of study throughout the school year. Blane left thinking these students were lucky to have teachers who took risks, integrated technology, and supported question 4 learners' critical thinking by enlisting them to help develop arguments, listening to them, and taking their suggestion to use the video game in class. These teachers' expectations were much higher than merely having students restate previously provided information from earlier in the unit. They wanted their learners to actually interact with the content, providing a much richer learning experience than what would have occurred without the technology.

INDIVIDUAL REFLECTION

Looking at your notes on the stories about integrating technology, what are three actions you can take in the next five days to increase your integration of technology with your learners?

Individual Reflection: Integrating Technology

On your own, rate yourself using the following reflection rubric. Use the following key: never is zero days, seldom is one to three days, often is four to six days, and consistently is seven to ten days.

Integrating Technology Definition: Technology integration is when teachers incorporate technology tools and technology-based practices into daily classroom routines. Technology tools include digital devices such as tablets, computers, laptop and desktop computers, and internet access and networking. Technology-based practices include collaborative work, communication, software- and app-based activities, and internet-based activities.	Today's Date:			
	Never	**Seldom**	**Often**	**Consistently**
A. I allow question 4 students to utilize technology in a meaningful and imaginative way.				
Notes:				
B. I design lessons for question 4 students which integrate technology in ways that challenge students to think deeper.				
Notes:				

page 1 of 2

	Never	Seldom	Often	Consistently
C. I reinforce critical reading, critical thinking, or management with technology in lessons for my question 4 students.				
Notes:				
D. I review district policies, local protocol, and laws when implementing technology.				
Notes:				

When They Already Know It © 2018 Solution Tree Press • SolutionTree.com
Visit **go.SolutionTree.com/PLCbooks** to download this free reproducible.

Collaborative Team Discussion: Integrating Technology

The following is intended for use in a standard forty-five- to fifty-minute collaborative team meeting.

As a team, define the ideal rating (never, seldom, often, or consistently) for each of the following actions involved in integrating technology. Is *consistently* ideal for A, B, C, and D? Is *often* the best choice? Record your collective team ideal rating for each action of integrating technology. Use the following key: never is zero days, seldom is one to three days, often is four to six days, and consistently is seven to ten days.

Integrating Technology Action	Ideal Rating
A. I allow for question 4 students to utilize technology in a meaningful and imaginative way.	
B. I design lessons which integrate technology in ways that challenge question 4 students to think deeper.	
C. I reinforce critical reading, critical thinking, or management with technology in lessons for my question 4 students.	
D. I review district policies, local protocol, and laws when implementing technology.	

Why are these the ideal ratings for each action?

How close are each of us to that ideal rating for each action?

How can we help each other get there?

For those of you who rated your actions as *often* or *consistent* on integrating technology, how does it feel for you, the teacher? What feedback do you hear from your students and their parents?

Integrating Technology Collaborative Team Formative Check

Directions: At regular intervals (such as once a grading period), collectively rate your team using the following formative check. Review your collaborative team results and support each other in progress toward an ideal rating. Use the following key: never is zero days, seldom is one to three days, often is four to six days, and consistently is seven to ten days.

Integrated Technology	Formative Check # _____			
Definition: Technology integration is when teachers incorporate technology tools and technology-based practices into daily classroom routines. Technology tools include digital devices such as tablets, computers, laptop and desktop computers, and internet access and networking. Technology-based practices include collaborative work, communication, software- and app-based activities, and internet-based activities.	Date:			
	Never	**Seldom**	**Often**	**Consistently**
A. I allow for question 4 students to utilize technology in a meaningful and imaginative way.				
Notes:				
B. I design lessons which integrate technology in ways that challenge question 4 students to think deeper.				
Notes:				

	Never	Seldom	Often	Consistently
C. I reinforce critical reading, critical thinking, or management with technology in lessons for my question 4 students.				
Notes:				
D. I review district policies, local protocol, and laws when implementing technology.				
Notes:				

How close are each of us to that ideal rating for each action?

How can we help each other get there?

Look at your ratings over time. Is your implementation of integrated technology the same over time? Different?

How have your actions around integrated technology changed over time?

CHAPTER 9

Bringing It All Together

Now that you have explored and reflected on the aspects of personalized learning and instructional strategies that support question 4 students, and how they might be implemented in a variety of classrooms, you and your team are ready to begin thinking about how to embed these elements in your lessons and instructional practices to extend learning for students who have already demonstrated proficiency with a learning target. You may be wondering where to begin this teamwork logistically. Let's revisit our sixth-grade mathematics team to understand its processes and team meeting conversations as an example of one way a team might attempt this work.

During the team's first meeting of the school year, the team members began discussing their goals for the upcoming year. The team leader quickly pulled out the recently released state testing data from the prior spring and began to talk about how their students had done over the past few years. In this team's state, teachers don't receive the state testing results until the fall after their students have moved on to the next grade. It is too late to do any corrective teaching to the students for whom they are reviewing; however, it helps them look at the trends that they see from their classroom over time. They saw that for the last four years, around 80 percent of their students were proficient on the state test. This was a solid ten points above their state's average and was one of the higher scores in their district. While they could have been satisfied by this result, one teacher on the team made an interesting comment that really caused the team members to think about how they work with their proficient students.

This teacher said, "I am really bothered by this information. While 80 percent proficient isn't bad, I do think we can do better. But, the thing that really strikes me is that our state testing data is about the same every year, but our class was so different this year. We knew when the school year started that we had some of the smartest and most talented mathematics students that we have ever had. And, when I think about it, we didn't do one thing different, for the most part, than we have done any other year. So we got the exact same scores as the year prior, and I don't think we did much of anything for our students who already knew the material when they walked in the door. I wonder how many were bored all year."

Another teacher looked down and said, "You know what, you are right! I had one student in my class who loves everything to do with statistics. I don't know many sixth-grade students who go to bed dreaming about this type of thing, but she does. This past winter, her parents met the head girls' basketball coach at one of our high schools, and, after learning about her passion, the coach asked the student to keep game statistics for the team. Not only did she embrace this role, she created a profile sheet of each game that showed all kinds of data for each player, and included mean, median, mode, and range from the various sets of data. When I look at the activities that I had her do when we studied these concepts last year, I feel a little embarrassed. She could have taught the unit. She could have spent class time actually applying what I was teaching."

A third teacher on the team shared a similar story about how he had a student who was considered to be autistic and had an IEP. At times, he struggled in class but just lit up when it came to mathematics class. He just got it and could really shine. The teacher shared that at the end of the year when they started their geometry unit, he started to include the student more and actually would meet with him prior to the whole-class lesson and figured out ways for him to actually co-teach. The teacher shared that this was a sight to behold, this student who struggled in other areas, up there with the teacher being a leader and explaining how to plot the location of an ordered pair in the coordinate plane while working problems for the whole class on the grease board. You could just see the student's confidence in the way he carried himself during the mathematics portion of the day as he demonstrated his talents and skills.

The first teacher indicated that this is exactly what she was talking about. She asked the group, "How do we do more of that?!" Together, they created a SMART goal that not only aimed to raise the group's proficient level as a whole but also developed goals for supporting students who already knew the material. They also had a thoughtful discussion about how their approach to this goal would not be based on the district's list of students who qualified for the gifted education program; they wanted to determine who the question 4 students were by unit. The teacher who spoke about the autistic student was adamant about this because you never know what area a student might bring a passion and knowledge base to. They also talked about how the question 4 students will many times be the same groups of students. They decided that while this is true, they would make it their own personal mission to discover opportunities for all students, at least once, to be considered the student who already knows it. One teacher said, "Who knows, maybe we will find that the things we do for the student who already knows it will be good for everyone."

Before the daily grind of the school year unfolded, the team worked diligently to determine the specific actions it would take to ensure it made progress toward its new goal. If the team members were to rely on this book, *When They Already Know It*, to begin their study, their work would look something like the following. They read the introduction and chapters 1 and 2 over the next two weeks and completed the reflection activities in these chapters. They noted in their reflections on chapter 1 that using personalized learning would require them to reframe some of their thinking. The thing that really stuck out to them was the need to let go of some of the control over the students. The team members collectively shared how not being in the driver's seat and allowing some students to do different activities than the rest of the class can be scary. After reading chapter 2, the team designated a good portion of the next reserved collaborative time to talk about the reasons for personalized learning presented in the book. One member discussed how the *myth of average* really resonated with him after his own ratings were disparate when reflecting on his personal rating exercise (see figure 2.1, page 38). Another member spoke about how she never thought about how technology prepared today's learners to expect personalization. As she shared, if everything else in their life is personalized, why wouldn't this be expected at school? Next, the team members took a week to read chapter 3 and commented on how they were a little more at ease because the strategies seemed to make sense and felt like something they could do.

After coming to a common understanding about the need for and benefits of personalized learning, the team members read and reflected on chapters 4–8 over the course of the next five weeks. In order to understand the vehicle of personalized learning, they followed the process of using one week to read and reflect about a new element of personalized learning, with the due date the next collaborative team meeting. Then, at the next meeting, the team members shared their reflections about the personalized learning element and the elementary and secondary stories. At each meeting, various team members made connections to activities they had previously done in their own classrooms. They also began reflecting on lessons they had done throughout the year, and when one of the examples from a classroom story would have been a good fit.

Once the team understood the five elements of personalized learning and instructional strategies that worked well in each, the members recognized it was time to begin planning. At the first collaborative meeting after completing the book, the team continued its focus on addressing the fourth critical question of a PLC to extend learning for proficient students and made a commitment to each other to devote time at each meeting to how to use personalized learning to respond to this question to increase these students' achievement. In fact, the team members developed a team norm to address personalized learning in some fashion at every weekly meeting—even if it is just for five minutes, they would not ignore this component of their practice.

One of the team members suggested that there was an upcoming unit in their mathematics class that had gotten pretty stale over the years where students learned about solving real-world problems involving ratios, unit rates, and percentages. In the past, the team members did a class discussion, which included samples and opportunities for students to practice, and then students spent time completing various problems on a worksheet. One team member suggested that they use this activity, which had traditionally taken five days of class time, to begin to develop personalized learning strategies in their classroom and use tiered assignments.

The district-developed curriculum maps were constructed using the Understanding by Design framework (Wiggins & McTighe, 2005)—which lists the standards, indicators, big ideas, guiding questions, and what a student will know and be able to do as a result of this unit—as a template. This document also suggested resources and a common district-developed assessment, which was mostly multiple choice and fill in the blank. The team felt very comfortable having flexibility in this unit and agreed that a good way to do some action research would be to analyze how students did on the final assessment this year compared to previous years with a more traditional instructional format.

To ensure there were no issues with this way of thinking, one member set up a meeting with an administrator to ensure the team's thinking did not infringe on any district requirements. After clarification of what was required and where flexibility was allowed, the team felt comfortable moving forward. The district administrator told the team members to follow the set pacing guide and ensure they were teaching the standards assigned to the course; however, they had latitude with how they developed the instructional model. They were also told that, while they had latitude, they needed to make sure that this new way of instruction produced similar or better results.

With this information and administration approval, the team used the planning form in figure 9.1 that it had obtained from a colleague in another district to begin thinking about the best place to begin.

Question 4 Planning Steps				
Will your extension experience be for:	What indicators will you cover?	What will the personalized learning components look like?	What instructional strategies will you use? How?	How will you formatively and summatively assess this work?
An activity ____ A lesson ____ A unit ____ Multiple units ____ A course ____		Knowing your learners: Allowing voice and choice: Implementing flexibility: Using data: Integrating technology:	Curriculum compacting: Flexible grouping: Product choices: Tiered assignments: Multilevel learning stations:	

Figure 9.1: Personalized learning plan.

*Visit **go.SolutionTree.com/PLCbooks** for a free reproducible version of this figure.*

By thinking about each of the areas listed in the planning form, and discussing and looking at examples from *When They Already Know It*, the team decided to develop a ten-day-long instructional unit that included personalized learning. As part of the unit, the team decided to create a lesson featuring flexible grouping, which focused on tiered assignments and multilevel learning stations, similar to the secondary classroom story in chapter 5 (page 111).

Prior to the start of the unit, the collaborative team worked to make a short preassessment for the content it would cover. The standards for which the team sought to evaluate students' understanding prior to the unit included the following (Nebraska Department of Education, 2015):

> MA 6.2.3.a Write equations (e.g., one operation, one variable) to represent real-world problems involving non-negative rational numbers.
>
> MA 6.2.3.b Solve real-world problems involving non-negative rational numbers.
>
> MA 6.2.3.c Solve real-world problems involving percents of numbers.
>
> MA 6.2.3.d Solve real-world problems using ratios and unit rates. (p. 21)

For each standard, the team developed three questions: a simple multiple-choice item, a more difficult problem that required solving a problem and describing how they came to the answer, and a final problem that would enable the student to show a mastery of the material by solving a problem that an individual might see outside of the school setting. Very quickly, the teachers could see the level with which their students were beginning this work.

The team quickly set up a spreadsheet to show how students performed on each of the standards, indicating if they scored a 0 (did not answer any question correctly), 1 (got the first question correct), 2 (got the first and second questions correct), and 3 (got all three questions correct). The team members then worked together to develop stations for each standard. For students who scored a 0 or 1, they would spend their first station with the teacher who led a traditional whole-group instruction lesson. Students with a 2 would have a choice of joining the session with the teacher-led group or working at a work station where they could watch a short instructional video the teachers had created. At this station, they could work at their own pace and demonstrate mastery at the end of the station with questions that looked similar to what was on the preassessment. The students who scored a 3 were given opportunities that looked a bit more personalized. If a student had a 3 on just one standard, he or she could choose from three options of how he or she might want to demonstrate his or her learning. Students who had a 3 on all of the items were given an opportunity to develop a final project that dealt with the standards involved.

During the actual lesson, the three team members were amazed at the students' activity level. While the teachers were skeptical about what it might look like in action, the students were really enjoying the flexibility and buzz they experienced in the classroom. Teachers also found this type of teaching demanding; they were constantly working with students, floating around the classroom, checking on student progress, and helping question 4 students meet their goals. At the end of the unit, the teachers were excited to see how the students performed on the final assessment.

After completing the unit, the team used its next meeting to discuss using its data protocol in this new format. In preparation, each teacher entered his or her student information into a spreadsheet with percentages of how the students performed on the questions tied to each of the four standards covered in the lesson. On a separate document, the teachers could see how students performed on this same unit in past years. To their pleasure, the data showed that overall, students performed better than in past years. In fact, on three of the standards, students' overall scores were 10 percent higher than in past years. Additionally, they reflected on how engaged their question 4 students were. One student who loves the stock market took data from the past performance of a popular shoe company's stock on the New York Stock Exchange and developed a chart to share her prediction of how it will perform in the next year. While it is unlikely that this prediction will prove to be correct, the teachers loved how engaged she was and how she talked three other students into helping her (and they became just as engaged). This student was so excited that she asked the teacher if she could start a stock market club after school.

In the last few minutes of their team meeting, they laughed, exchanged high fives, and talked about how much fun they had in this venture. It was clear to the team members that not only were students energized and excited about learning but also they were! They couldn't wait to repeat the process and have new successes to share with others in a future unit.

The team committed to repeat this process with activities and units continually throughout the year until it had a full personalized learning units library, which would offer lessons and activities to challenge question 4 students. The team members were so excited, they even set up a time to visit with the principal to request time at an upcoming staff meeting to share what they had learned and to become resources for others who looked to have the same journey.

The team members had a great deal of energy around this process and wanted to ensure that the momentum moved forward in subsequent years as well. They used the reproducible reflection tools at the ends of chapters 4–8 at least once a quarter to rate themselves on how often they implemented each of the actions or indicators for each element of personalized learning in the past ten days, and then talked through the results together. From these discussions, they reflected, pushed, and challenged each other to ensure the elements became more and more a part of their collaborative team conversations and frequent instructional practice. Over time, they hope to track their progress and see that they are consistently growing and using the five elements more and more frequently with greater success.

Next Steps for Your Team

Every collaborative team interested in this work will enter at a different place and continue at a different pace. In many ways, it seems wrong to suggest implementing something as fluid and natural as personalized learning, and then providing a rigid approach to do it. Everyone's approach can and should look different. The scenario we describe with this sample team is just one way you and your team may choose to move forward in your work.

In summary, our scenario provides an example one team might use as it completes the following activities.

- Learn the five elements of personalized learning.

- Determine and discuss the reframing teachers need to consider for successful implementation.

- Learn the instructional strategies for working with question 4 students.

- Determine where personalization elements fit into the curriculum.

- Commit to making personalized learning a part of your weekly collaborative team meetings.

- Find a comfortable entry point for implementation.

- Learn by (doing) implementing your plan.

- Plan for reflection and make adjustments.

- Make a commitment to ensuring that proficient students are challenged as much as students who are still working toward proficiency.

It is important to determine implementation steps that make sense for your team. Use the tool in figure 9.2 to indicate what your team feels it needs to do next, how you will go about completing this task, how much time you anticipate it taking, who will be responsible, and your key findings. As with any task collaborative teams face, there is no single correct way to go about this task; you and your team will need to take some time to determine how you want to proceed. The important thing for you and your team to do is to start. Don't worry about it being perfect—learn by doing. Refer to figure 9.3 (pages 216–217) for the sixth-grade mathematics team's completed form. Use all, some, or none of the items described in this chapter and listed in the team's sample form. These are intended as an example and a template that *might* serve to guide your team.

Items to Complete	Plan of Action	Estimated Time	Who Is Responsible	Key Findings

Figure 9.2: Collaborative team planning form template.

Visit go.SolutionTree.com/PLCbooks for a free reproducible version of this figure.

Items to Complete	Plan of Action	Estimated Time	Who Is Responsible	Key Findings
Learn about why teams should think about responding to question 4 and why personalized learning is an important consideration.	Read *When They Already Know It* introduction and chapters 1 and 2.	Two weeks	All team members	The team agreed with the philosophy of making extending learning for question 4 students a priority.
Determine why the team wants to use the elements of personalized learning.	Engage in conversation about the introduction and chapters 1 and 2.	One team meeting after the initial assignment	All team members individually reflect and then share as a team.	The team agreed the myth of average and students' use of technology were its grounding arguments.
Learn about and reflect on the instructional strategies recommended for high-achieving learners.	Engage in conversation about chapter 3.	One team meeting after the initial assignment	All team members individually reflect and then share as a team.	The team highlighted the activity that they would feel most comfortable implementing and discussed what this would look like in the classroom.
Determine "load-bearing walls" within existing curriculum maps and guides.	Meet with district curriculum director to ask about flexibility.	Two weeks to set appointment and get back to the team	Collaborative team leader	Team learned it had flexibility around instruction; pacing and standards are load-bearing walls. It also learned that using preassessments for students and then allowing for more personalized learning is supported by the school.
Learn the five elements of personalized learning.	Read, reflect on, and discuss chapters 4–8.	Reserve time over five weeks to discuss one element at each meeting.	All team members	Team learned the five elements of personalized learning is a way to extend learning for students who are already proficient on a target.

Commit to making personalized learning a part of the weekly team meetings.	Include personalized learning on weekly collaborative agenda document.	One meeting	All team members (collaborative team leader adjusts weekly document)	By including an item on the weekly document, the team held itself accountable for addressing personalized learning to respond to question 4.
Determine where personalization fits into the curriculum.	Complete the personalized learning plan (figure 9.1).	One or two meetings	All team members	Team completed plans for implementation.
Learn by doing.	Implement plan.	Ten days	All team members	Team found that implementing the five elements engaged students and students were also more successful on assessments.
Plan for reflection and adjustments.	Schedule reflection time in the collaborative meeting.	Part of the collaborative meeting following unit completion (minimum of fifteen minutes)	All team members	Team analyzed data of all students and final products of question 4 students, made adjustments for the next year, and collectively analyzed effectiveness of instructional approaches used for question 4 students.
Plan ways to make extending students' learning the culture of the team.	Meet with the principal or share at staff meetings. Regularly assess progress on a reflection document.	Schedule a thirty-minute meeting to ask to present for fifteen minutes at a staff meeting. Spend fifteen to twenty minutes on quarterly reflections.	All team members	Team continued to grow and consider ways to incorporate the five elements of personalized learning to respond to question 4.

Figure 9.3: Sample completed collaborative team planning form.

Conclusion

We thank the educators and team members who have read this book; we sincerely hope you individually and as a team see the concepts outlined in the five elements of personalized learning as tools for addressing the fourth critical question of a PLC in a manner that impacts your students.

If you have followed this book from beginning to end, you have a plan to make the five elements of personalized learning and the instructional strategies for question 4 students come to life. When students come to your classroom already knowing the material, you will have a plan to extend their learning and engage them in their learning. We challenge you to get started and—as our PLC heroes would say—learn by doing! We have no doubt that by implementing these ideas in your own classroom at a pace you find comfortable, students will be engaged and joyful in their learning; the school culture will be one where inquiry and innovation are the norms; and you, personally, will find new sparks in your work. We thank you for your interest in personalized learning and can't wait to hear your wonderful implementation stories.

References and Resources

Achieve. (2013). *DCI arrangements of the Next Generation Science Standards*. Accessed at www.nextgenscience.org/sites/default/files/AllDCI.pdf on November 6, 2017.

AllThingsPLC. (2016). *Glossary of key terms and concepts*. Accessed at www.allthingsplc .info/files/uploads/Terms.pdf on February 15, 2018.

Ambady, N., Paik, S. K., Steele, J., Owen-Smith, A., & Mitchell, J. P. (2004). Deflecting negative self-relevant stereotype activation: The effects of individuation. *Journal of Experimental Social Psychology, 40*(3), 401–408.

Anania, J. (1982). The effects of quality of instruction on the cognitive and affective learning of students. (Doctoral dissertation, University of Chicago, 1981). *Dissertation Abstracts International, 42*, 4269A.

Anania, J. (1983). The influence of instructional conditions on student learning and achievement. *Evaluation in Education: An International Review Series, 7*(1), 1–92.

Assor, A., Kaplan, H., & Roth, G. (2002). Choice is good, but relevance is excellent: Autonomy-enhancing and suppressing teacher behaviours predicting students' engagement in schoolwork. *British Journal of Educational Psychology, 72*, 261–278.

Babad, E. (1995). The "teacher's pet" phenomenon, students' perceptions of teachers' differential behavior, and students' morale. *Journal of Educational Psychology, 87*(3), 361–374.

Bailey, K., & Jakicic, C. (2012). *Common formative assessment: A toolkit for Professional Learning Communities at Work*. Bloomington, IN: Solution Tree Press.

Balow, C. (2017, June 15). The "effect size" in educational research: What is it & how to use it? *Illuminate Education*. Accessed at www.illuminateed.com/blog/2017/06/effect -size-educational-research-use on April 12, 2018.

Banaji, M., & Greenwald, A. (2013). *Blindspot: Hidden biases of good people*. New York: Delacorte Press.

Baroutsis, A., McGregor, G., & Mills, M. (2016). Pedagogic voice: Student voice in teaching and engagement pedagogies. *Pedagogy, Culture and Society, 24*(1), 123–140.

Beach, D., & Dovemark, M. (2009). Making "right" choices? An ethnographic account of creativity, performativity and personalised learning policy, concepts and practices. *Oxford Review of Education, 35*(6), 689–704.

Bell, B., & Cowie, B. (2001). The characteristics of formative assessment in science education. *Science Education, 85*(5), 536–553.

Bill and Melinda Gates Foundation. (2014). *Early progress: Interim research on personalized learning.* Seattle, WA: Author. Accessed at http://k12education.gatesfoundation.org /resource/early-progress-interim-research-on-personalized-learning on September 25, 2017.

Bloom, B. S. (Ed.). (1956). *Taxonomy of educational objectives: The classification of educational goals.* New York: Longman, Green.

Bloom, B. S. (1984). The 2 sigma problem: The search for methods of group instruction as effective as one-to-one tutoring. *Educational Researcher, 13*(6), 4–16.

Bray, B., & McClaskey, K. (2015). *Make learning personal: The what, who, WOW, where, and why.* Thousand Oaks, CA: Corwin Press.

Bray, B., & McClaskey, K. (2017). *How to personalize learning: A practical guide for getting started and going deeper.* Thousand Oaks, CA: Corwin Press.

Brookhart, S. M. (2014). *The essence of formative assessment: Creating a common understanding of the formative assessment process* (Part one of a three-part series) [Archived webinar]. Washington, DC: U.S. Department of Education. Accessed at www.relcentral.org/news-and-events/the-essence-of-formative-assessment-creating-a -common-understanding-of-the-formative-assessment-process on April 5, 2017.

Brooks, J. G., & Brooks, M. G. (1993). *In search of understanding: The case for constructivist classrooms.* Alexandria, VA: Association for Supervision and Curriculum Development.

Buckner, R., & Vincent, J. L. (2007). Unrest at rest: Default activity and spontaneous network correlations. *NeuroImage, 37*(4), 1091–1096.

Burke, A. J. (1984). Students' potential for learning contrasted under tutorial and group approaches to instruction. (Doctoral dissertation, University of Chicago, 1983). *Dissertation Abstracts International, 44,* 2025A.

Cain, S. (2012). *Quiet: The power of introverts in a world that can't stop talking.* New York: Crown.

California Department of Education. (2017). *Taking center stage—Act II.* Accessed at www.cde.ca.gov/ci/gs/mg/cefmgtcsii.asp on April 13, 2018.

Center for Elementary Mathematics and Science Education. (n.d.) *Everyday Mathematics: Overview of preK–6 grade-level goals.* Accessed at http://everydaymath.uchicago.edu /about/understanding-em/glg_overview_ccss.pdf on April 2, 2018.

Chan, K. W., Wong, A., & Lo, E. (2012). Relational analysis of intrinsic motivation, achievement goals, learning strategies and academic achievement for Hong Kong secondary students. *Asia-Pacific Education Researcher, 21*(2), 230–243.

The Children's Online Privacy Protection Act, 15 U.S.C. 6501–6506. (1998).

Christensen, C. M., Horn, M. B., & Johnson, C. W. (2008). *Disrupting class: How disruptive innovation will change the way the world learns*. New York: McGraw-Hill.

Clynes, T. (2016, September 7). How to raise a genius: Lessons from a 45-year study of super-smart children. *Nature*. Accessed at https://www.nature.com/news/how-to -raise-a-genius-lessons-from-a-45-year-study-of-super-smart-children-1.20537 on April 4, 2018.

Corning, A. F., & Myers, D. J. (2002). Individual orientation toward engagement in social action. *Political Psychology, 23*, 703–729.

Cox, J. (n.d.). *Flexible grouping as a differentiated instruction strategy*. Accessed at www .teachhub.com/flexible-grouping-differentiated-instruction-strategy on March 29, 2018.

Crandal, B., Klein, G., & Hoffman, R. R. (2006). *Working minds: A practitioner's guide to cognitive task analysis*. Cambridge, MA: MIT Press.

Csikszentmihalyi, M. (2008). *Flow: The psychology of optimal experience* (Harper Perennial Modern Classics ed.). New York: HarperCollins.

Damasio, A. (1999). *The feeling of what happens*. New York: Harcourt Brace.

Darling-Hammond, L., Herman, J., Pellegrino, J., et al. (2013). *Criteria for high-quality assessment*. Stanford, CA: Stanford Center for Opportunity Policy in Education. Accessed at www.hewlett.org/wp-content/uploads/2016/08/Criteria_for_High _Quality_Assessment_June_2013.pdf on April 6, 2018.

Deed, C., Lesko, T. M., & Lovejoy, V. (2014). Teacher adaptation to personalized learning spaces. *Teacher Development, 18*(3), 369–383.

dek2635. (2011, September 27). *Similar triangles* [Video file]. Accessed at https://youtu.be /gQoNjgayoLI on November 4, 2017.

Doorley, S., & Witthoft, S. (2012). *Make space: How to set the stage for creative collaboration*. Hoboken, NJ: Wiley.

Duckworth, A. (2016). *Grit: The power of passion and perseverance*. New York: Scribner.

Duckworth, A. (2017, February 1). Speech presented at the Phoenix Academy Scholarship Luncheon, Omaha, NE.

Duckworth, A., Peterson, C., Matthews, M. D., & Kelly, D. R. (2007). Grit: Perseverance and passion for long-term goals. *Journal of Personality and Social Psychology, 92*(6), 1087–1101.

DuFour, R., DuFour, R., Eaker, R., & Karhanek, G. (2010). *Raising the bar and closing the gap: Whatever it takes*. Bloomington, IN: Solution Tree Press.

DuFour, R., DuFour, R., Eaker, R., Many, T. W., & Mattos, M. (2016). *Learning by doing: A handbook for Professional Learning Communities at Work* (3rd ed.). Bloomington, IN: Solution Tree Press.

DuFour, R., & Eaker, R. (1998). *Professional Learning Communities at Work: Best practices for enhancing student achievement.* Bloomington, IN: Solution Tree Press.

Duke, N. K. (2000). For the rich it's richer: Print experiences and environments offered to children in very low- and very high-socioeconomic status first-grade classrooms. *American Educational Research Journal, 37*(2), 441–478.

Dweck, C. S. (2006). *Mindset: The new psychology of success.* New York: Random House.

Dweck, C. S. (2007). Boosting achievement with messages that motivate. *Education Canada, 47*(2), 6–10.

Dweck, C. S. (2015). Growth. *British Journal of Educational Psychology, 85*(2), 242–245.

Easton, A. (2016). *District 66 personalized learning element #2: Voice and choice* [Video file]. Accessed at www.youtube.com/watch?v=h0sSr2SG-vE on April 4, 2018.

Education Elements. (2015). *Jaime Casap's keynote at the Education Elements Personalized Learning Summit 2015* [Video file]. Accessed at www.youtube.com/watch?list =PLpJvMT3yigZmslHkBQ47lsnjYjnck2-vC&time_continue=31&v=ClqlcctqZTk on April 5, 2018.

El Bouhdidi, J., Ghailani, M., & Fennan, A. (2013). A probabilistic approach for the generation of learning sessions tailored to the learning styles of learners. *International Journal of Emerging Technologies in Learning, 8*(6), 42–49.

Elliot, A. J., & Dweck, C. S. (Eds.). (2005). *Handbook of competence and motivation.* New York: Guilford Press.

Elliot, A. J., & McGregor, H. A. (2001). A 2 x 2 achievement goal framework. *Journal of Personality and Social Psychology, 80*(3), 501–519.

Elliott, E. S., & Dweck, C. S. (1988). Goals: An approach to motivation and achievement. *Journal of Personality and Social Psychology, 54*(1), 5–12.

Esposito, F., Bertolino, A., Scarabino, T., Latorre, V., Blasi, G., Popolizio, T., Tedeschi, G., Cirillo, S., Goebel, R., & Di Salle, F. (2006). Independent component model of the default-mode brain function: Assessing the impact of active thinking. *Brain Research Bulletin, 70*(4–6), 263–269.

Evans, M., & Boucher, A. R. (2015). Optimizing the power of choice: Supporting student autonomy to foster motivation and engagement in learning. *Mind, Brain, and Education, 9*(2), 87–91.

Farrington, C. A., Roderick, M., Allensworth, E., Nagaoka, J., Keyes, T. S., Johnson, D. W., et al. (2012). *Teaching adolescents to become learners: The role of noncognitive factors in shaping school performance—A critical literature review.* Chicago: The University of Chicago Consortium on Chicago School Research.

Ferriter, B. (2015, November). *Singletons in a PLC.* Presentation at the Solution Tree PLC associate retreat, Salt Lake City, UT.

Field, G. (2013, June). *Schoolwide enrichment.* Session presented at Westside Community Schools Summer Learning Series, Omaha, NE.

Fischer, K., & Bidell, T. (1998). Dynamic development of psychological structures in action and thought. In W. Damon (Editor-in-Chief) & R. Lerner (Vol. Ed.), *Handbook of child psychology: Vol. 1. Theoretical models of human development* (5th ed., pp. 467–561). New York: Wiley.

Fisher, D., & Frey, N. (2014). *Better learning through structured teaching: A framework for the gradual release of responsibility* (2nd ed.). Alexandria, VA: Association for Supervision and Curriculum Development.

Fisher, D., & Frey, N. (2017, February 15). *That pesky fourth PLC question* [Blog post]. Accessed at www.solutiontree.com/blog/that-pesky-fourth-plc-question on September 25, 2017.

Fleming, N. D. (2006). *V.A.R.K. visual, aural/auditory, read/write, kinesthetic.* New Zealand: Bonwell Green Mountain Falls.

Flowerday, T., & Schraw, G. (2000). Teacher beliefs about instructional choice: A phenomenological study. *Journal of Educational Psychology, 92*(4), 634–645.

Fountas, I., C., & Pinnell, G. S. (2016). *Benchmark assessment system* (3rd ed.). Portsmouth, NH: Heinemann.

Fox, J., & Hoffman, W. (2011). *The differentiated instruction book of lists.* San Francisco: Jossey-Bass.

Fox, M. D., Snyder, A. Z., Vincent, J. L., Corbetta, M., Van Essen, D. C., & Raichle, M. E. (2005). The human brain is intrinsically organized into dynamic, anti-correlated functional networks. *Proceedings of the National Academy of Sciences of the United States of America, 102*(27), 9673–9678.

France, P. E. (2017). Is standardization the answer to personalization? *Educational Leadership, 74*(6), 40–44.

Gardner, H. (2011). *Frames of mind: The theory of multiple intelligences.* New York: Basic Books.

Gentry, M. (1996). Total school cluster grouping: An investigation of achievement and identification of elementary school students. *The National Research Center on the Gifted and Talented 1996 Spring Newsletter.* Accessed at https://nrcgt.uconn.edu /newsletters/spring964/ on May 24, 2018.

Gentry, M. (1999). *Promoting student achievement and exemplary classroom practices through cluster grouping: A research-based alternative to heterogeneous elementary classrooms* (RM99138). Storrs, CT: National Research Center on the Gifted and Talented.

Gentry, M. (2014). *Total school cluster grouping and differentiation: A comprehensive, research-based plan for raising student achievement and improving teacher practices* (2nd ed.). Waco, TX: Prufrock Press.

Gentry, M., & Gable, R. K. (2001). From the student's perspective: My class activities— An instrument for use in research and evaluation. *Journal for the Education of the Gifted, 24*(4), 322–343.

Gentry, M., & Owen, S. V. (2004). Secondary student perceptions of classroom quality: Instrumentation and differences between advanced/honors and nonhonors classes. *Journal of Secondary Gifted Education*, *16*(1), 20–29.

Given, L. (2008). *The SAGE encyclopedia of qualitative research methods*. Los Angeles: SAGE Publications.

Godsey, M. (2015, September 28). When schools overlook introverts. *The Atlantic*. Accessed at www.theatlantic.com/education/archive/2015/09/introverts-at-school-overlook/407467 on April 4, 2018.

Graham, P., & Ferriter, B. (2008). One step at a time. *Journal of Staff Development*, *29*(3), 38–42.

Haimovitz, K., & Dweck, C. S. (2017). The origins of children's growth and fixed mindsets: New research and a new proposal. *Child Development*, *88*(6), 1849–1859.

Hart, S., Dixon, A., Drummond, M. J., & McIntyre, D. (2004). *Learning without limits*. Maidenhead, England: Open University Press.

Hattie, J. A. C. (2009). *Visible learning: A synthesis of over 800 meta-analyses relating to achievement*. New York: Routledge.

Hattie, J. A. C. (2015). The applicability of visible learning to higher education. *Scholarship of Teaching and Learning in Psychology*, *1*(1), 79–91.

Hattie, J. A. C., & Donoghue, G. M. (2016, December). Learning strategies: A synthesis and conceptual model. *npj Science of Learning*, *1*(16013). Accessed at www.nature.com/articles/npjscilearn201613 on April 16, 2018.

Heacox, D. (2002). *Differentiating instruction in the regular classroom*. Minneapolis, MN: Free Spirit Publishing.

Hernandez, A. (2016). *Stop trying to define personalized learning*. Accessed at www.edsurge.com/news/2016-05-11-stop-trying-to-define-personalized-learning on September 25, 2017.

Herold, B. (2017, November 7). The case(s) against personalized learning. *Education Week*. Accessed at www.edweek.org/ew/articles/2017/11/08/the-cases-against-personalized-learning.html on April 6, 2018.

Hollander, R. (2018). Augmented reality apps are seeing fast success on iOS. *Business Insider*. Accessed at www.businessinsider.com/augmented-reality-success-ios-2018-3 on April 3, 2018.

Hunter, R. (2004). *Madeline Hunter's mastery teaching: Increasing instructional effectiveness in elementary and secondary schools* (Rev. and updated ed.). Thousand Oaks, CA: Corwin Press.

Immordino-Yang, M. H. (2016). *Emotions, learning, and the brain: Exploring the educational implications of affective neuroscience*. New York: Norton.

Iyengar, S. S., & Lepper, M. R. (2000). When choice is demotivating: Can one desire too much of a good thing? *Journal of Personality and Social Psychology*, *79*(6), 995–1006.

Kallick, B., & Zmuda, A. (2017). *Students at the center: Personalized learning with habits of mind*. Alexandria, VA: Association for Supervision and Curriculum Development.

Karampiperis, P., Lin, T., & Sampson, D. S. (2006). Adaptive cognitive-based selection of learning objects. *Innovations in Education & Teaching International, 43*(2), 121–135.

Kashdan, T. B., Gallagher, M. W., Silvia, P. J., Winterstein, B. P., Breen, W. E., Terhar, D., et al. (2009). The curiosity and exploration inventory-II: Development, factor structure, and psychometrics. *Journal of Research in Personality, 43*(6), 987–998.

Kelly, K. (2016). *The inevitable: Understanding the 12 technological forces that will shape our future*. New York: Viking.

Killian, S. (2017, September). Hattie's 2017 updated list of factors influencing student achievement. *The Australian Society for Evidence Based Teaching*. Accessed at www .evidencebasedteaching.org.au/hatties-2017-updated-list on April 17, 2018.

King, A. (1993). From sage on the stage to guide on the side. *College Teaching, 41*(1), 30–35.

Klute, M., Apthorp, H., Harlacher, J., & Reale, M. (2017). *Formative assessment and elementary school student academic achievement: A review of the evidence* (REL 2017– 259). Washington, DC: U.S. Department of Education, Institute of Education Sciences, National Center for Education Evaluation and Regional Assistance, Regional Educational Laboratory Central.

Koh, J. (2015). The more, the better? Examining choice and self-regulated learning strategies. *International Journal of Learning: Annual Review, 21*, 13–32.

Kolano, L. (2016). Smartness as cultural wealth: An AsianCrit counterstory. *Race, Ethnicity and Education, 19*(6), 1149–1163.

Lahey, J. (2015). *The gift of failure: How the best parents learn to let go so their children can succeed*. New York: Harper.

Lee's Summit R–7 School District. (2014). *3rd grade mathematics curriculum year-at-a-glance*. Accessed at www.lsr7.org/wp-content/uploads/2012/09/3rd-Grade -Mathematics-Curriculum-Year-At-A-Glance-14-15.pdf on April 12, 2018.

Liem, G. D., & Martin, A. J. (2012). The Motivation and Engagement Scale: Theoretical framework, psychometric properties, and applied yields. *Australian Psychologist, 47*(1), 3–13.

Liesveld, R., & Miller, J. A. (2005). *Teach with your strengths: How great teachers inspire their students*. New York: Gallup Press.

Long, C. (2013, September 18). Are we failing gifted students? *NEA Today*. Accessed at http://neatoday.org/2013/09/18/are-we-failing-gifted-students-2 on April 4, 2018.

Long Beach Unified School District. (2008). *Elementary school educational specifications*. Accessed at http://lbschoolbonds.net/pdfs/lbusd_ES_ed_spec_final.pdf on April 13, 2018.

Marzano, R. J. (2003). *What works in schools: Translating research into action*. Alexandria, VA: Association for Supervision and Curriculum Development.

Marzano, R. J. (2009). Setting the record straight on "high-yield" strategies. *Phi Delta Kappan, 91*(1), 30–37.

Mateusz, M. (2014, September 15). *Unbroken* [Video file]. Accessed at https://youtube .com/watch?v=26U_seo0a1g on November 16, 2017.

Mertler, C. (2017). *Classroom assessment: A practical guide for educators.* London: Routledge.

Midgley, C., Maehr, M., Hruda, L., Anderman, E., Anderman, L., Freeman, K., Gheen, M., Kaplan, A., Kumar, R., Middleton, M., Nelson, J., Roeser, R., & Urdan, T. (2000). *Manual for the patterns of adaptive learning scales.* Ann Arbor: University of Michigan. Accessed at www.umich.edu/~pals/PALS%202000_V13Word97.pdf on April 2, 2018.

Muhammad, A. (2015). *Overcoming the achievement gap trap: Liberating mindsets to effect change.* Bloomington, IN: Solution Tree Press.

Murray, T. (2017, April). *Future Ready Schools: A framework for transformation.* Symposium conducted at the Nebraska Technology Educators Spring Conference, Omaha, NE.

The Myers & Briggs Foundation. (2018). *Extraversion or introversion.* Accessed at www .myersbriggs.org/my-mbti-personality-type/mbti-basics/extraversion-or-introversion .htm?bhcp=1 on April 2, 2018.

National Association for Gifted Children. (n.d.). *Curriculum compacting.* Accessed at www.nagc.org/resources-publications/gifted-education-practices/curriculum -compacting on February 27, 2018.

National Center for Education Statistics. (n.d.). *Fast facts.* Accessed at https://nces.ed.gov /fastfacts/display.asp?id=28 on April 3, 2018.

National Council of Teachers of Mathematics. (n.d.). *Benefits of formative assessment.* Accessed at www.nctm.org/Research-and-Advocacy/Research-Brief-and-Clips /Benefits-of-Formative-Assessment on April 5, 2017.

National Governors Association Center for Best Practices & Council of Chief State School Officers. (2010a). *Common Core State Standards for English language arts and literacy in history/social studies, science, and technical subjects.* Washington, DC: Authors. Accessed at www.corestandards.org/assets/CCSSI_ELA%20Standards.pdf on April 6, 2018.

National Governors Association Center for Best Practices & Council of Chief State School Officers. (2010b). *Common Core State Standards for mathematics.* Washington, DC: Authors. Accessed at www.corestandards.org/assets/CCSSI_Math%20Standards .pdf on November 10, 2017.

Nebraska Department of Education. (2014). *2014 Nebraska college- and career-ready ELA standards.* Accessed at https://2x9dwr1yq1he1dw6623gg411-wpengine.netdna-ssl .com/wp-content/uploads/2017/07/2014_ELA_Standards.pdf on April 13, 2018.

Nebraska Department of Education. (2015). *Mathematics standards.* Accessed at https:// 2x9dwr1yq1he1dw6623gg411-wpengine.netdna-ssl.com/wp-content/uploads

/2017/07/2015_Nebraska_College_and_Career_Standards_for_Mathematics
_Vertical.pdf on April 4, 2018.

Nedungadi, P., & Raman, R. (2012). A new approach to personalization: Integrating
e-learning and m-learning. *Educational Technology Research and Development*, *60*(4),
659–678.

Nelson, N., Fien, H., Doabler, C., & Clarke, B. (2016). Considerations for realizing the
promise of educational gaming technology. *Teaching Exceptional Children*, *48*(6),
293–300.

Nilsson, J. E., Marszalek, J. M., Linnemeyer, R. M., Bahner, A. D., & Misialek, L. H.
(2011). Development and assessment of the Social Issues Advocacy Scale. *Educational
& Psychological Measurement*, *71*(1), 258–275.

Oakes, J. (1986). Keeping track, part 1: The policy and practice of curriculum inequality.
Phi Delta Kappan, *68*(1), 12–17.

Oakes, J. (2005). *Keeping track: How schools structure inequality* (2nd ed.). New Haven,
CT: Yale University Press.

Oakes, J., & Lipton, M. (1990). Tracking and ability grouping: A structural barrier to
access and achievement. In J. I. Goodlad & P. Keating (Eds.), *Access to knowledge:
An agenda for our nation's schools* (pp. 187–204). New York: College Entrance
Examination Board.

Ohio Department of Education. (2010). *Ohio's new learning standards: Social studies
standards*. Accessed at http://education.ohio.gov/getattachment/Topics/Ohio-s-New
-Learning-Standards/Social-Studies/SS-Standards.pdf.aspx on April 13, 2018.

Olentangy Local Schools. (n.d.). *Social studies eighth grade curriculum blueprint*. Accessed
at https://docs.google.com/document/d/1nrdKdXKRQjd2IVawGh90xURI
_AQbFERB6oKGLN22GdY/edit on April 13, 2018.

O'Neill, J., & Conzemius, A. E. (2006). *The power of SMART goals: Using goals to improve
student learning*. Bloomington, IN: Solution Tree Press.

Orehek, E., & Human, L. J. (2016). Self-expression on social media: Do tweets present
accurate and positive portraits of impulsivity, self-esteem, and attachment style?
Personality and Social Psychology Bulletin, *43*(1), 60–70.

Ostler, E., & Flesch, M. (2012). Using dynamic solution exercises to achieve vertical
course alignment. *MathAMATYC Educator*, *3*(3), 10–16.

Pane, J. F., Steiner, E. D., Baird, M. D., & Hamilton, L. S. (2015). *Continued progress:
Promising evidence on personalized learning*. Santa Monica, CA: RAND Corporation.
Accessed at http://k12education.gatesfoundation.org/resource/continued-progress
-promising-evidence-on-personalized-learning-2 on September 25, 2017.

Pane, J. F., Steiner, E. D., Baird, M. D., Hamilton, L. S., & Pane, J. D. (2017). *Informing
progress: Insights on personalized learning implementation and effects*. Accessed at www
.rand.org/pubs/research_reports/RR2042.html on June 1, 2018.

Park, G., Lubinski, D., & Benbow, C. P. (2013). When less is more: Effects of grade skipping on adult STEM accomplishments among mathematically precocious youth. *Journal of Educational Psychology, 105*(1), 176–198.

Paul, R., & Elder, L. (2006). *The miniature guide to critical thinking concepts and tools* (4th ed.). Tomales, CA: Foundation for Critical Thinking.

Peterson, K., & Kolb, D. (2017). *How you learn is how you live: Using nine ways of learning to transform your life*. Oakland, CA: Berrett-Koehler.

Pintrich, P. (2004). A conceptual framework for assessing motivation and self-regulated learning in college students. *Educational Psychology Review, 16*(4), 385–407.

Powell, W., & Kusuma-Powell, O. (2011). *How to teach now: Five keys to personalized learning in the global classroom*. Alexandria, VA: Association for Supervision and Curriculum Development.

Prain, V., Cox, P., Deed, C., Dorman, J., Edwards, D., Farrelly, C., et al. (2013). Personalised learning: Lessons to be learnt. *British Educational Research Journal, 39*(4), 654–676.

Public Profit. (n.d.). *Dabbling in the data: A hands-on guide to participatory data analysis*. Oakland, CA: Author. Accessed at www.publicprofit.net/content/common/common .download_file.php?action_special=download_file&sid=becc4648297174eea4a5 bfe6c4e32f15&download_file_id=843659 on November 2, 2017.

Puentedura, R. (2014). *SAMR: First steps*. Accessed at www.hippasus.com/rrpweblog /archives/2014/11/13/SAMR_FirstSteps.pdf on April 13, 2018.

Raichle, M., MacLeod, A., Snyder, A., Powers, W., Gusnard, D., & Shulman, G. (2001). A default mode of brain function. *Proceedings of the National Academy of Sciences of the United States of America, 98*(2), 676–682.

Rattan, A., Savani, K., Chugh, D., & Dweck, C. S. (2015). Leveraging mindsets to promote academic achievement: Policy recommendations. *Perspectives on Psychological Science, 10*(6), 721–726.

Reis, S. M., Burns, D. E., & Renzulli, J. S. (1992). *Curriculum compacting: The complete guide to modifying the regular curriculum for high-ability students*. Mansfield Center, CT: Creative Learning Press.

Reis, S. M., Gentry, M., & Park, S. (1995). *Extending the pedagogy of gifted education to all students* (Research Monograph 95118). Storrs: University of Connecticut, The National Research Center on the Gifted and Talented.

Reis, S. M., & Renzulli, J. S. (n.d.). *Curriculum compacting: A systematic procedure for modifying the curriculum for above average ability students*. Accessed at https://gifted .uconn.edu/schoolwide-enrichment-model/curriculum_compacting on April 4, 2018.

Reis, S. M., & Renzulli, J. S. (2015). Compass white paper on the five dimensions of differentiation. *Gifted Education Press Quarterly, 29*(3), 2–9.

Reis, S. M., & Renzulli, J. S. (2016). The schoolwide enrichment model: A focus on student strengths and interests. In S. M. Reis (Ed.), *Reflections on gifted education:*

Critical works by Joseph S. Renzulli and Colleagues (pp. 251–270). Waco, TX: Prufrock Press.

Renzulli, J. S. (n.d.a). *The definition of high-end learning.* Accessed at https://gifted.uconn .edu/schoolwide-enrichment-model/high-end_learning on April 5, 2018.

Renzulli, J. S. (n.d.b). *How to develop an authentic enrichment cluster.* Accessed at https:// gifted.uconn.edu/schoolwide-enrichment-model/authentic_enrichment_cluster on April 17, 2018.

Renzulli, J. S. (1977). *The enrichment triad model: A guide for developing defensible programs for the gifted and talented.* Wethersfield, CT: Creative Learning Press.

Renzulli, J. S. (1997). *Interest-A-Lyzer family of instruments: A manual for teachers.* Waco, TX: Prufrock Press.

Renzulli, J. S., & Reis, S. M. (n.d.a). *The Schoolwide Enrichment Model executive summary.* Accessed at https://gifted.uconn.edu/schoolwide-enrichment-model/semexec on March 30, 2018.

Renzulli, J. S., & Reis, S. M. (n.d.b). *SEM third edition resources and forms.* Accessed at http://gifted.uconn.edu/schoolwide-enrichment-model/sem3rd on October 27, 2017.

Renzulli, J. S., & Reis, S. M. (2016). Defensible and doable: A practical, multiple-criteria gifted program identification system. In S. M. Reis (Ed.), *Reflections on gifted education: Critical works by Joseph S. Renzulli and Colleagues* (pp. 91–128). Waco, TX: Prufrock Press.

Responsive Classroom. (2018). *Principles & practices.* Accessed at www.responsive classroom.org/about/principles-practices on April 5, 2018.

Richards, M. R. E., & Omdal, S. N. (2007). Effects of tiered instruction on academic performance in a secondary science course. *Journal of Advanced Academics, 18*(3), 424–453.

Rickabaugh, J. (2016). *Tapping the power of personalized learning: A roadmap for school leaders.* Alexandria, VA: Association for Supervision and Curriculum Development.

Rose, D. H., & Meyer, A. (2002). *Teaching every student in the digital age: Universal design for learning.* Alexandria, VA: Association for Supervision and Curriculum Development.

Rose, T. (2016). *The end of average: How we succeed in a world that values sameness.* New York: HarperCollins.

Rosenthal, H. S., & Crisp, R. J. (2006). Reducing stereotype threat by blurring intergroup boundaries. *Personality and Social Psychology Bulletin, 32*(4), 501–511.

Rotter, J. B. (1954). *Social learning and clinical psychology.* Englewood Cliffs, NJ: Prentice Hall.

Saeed, S., & Zyngier, D. (2012). How motivation influences student engagement: A qualitative case study. *Journal of Education and Learning, 1*(2), 252–267.

Schwartz, K. (2017, June). How do you know when a teaching strategy is most effective? John Hattie has an idea. *Mind/Shift.* Accessed at https://ww2.kqed.org/mindshift

/2017/06/14/how-do-you-know-when-a-teaching-strategy-is-most-effective-john
-hattie-has-an-idea on April 17, 2018.

Seeley, W. W., Menon, V., Schatzberg, A. F., Keller, J., Glover, G. H., Kenna, H., Reiss, A. L., & Greicius, M. D. (2007). Dissociable intrinsic connectivity networks for salience processing and executive control. *Journal of Neuroscience, 27*(9), 2349–2356.

Senge, P. (2000). *Schools that learn: A fifth discipline fieldbook for educators, parents, and everyone who cares about education.* New York: Doubleday.

Sheninger, E., & Murray, T. C. (2017). *8 keys to designing tomorrow's schools, today.* Accessed at https://edsurge.com/news/2017-05-31-8-keys-to-designing-tomorrow-s -schools-today on September 25, 2017.

Slavin, R. E. (1987). Ability grouping and student achievement in elementary schools: A best-evidence synthesis. *Review of Educational Research, 57*(3), 293–336.

Spencer, J. (2017). The genius of design. *Educational Leadership, 74*(6), 16–21.

Stamps, L. S. (2004). The effectiveness of curriculum compacting in first grade classrooms. *Roeper Review, 27*(1), 31.

Steele, C. M. (1998). Stereotyping and its threat are real. *American Psychologist, 53*(6), 680–681.

Steele, C. M. (2011). *Whistling Vivaldi: How stereotypes affect us and what we can do.* New York: Norton.

Stefanou, C. R., Perencevich, K. C., DiCintio, M., & Turner, J. C. (2004). Supporting autonomy in the classroom: Ways teachers encourage student decision making and ownership. *Educational Psychologist, 39*(2), 97–110.

Swinke, T. (2012). A unique, culture-aware, personalized learning environment. *International Journal of Emerging Technologies in Learning, 7*(2), 31–36.

The Teaching Center. (2016). *Reducing stereotype threat: Strategies for instructors.* Accessed at http://teachingcenter.wustl.edu/resources/inclusive-teaching-learning/reducing -stereotype-threat on April 2, 2018.

TEDx Talks. (2009, September 28). *Start with why: How great leaders inspire action— Simon Sinek TEDxPugetSound* [Video file]. Accessed at https://youtu.be/u4ZoJKF _VuA on September 25, 2017.

TEDx Talks. (2013, June 19). *The myth of average: Todd Rose at TEDxSonoma County* [Video file]. Accessed at https://youtu.be/4eBmyttcfU4 on September 25, 2017.

Thalmann, S. (2014). Adaptation criteria for the personalised delivery of learning materials: A multi-stage empirical investigation. *Australasian Journal of Educational Technology, 30*(1), 45–60.

Thompson, G. L. (2004). Playing God with other people's children. *High School Journal, 87*(3), 54–62.

Tomlinson, C. A. (2001). *How to differentiate instruction in mixed-ability classrooms* (2nd ed.). Alexandria, VA: Association for Supervision and Curriculum Development.

Tomlinson, C. A. (2014). *The differentiated classroom: Responding to the needs of all learners* (2nd ed.). Alexandria, VA: Association for Supervision and Curriculum Development.

Tomlinson, C. A. (2017). Let's celebrate personalization: But not too fast. *Educational Leadership, 74*(6), 10–15.

Tucker, C. (2017). Stations: A shift that's worth it. *Educational Leadership, 74*(6), 86–87.

University of Minnesota. (2018). *The student engagement instrument.* Accessed at http://checkandconnect.umn.edu/research/engagement.html on April 3, 2018.

Van Deur, P. (2004). Gifted primary students' knowledge of self-directed learning. *International Education Journal, 4*(4), 64–74.

VARK Learn. (n.d.). *The VARK modalities.* Accessed at http://vark-learn.com/introduction-to-vark/the-vark-modalities on November 10, 2017.

Visible Learning. (n.d.a). *Glossary of Hattie's influences on student achievement.* Accessed at https://visible-learning.org/glossary on February 17, 2018.

Visible Learning. (n.d.b). *Hattie effect size list: 195 influences related to achievement.* Accessed at https://visible-learning.org/hattie-ranking-influences-effect-sizes-learning-achievement on February 17, 2018.

Vygotsky, L. S. (1978). *Mind in society: The development of higher psychological processes* (M. Cole, V. John-Steiner, S. Scribner, & E. Souberman, Eds.). Cambridge, MA: Harvard University Press.

Wehby, J. H., Symons, F. J., & Shores, R. E. (1995). A descriptive analysis of aggressive behavior in classrooms for children with emotional and behavioral disorders. *Behavioral Disorders, 20*(2), 87–105.

Wiggins, G., & McTighe, J. (2005). *Understanding by design* (2nd ed.). Alexandria, VA: Association for Supervision and Curriculum Development.

Willard-Holt, C. (2003, October). Raising expectations for the gifted. *Educational Leadership, 61*(2), 72–75.

Wilusz, B., & Templeton, K. (2017). A personalized approach to equity. *Educational Leadership, 74*(6). Accessed at www.ascd.org/publications/educational-leadership/mar17/vol74/num06/A-Personalized-Approach-to-Equity.aspx on November 28, 2017.

Wisconsin Department of Public Instruction. (2011a). *Wisconsin foundations of English language arts.* Accessed at https://dpi.wi.gov/sites/default/files/imce/cal/pdf/ela-majorshifts.pdf on April 19, 2018.

Wisconsin Department of Public Instruction. (2011b). *Wisconsin standards for English language arts.* Madison, WI: Author. Accessed at https://dpi.wi.gov/sites/default/files/imce/standards/pdf/ela-stds-app-a-revision.pdf on April 6, 2018.

Wolfe, P. (1987). What the "seven-step lesson plan" isn't! *Educational Leadership, 44*(5), 70–71.

Yaluma, C. B., & Tyner, A. (2018, January). *Is there a gifted gap? Gifted education in high-poverty schools.* Accessed at https://edexcellence.net/publications/is-there-a-gifted-gap on April 4, 2018.

Index

Personalizing Learning Through Voice and Choice
Adam Garry, Amos Fodchuk, and Lauren Hobbs
This practical resource introduces personalized learning and breaks down what it looks and feels like in the classroom. The authors reveal structures that empower student voice and choice and share stories about real students with the life-changing opportunity to design their own learning experiences.
BKF657

Personalized Learning in a PLC at Work®
Timothy S. Stuart, Sascha Heckmann, Mike Mattos, and Austin Buffum
Rely on this resource to help you build a highly effective learning-progressive school. You will learn how to engage students in personalized learning experiences and empower them to take ownership of the four critical questions of the PLC at Work® process.
BKF703

A Handbook for Personalized Competency-Based Education
Robert J. Marzano, Jennifer S. Norford, Michelle Finn, and Douglas Finn III
Ensure all students master content by designing and implementing a personalized competency-based education (PCBE) system. Explore examples of how to use proficiency scales, standard operating procedures, behavior rubrics, personal tracking matrices, and other tools to aid in instruction and assessment.
BKL037

Learning by Doing, Third Edition
Richard DuFour, Rebecca DuFour, Robert Eaker, Thomas W. Many, and Mike Mattos
Discover how to transform your school or district into a high-performing PLC. The third edition of this comprehensive action guide offers new strategies for addressing critical PLC topics, including hiring and retaining new staff, creating team-developed common formative assessments, and more.
BKF746

"Tremendous, tremendous, tremendous!

The speaker made me do some very deep internal reflection about the **PLC process** and the personal responsibility I have in making the school improvement process work **for ALL kids.**"

—Marc Rodriguez, teacher effectiveness coach, Denver Public Schools, Colorado

PD Services

Our experts draw from decades of research and their own experiences to bring you practical strategies for building and sustaining a high-performing PLC. You can choose from a range of customizable services, from a one-day overview to a multiyear process.

Book your PLC PD today!
888.763.9045

Solution Tree